Changing Song

Nakano Shigeharu in his study, circa 1937. (Courtesy of Hara Izumi.)

Changing Song

THE MARXIST MANIFESTOS OF NAKANO SHIGEHARU

Miriam Silverberg

PRINCETON UNIVERSITY PRESS

PRINCETON, NEW JERSEY

Copyright ©1990 by Miriam Silverberg
Published by Princeton University Press, 41 William Street,
Princeton, New Jersey 08540
In the United Kingdom: Princeton University Press, Oxford

Library of Congress Cataloging-in-Publication Data

Silverberg, Miriam Rom, 1951–
Changing song : the Marxist manifestos of Nakano Shigeharu / Miriam Silverberg.
p. cm.
Bibliography: p.
Includes index.
1. Nakano, Shigeharu, 1902–   —Political and social views.   2. Communism and
literature—Japan.   3. Communism and culture—Japan.   I. Title.
PL834.A527Z825   1990   895.6'142—dc20   89-34627

ISBN 0-691-06816-X (alk. paper)

This book has been composed in Linotron Sabon

Princeton University Press books are printed on acid-free paper,
and meet the guidelines for permanence and durability of the
Committee on Production Guidelines for Book Longevity of the
Council on Library Resources

Printed in the United States of America by Princeton University Press,
Princeton, New Jersey

10 9 8 7 6 5 4 3 2 1

To my teachers

Contents

viii · Contents

Illustrations

Acknowledgments

I COULD NOT have moved through the stages of this work without the continued support of many. At the University of Chicago, Harry Harootunian and Tetsuo Najita inspired me to listen and to challenge, Bill Sibley showed how the grace and power of language need not be lost in translation, and Masao Miyoshi forged connections that others could not dare to imagine. In Japan, Nimura Kazuo, of the Ohara Institute for Social Research at Hosei University, wryly and generously opened up the archives and helped explicate the canon of Japanese Marxism; the insights of Fujita Shōzō demonstrated how anger and mirth could coexist in Taishō Japan; and Ryūsawa Takeshi introduced me to the dialogue made possible by the poetry of Nakano Shigeharu. Moreover, the late Maeda Ai exchanged notes on Kagurazaka; Takayama Yoshiki introduced me to Hara Izumi, who showed me her photographs; and Miyagi Kimiko took me out to dinner. During the final stages of research, Mitsuta Ikuo discussed problems of interpretation; and Nakano's friends, Sata Ineko—who remembers and smiles—and Ishidō Kiyotomo, the scholar even now committed to translating the Japanese revolutionary experience into history, shared treasured memories.

Over the past few years of reading and writing, Anne Walthall has been the finest of *senpai*; Susan Griswold was always a loving colleague; and Elizabeth Young-Bruehl, Sam Kassow, and Caryl Emerson helped me frame the big questions. Research and writing were made possible by grants from the Fulbright-Hayes Foundation; the Social Science Research Council; and the Mellon Foundation, which allowed me to affiliate with the Asian Studies Department of Cornell University; and through the continued assistance of the staff of the Ohara Institute. Appreciation is owed to Brett DeBary and Thomas Havens for readings of the initial manuscript and to Margaret Case and Beth Gianfagna of Princeton University Press for their editorial assistance. Special gratitude is due to Norma Field and Harry Harootunian for rereading the changes at all stages, to Yōko Kuki of the University of Chicago Library, and to Miwako Kimura.

Circles of friends in Ithaca, New York, and at Hamilton College helped me see this project to the end, as did the wise counsel of Deborah Neipris, Peter Agree, Peter Rabinowitz, Gail Bernstein, Harry Wessel, Willo Pequegnat, Mike Frame, Kyoko Selden, Steve Caton, and Agha Shahid Ali; the unfailing labors of Valerie Hing; and the warm support of my colleagues in the History Department of Hamilton College. Jim Fujii has at all times been there to listen and respond. I thank him and all of the others for their company.

Clinton, New York
December 3, 1988

Changing Song

Reclaiming Nakano Shigeharu

NAKANO SHIGEHARU left his readers a photograph. At first glance the picture appears to be a portrait of a dignified yet relaxed figure. This is a man of letters in traditional kimono seated before his books and curios. The sparsely exhibited treasures on display are the books and a small Buddha-like figurine placed atop a wooden folk-chest. The observer is almost forced to respond, "Ahh. The artist in repose." And yet Nakano Shigeharu is not in repose. He has broken the strictures of decorum—and not only by perching himself on the ledge of the *tokonoma*, the recessed space in the Japanese sitting room meant only for venerated objects of art. He is also challenging tradition by his stance. The folds of his kimono hang gracefully, and one arm grasps the other in a centering motion parallel to the front fold of the robe. But the image is askew, for the artist does not have both feet on the tatami. One foot is half off the floor. It turns outward, away from center, as does Nakano. He refuses to return the camera's gaze, to confirm that yes, he is the man of letters seated before his books and his art and his audience. Rather he directs the attention of the viewer elsewhere; he hints that there is another subject to be seen. He asks his readers to take a second look.

That same stance informs this book. It calls for a new perspective on Nakano Shigeharu (1902–1979), the man of letters, the poet, the revolutionary. It offers an image of Nakano Shigeharu as Marxist critic, and in the process it suggests a new way of positioning the Japanese Marxist vision within the prewar culture of Taishō Japan. This is not a biography. It is a history of the changing consciousness of one Japanese Marxist, whose life spanned the three imperial reigns of Japan's modern era, the Meiji (1868–1912), Taishō (1912–1926), and Shōwa (1926–1989) years. Nakano Shigeharu, the premier poet and leading organizer of the Communist wing of the prewar revolutionary literature movement of the 1920s, who maintained a position of both political and intellectual leadership after the Second World War, wrote novels about his place in the prewar Culture Movement, but there are no memoirs. Possibly unwittingly, Nakano did leave fragments that allow a history of Japanese Marxist thought and Japanese cultural revolution to emerge. These parts have been pieced together to interpret Nakano's turn to Marxism and his ensuing critique of Taishō culture, an astute analysis of the rapid cultural and political transitions in Japan during the decade beginning in the second half of the 1920s. Rather than presume that the autobiographical fiction produced by Nakano after the fact reproduces his life and times, this study relies on writings from the 1920s and early 1930s. It makes use of classics from the Japanese and Western Marxist canon, essays on Japanese history and culture, poetry, letters, and stories. Political and social theory, the imagery of verse, the ideology in song, the fact in fiction, the epistolary form of the letter, and the polemic of the manifesto are put to use so that a moment in modern Japanese history, the Marxist moment, may be illuminated. The fragments have been put into one unified process of changing song.

The conceit of changing song, taken from the Japanese term "changed song" (*kaeuta*), takes on different meanings in this study of the thought of Nakano Shigeharu. In the Japanese tradition the word *uta* means both song and poem, and *kaeuta* simply refers to a newly conceived song combining the melody of an original song or *motouta* with different lyrics. This is the way in which Nakano used the term. But Nakano also used the idea—he actually changed his song or poetry in several stages during the years between the two world wars—when, as the authoritative voice of the revolutionary poetry movement, he combined lyric power with an eloquent and angry demand for resistance and social transformation. His poetry is "changed song" for three reasons. Not only did the young writer abandon the constriction of the traditional thirty-one–syllable *tanka* verse form; in addition, the intent and subject matter of his song shifted as his lyric poetry was transformed to political poetry after he turned to Marxism. Finally and most importantly, in the context of this reading of Nakano the focus of the revolutionary Marxist poetry continued to change.

Both a biography of Nakano's life, which could illuminate the history of Japanese intellectual life over the past half-century, and a literary history of Nakano's poetry, placing him within the Japanese poetic tradition, remain to be written. This book is neither of those works. What follows is one answer to two large historical questions. First, why was Marxism adopted as the dominant method of intellectual inquiry for Japanese thinkers during the transition between the Taishō and Shōwa eras? Second, how should the Taishō era be placed within the narrative of Japanese history? The dialogue surrounding this question has hitherto centered on one of two choices—either something "went wrong" with the forward course of history, or "nothing really changed" as the structuring of Meiji political history determined the character of the Taishō and Shōwa eras. Until recently the period has been seen either as a democratic interlude preceding the repression of the 1930s and 1940s, or as a stage in the consolidation of a progressively belligerent imperial system. Within these schemas the question of cultural change has received scant notice.[1] This interpretation and contextualization of the changed song of Nakano Shigeharu allows for an answer to the first question, and Nakano's critique of his own culture provides a third alternative to the dominant interpretations of Taishō Japan. (It must be noted at the outset that while the Taishō imperial reign is officially bracketed between the years 1912 and 1926, the stages of Nakano's changed song accompanied the dizzying changes in Japanese urban society after the Tokyo earthquake of 1923 and before Japan's advance into China. Therefore, the term Taishō, as dictated by the focus on Nakano's cultural context, will hereafter refer to the 1920s and the first years of the 1930s.)

The cultural shift in Japan during the 1920s was part of a worldwide reorientation of mass production, mass consumption, and mass politics. During these years the direction of Marxism was shifting in Europe as thinkers confronting the power of cultural symbols and institutions reassessed the role of consciousness in making revolution. The new canon of writings emerging from this process has been subsumed under the rubric of "Western Marxism."[2] In the following pages, Nakano's Marxist critique of Taishō culture will be placed alongside the formulations of the leading Marxist theorists of culture in the West, because his changed Marxism bears strong resemblances to the new directions charted by such theorists as Georg Lukács, Walter Benjamin, and Antonio Gramsci. Nakano's Marxism derived from the Marxism of Marx and was also informed by the theory of consciousness set forth by Lukács in the early 1920s. To the extent that the present work can convince the reader that Nakano Shigeharu's criticism of modern culture was Marxist, it is a com-

---

[1] See Edwin O. Reischauer, "What Went Wrong?" in *Dilemmas of Growth in Prewar Japan*, ed. James Morley (Princeton: Princeton University Press, 1971), pp. 489–510. Most Japanese scholarship, based on a Marxist conceptual language, has taken the second position. See Matsuo Takayoshi, *Taishō demokurashii* (Iwanami shoten, 1974). See also Shinobu Seizaburō, *Taishō demokurashii shi* (Nihon hyōronsha, 1958) and the group effort *Shimpojiumu, Taishō demokurashii*, Nihon rekishi, no. 20 (Gakuseisha, 1969). On Taishō culture, see Minami Hiroshi, *Taishō bunka* (Keisō shobō, 1965), Takemura Tamio, *Taishō bunka* (Kōdansha, 1980), and Tsurumi Shunsuke, "Taishōki no bunka," *Gendai* 19, no. 2, *Iwanami kōza Nihon rekishi* (Iwanami shoten, 1963), pp. 288–323.

For an important reworking of the terms of the discussion that shifts the focus away from "Taishō democracy" to a topic that might more appropriately be termed "Taishō bureaucracy," see Bernard Silberman, "The Bureaucratic State in Japan: The Problem of Authority and Legitimacy," in *Conflict in Modern Japanese History: The Neglected Tradition*, ed. Tetsuo Najita and J. Victor Koschmann (Princeton: Princeton University Press, 1982), pp. 226–57.

[2] For the historiography of the term "Western Marxism," which includes a critique, see the Introduction, "The Topography of Western Marxism," to Martin Jay, *Marxism and Totality: The Adventures of a Concept from Lukács to Habermas* (Berkeley: University of California Press, 1984), pp. 1–20.

parative history. But it must be underscored that Nakano is being placed in relation to, and not in actual dialogue with, the other Marxist thinkers who were his contemporaries. With the exception of the work of Lukács, the writings of the Western Marxists were not available to him until after the war. No other study has placed him or his colleagues in such a context, but he does share a history with these non-Japanese Marxist members of his generation. Although this history was not premised on any familiarity with their work, it was derived from a shared set of theoretical and political questions. Nakano was a Marxist thinker schooled in the same canon of intellectual and cultural history, but, like his peers, he was also a Marxist revolutionary working to place his theory of culture into political practice during a historical moment when the politics of culture had been transformed by modern technologies blind to national or historical boundaries.

It will be argued that as a Marxist, Nakano's concerns were in part transnational. To deny him brotherhood with the European writers of his generation is to deny the cosmopolitan nature of Japanese culture in the 1920s. It also denies the importance of Nakano's insights into the culture of the twentieth century, which is blind to contrasting historical traditions. As a Marxist cultural critic he recognized the revolutionary transformation in the production and consumption of words and pictures during the Taishō era. He saw that in the context of modern Japanese history, the colonizing power of culture moved in two directions: the imposition of Western attitudes and the Western invention of Japanese tradition worked internally to create a consciousness in Japan, in tandem with the imposition of cultural controls by Japan on the Asian continent. By bestowing upon him the title of "Western Marxist," the historian can only commit yet another instance of the cultural imperialism denounced by Nakano in such powerful statements as his sarcastic indictment of the French Orientalist, Paul Claudel, and his farewell poem to Korean colleagues deported home to the Japanese possession. To call him a Western Marxist would also be to deny the specificity in Japanese history that he affirmed, for as a Marxist, Nakano respected both the tradition and the transformation of Japanese culture. This is most evident in his celebration in theoretical prose and poetic practice of the richness of the Japanese language.

During the decade under consideration, Nakano's writing changed, but it was also informed by continuities. The city, the photograph, and the central role of dialogue in social action remained constant concerns for Nakano during the Taishō years, when the state was beginning to silence all alternative cultural expression. Like his German contemporary Walter Benjamin, Nakano Shigeharu formulated a theory of the place of the artist as producer in capitalist culture. And like Benjamin's nineteenth-century hero Baudelaire, Nakano was a "social poet" negotiating the crowds in an emerging urban landscape. But Nakano's approach to culture is also reminiscent of the work of his contemporary Mikhail Bakhtin, because Nakano, like Bakhtin, rendered meaningful the social significance of the relationships among a multiplicity of languages coexisting at one synchronous moment. The words of Bakhtin about his hero, Dostoyevsky, apply equally to Nakano Shigeharu. According to Bakhtin, Dostoyevsky heard his epoch as "a great dialogue" and was able to hear not only individual voices, "but precisely and predominantly the *dialogic relationship* among voices, their dialogic *interaction.*" The same can be said for Nakano, who also "heard both the loud, recognized, reigning voices of the epoch" and the "voices still weak."[3]

This treatment of the ideas of Nakano Shigeharu acknowledges him as one of the many Marxist voices of the modern epoch of the 1920s and early 1930s. It recognizes that his Marxist vision of the production of Taishō culture emerged at a moment in the history of Marxism when intellectuals were just beginning to ponder the production and power of culture. In that context, the voices of his European colleagues will be heard in the following pages. But of central concern is Nakano's ability, as a Marxist, to capture the interaction of Japanese voices. According to Caryl Emerson, the eloquent interpreter of Bakhtin's theory of the dialogic, the vocal pluralism advocated by Bakhtin appears to be directed toward "Bakhtin's ultimate task: to make a unified truth compatible with multiple consciousnesses." This can also be said to have been Nakano's ultimate task as a Marxist cultural revolutionary writing in many voices. Bakhtin believed that the author must "define and shape others in a way in which they cannot define and shape themselves."[4] Writing from a perspective in the 1980s that takes into account Marxist voices not accessible to Nakano during the 1920s and Marxist interpretations not articulated by him, I aim here at such an authoring of Nakano. It is an authoring based on translation, a problem respected by Bakhtin, who recognized that not only must the languages of different nations be translated, but that the languages within one national, linguistically defined culture also require translation.

According to Nakano, songs change because historical actors create new forms of culture within social and economic structures; changed song implies the active process of changing song. In this context he chose to reenact the voices of Taishō Japan to promote revolutionary change by revealing the historical process of the contestation among historically, so-

---

[3] Mikhail Bakhtin, *Problems of Dostoevsky's Poetics*, ed. and trans. Caryl Emerson, in *Theory and History of Literature* (Minneapolis: University of Minnesota Press, 1984), 8:90.

[4] See Caryl Emerson, "The Tolstoy Connection in Bakhtin," *Publications of the Modern Language Association of America* 100, 1 (January 1985): 70–72.

cially created voices. Nakano Shigeharu's revolutionary impulse has been duly noted in numerous histories of his work and his political movement, but it is never analyzed as a *Marxist* stance. An early essay by Nakano on his predecessor Ishikawa Takuboku, the writer who recorded the transition from Meiji to Taishō politics and culture, provides a method out of this silence. In "Takuboku ni kansuru danpen" (A fragment on Takuboku),[5] written in 1926, Nakano explained that while Takuboku had lived in close proximity to Nakano's own era and had left behind powerful, positive views on life and social organization, his true identity had been lost within the interpretations of his followers. Nakano's goal, therefore, was to take back the revolutionary poet from his erring followers by reexamining the true Takuboku. My goal also is to "take back" a revolutionary poet, because Nakano Shigeharu, like Ishikawa Takuboku, has been a captive of rigid schematizing. According to Nakano, the interpretations of Takuboku discounted his socialism by claiming that he had "graduated" from his socialist position. Nakano's thought and actions have likewise been circumscribed by the uniform historical accounts of the lyric poet turned revolutionary who espoused hard-line political views as he gained leadership of one branch of the revolutionary literature movement. Nakano's method for reclaiming Ishikawa Takuboku as a revolutionary poet was to seek the transitions in Takuboku's thought in order to free the thinker to emerge as a romantic, a lyric poet, a critic of art and its relation to life and social organization, and a socialist. I have adopted a similar method.

Nakano's changing consciousness is framed in this book within the four prewar stages of his changing song. The first two chapters provide the context. Chapter 1, "Fragments from a Life," challenges the standard treatment of Nakano's early years. It introduces the four stages by tracing how they are inscribed in *Nashi no hana* (Pear flowers), Nakano's novel about growing up in late Meiji Japan, and provides the biographical context of Nakano's integration of politics with culture during his youth. Chapter 2, "A World Split in Two," reclaims Nakano as one of the numerous Japanese producers of a Marxist discourse informed by the imagery and historiography of the *Communist Manifesto*. It revises the common representation of Nakano as an adherent of Leninist theorist Fukumoto Kazuo by analyzing the poet's earliest Marxist essays on art as a series of Marxist manifestos. Chapter 3, "Song I: The Discovery of History," covers the first of Nakano's four stages of song. It traces his discovery of a Marxist theory of historical transformation during the years

[5] Nakano Shigeharu, "Takuboku ni kansuru danpen," *Nakano Shigeharu zenshū* [hereafter referred to as *NSZ*] (Tokyo: Chikuma Shobō, 1977), 16:3–12 [*Roba* 11/26]. See the introductory note to the present book's bibliography for further explanation.

1924–1926, through a close reading of his earliest Marxist poems. It also examines his idea of intellectual production, relating it to a reconceptualization of Nakano's much-cited relationship with modernist writer Akutagawa Ryūnosuke. Chapter 4, "Song II: The Reproduction of Taishō Culture," views Nakano's critique of mass culture from 1926 through 1928 during the second stage of his changing song. It is a reading of Nakano's critique of his surroundings as shaped by "the reproduction of culture" by capitalists and orientalists appropriating Japanese tradition for new ends, and by a "culture of reproduction" produced in the mass press. Chapter 5, "Song III: The Dialogue of Revolution," follows Nakano's publications from 1928 to 1932, during the years when a Japanese Marxist canon was being consolidated, the Culture Movement was in retreat, and Nakano's poetic production was coming to an end. His poetry, charting apocalyptic violence and contending revolutionary, colonial, and colonizing voices, offers a contrasting polemic response to escalating state repression, and his literary criticism is placed within the newly consolidated indigenous Marxist canon. Chapter 6, "Song IV: Closing Song," based on a reading of prison letters and essays produced after Nakano's release from prison in 1934, focuses on the silencing of his revolutionary voice during the early 1930s. In conclusion, "Marxism Addresses the Modern" returns to the two questions posed at the outset: Why the appeal of Marxism? and How are the interwar years in Japan to be conceptualized?

After Nakano Shigeharu was released from prison in 1934 he continued to write social and cultural criticism and prose fiction. The twenty-eight volumes of his oeuvre attest to his unceasing commitment to the printed word and to revolutionary change after the war, when he helped to revive the literary left and served as an editor of the Communist newspaper *Akahata*. He continued to engage in cultural politics as a leader of the literary left and as representative of the Japanese Communist Party in the National Diet from 1947 until 1950. Following his expulsion from the party in 1964 he produced scathing commentary on world affairs, the use of the Japanese language, and his own prewar past. This history is not part of the narrative constituted by the changes in Nakano's song, and not only because his poetry had ended. During the 1920s Nakano recorded how his work as a cultural revolutionary was both made possible and manipulated by a mass culture poised in an ambiguous relationship with the state. By the end of the 1930s all such ambiguities would be absent, and after the war the Communist left was incorporated into public and private bureaucratic structures. Nakano's postwar writings cannot be read as defiant manifestos demanding immediate social revolution; they are part of another history.

Nakano Shigeharu succeeded in taking back Ishikawa Takuboku as a revolutionary poet whose critique of the Japanese state expressed a recognition that Japanese society was, at the beginning of the Taishō era, on the edge of profound repression. His own revolutionary poetry came out of a similar moment in Japanese history, for Nakano changed song at the end of the Taishō era, when, for the second time in the twentieth century, the Japanese intellectual's belief in revolutionary possibility was destroyed by the state. If this book can reclaim the transitions in the thought of Nakano Shigeharu, the poet, the vocal critic of Taishō society and culture, and the Marxist revolutionary, it will have reclaimed Nakano as a witness to that moment. For the words of Nakano Shigeharu produced in the 1920s and early 1930s were an angry indictment of modernity, a passionate voicing of revolutionary vision, and an augury of the era in modern Japanese history when poetry, conflict, and all other dialogic encounters would be silenced.

CHAPTER ONE

Fragments from a Life

THE MAKINGS OF BIOGRAPHY

Before Nakano Shigeharu can be reclaimed he must be found. And he is easily found in the histories of prewar Japanese revolutionary literature and thought: he is the brash young man who harnessed his talents as a lyric poet to the dictates of Leninism. According to most accounts, the problematic governing his work as writer and political organizer was the tension between politics and culture,[1] but in fact the young Nakano determined that the two were inseparable. As a Marxist poet and critic, he integrated and continually reintegrated politics with culture.

There is no biography of Nakano Shigeharu to aid in the process of piecing together his life. Instead there is the chronology found in the Japanese world of letters, the detailed personal *nenpu* for every year of the author's life provided at the end of the last volume of the collected works of all modern Japanese writers considered sufficiently prominent to merit canonization. When the information provided by the *nenpu* is reordered in columns under the three headings "everyday life" (in reference to place of residence, school, work, family situation, and other social structures), "literary production" (with subcolumns of poetry, fiction, and essays), and "political activism" (providing a place for revolutionary politics), the details take on new meaning. Although Nakano and others have argued that the form of the newspaper isolates events and obscures connections, this use of a similar format of columns reveals how the young activist was forging politics with culture. It tells which essays accompanied which poems in time, how school life at Tokyo Imperial University from the spring of 1924 through the spring of 1927 was one part of a life structured to include activity in more than one type of political organization, and how

---

[1] Hirano Ken's conceptualization of the politics versus culture dichotomy is most often cited. See Hirano Ken, "Hito to bungaku," in *Nakano Shigeharushū*, Chikuma gendai bungaku taikei, no. 35 (Chikuma shobō, 1979), pp. 499–500. Kimura Hideo suggests that the tension in Nakano's youth lay not in the contradiction between politics and literature, but in Nakano's close association in early life with the Japanese literary tradition of Taishō and his unification, in the latter half of his youth, of politics and literature in political and literary self-transformation. Kimura Hideo, *Nakano Shigeharuron: shi to hyōron* (Ōfūsha, 1979), pp. 235–36, 246–51. Kuno Osamu eschews any binarism, emphasizing Nakano's politicization of culture. Kuno Osamu, "Nakano Shigeharu san no eikyōryoku," *Geppō* 1 (September 1976) [appendix to *NSZ*] (Chikuma shobō, 1976), p. 3.

the writer's production coincided with his half-dozen incarcerations between 1928 and 1932. Within this grid, the breaks in Nakano's life are separated from the continuities. In these three columns one can find when the poetry began and ended and how themes of self-absorption were replaced by conceptualizations of social change and utopian transformation. The pieces in the reordered chronology show that by 1932 a boy born in a village on the Japan seacoast and educated at the elite Fourth Higher School in Kanazawa and the Imperial University at the turn of the century had published over fifty poems, almost thirty short stories, and seventy essays.[2] He had also edited four successive journals of the Communist literary left and had joined the Communist Party (during the summer of 1931). All of this activity was sufficiently threatening to the Japanese state to cause his longest incarceration, an imprisonment of two years between 1932 and 1934.

Biographies begin at the beginning with due respect for lineage and domicile articulated in the first of the segments of Nakano's *nenpu*, a form of biography that begins with the heading for 1902, the thirty-fifth year of Meiji, and proceeds to frame one lifetime within 120 pages of staccato prose ending with the entry for 1979, the fifty-fourth year of Shōwa, which was the year of Nakano's death. The abbreviated family history in the early entries serves to place the earliest years of Nakano's everyday life within the social and political context of the sweeping historical transformation following the Meiji Restoration of 1868. It allows for the interpretation that Nakano's father, after his adoption into the family of tenant-farmer commoners who owned small holdings of land, positioned himself within the process of expansion of the newly constituted state. (He worked for the Taiwan Government General and for the state-run Tobacco Monopoly Bureau before being transferred to the Korean Government General after the annexation of Korea in 1910.) Thus Nakano Shigeharu's earliest years of family life were governed by his father's advancement through the bureaucracy, as his parents and siblings moved in and out of the village of Ipponden where he stayed with his grandparents. The shorter *nenpu* entries for the years preceding Nakano's move to enter high school in Kanazawa, at the age of seventeen, mention the use of postcards as a means of maintaining family bonds amidst geographic separation caused by the exigencies of state business. The same means of dialogue was to be repeated two decades later when state regulations would forbid Nakano to contact those closest to him in any way other than the brief messages allowed on prison postcards.

The *nenpu* does not mention the Russo-Japanese War in Nakano's

[2] Nakano's "complete works" contain sixty-one poems, twenty-eight short stories, and seventy essays for the years between 1926 and 1932.

third year, the annexation of Korea five years later, the First World War, or its domestic repercussions. It gives only births, deaths, and changes of address. For example, Nakano's transition away from his childhood surroundings in 1914, at the age of twelve, is phrased in institutional terms listing, among other facts, the names of his reading and arithmetic teachers, and his move to lodgings at a nearby temple.

What is absent from this form of biography is a child's consciousness—Nakano's own experience of the structures and family relationships so conscientiously catalogued, although Nakano did make memories about his earliest attachments available. In an essay written in 1976 he distanced himself from his colleagues in the world of letters, claiming that literature as usually conceived had played no part in his childhood, but that he had cherished access to magazines left about the house by his older brother, bought on occasion at the local bookstore, or handed down to him by an older cousin. This cousin, in a fit of filial guilt for behavior inappropriate to the son of farmers, after a bout of illness had passed on the remainder of his subscription to *Shōnen sekai* (Boy's world). In this memoir Nakano also confessed that until the sixth grade he had no familiarity with the world of fairy tales. Nonetheless, the old tales he did know, the stories told to him by his toothless grandmother, provided a foundation for his fascination with the adventure and detective stories in the monthly magazines.[3]

There is no way to authenticate this memoir, although the recollection does repeat a theme Nakano first voiced in an essay written in 1936, entitled "Waga bungakuteki jiden" (My literary autobiography).[4] In this essay, which opens with the confessional statement, "Magazines gave me my first literary education," Nakano recalled how as a child he had been drawn to the illustrations even more strongly than to the stories he had relished in the pages of *Shōnen sekai* and *Nihon shōnen* (Boys of Japan). He had at that early age realized that the work of an author changes over time, and that the world of pictures has its own history, as he followed the production of favorite authors. In this essay he shared stories from the boy's magazines, such as the narrative about elementary school students who are informed of their teacher's death in the Russo-Japanese War. In his memoir Nakano recalled that this story of heroism, which contained "no smell of jingoism," had elicited in him a different response from the other stories about valor relayed in school textbooks and in ethics classes. As a child reading this tale he had felt privy to a "correct suggestion as to what a human being should respect." This ambiguous

[3] Nakano, "Chosha ushirogaki: seiriteki yōshōnenki to bungakuteki shōnenki," *NSZ* 1:485–91.
[4] Nakano, "Waga bungakuteki jiden," *NSZ* 22:3.

commentary, supporting the martyred teacher while at the same time criticizing the standardized ethics instruction in the classrooms, was undoubtedly as much a statement about the 1930s, when the memory was
first published, as a nostalgic recollection of the journalism produced for
juvenile readership during his childhood at the end of the Meiji era.

Nakano's account of the children's story, which indirectly associates
present with past, is but one illustration of the truism that autobiography
of one era must inevitably be filtered through the memories of other
times. Such is also the case with *Pear Flowers*,[5] Nakano Shigeharu's remembrance of his childhood in a village on the Japan seacoast during the
closing years of the Meiji era. When *Pear Flowers* appeared in serialized
form in the popular magazine *Shinchō* in 1957 and 1958, the postwar
Japanese intellectual world, engaged in the heated process of assessing its
collective history, was at first disappointed.[6] They despaired that instead
of erasing the autobiographical lacuna caused by the gap between his
three novellas about his high school and college days—*Uta no wakare* (A
farewell to song, 1939), *Machi aruki* (City walks, 1940), and *Muragimo*
(Churning, 1954)—and his confessional account of the homecoming of a
young Communist after release from prison following a statement of
apostasy—*Mura no ie* (The house in the village, 1954), the author had
chosen to go back to the earliest era of his life. It was true that Nakano
had not provided an account of the everyday life of a Japanese Communist cultural revolutionary of the 1920s, but the disappointment within
the literary establishment was soon replaced by superlatives proclaiming
the autobiographical veracity and literary power of *Pear Flowers*.[7]

[5] Nakano, *Nashi no hana*, NSZ 6 [*Shinchō* 1/57–12/58].

[6] The most ambitious endeavor to place the Japanese intellectual in recent political history
is the three-volume group effort on apostasy. See Shisō no Kagaku Kenkyūkai, ed. *Tenkō*,
3 vols. (Heibonsha, 1959–1962). Other representative works are the collaboration by Kuno
Osamu and Tsurumi Shunsuke, *Gendai Nihon no shisō* (Iwanami shoten, 1956), and the
classic by Maruyama Masao, *Nihon no shisō* (Iwanami shoten, 1961), comprising essays
published between 1957 and 1959.

[7] Nakano, *Uta no wakare*, NSZ 5:3–95 [*Kakushin* 4/39; 5/39; 7/39; 8/39]; *Machi aruki*,
NSZ 5:99–121 [*Shinchō* 6–7/40]; *Muragimo*, NSZ 125–404 [*Gunzō* 1–7/54]; *Mura no ie*,
NSZ 2:64–89 [*Keizai ōrai* 5/35]. Based on discussion with literary historian Mitsuta Ikuo,
I have translated the allusion to emotional turmoil implied by the term *muragimo* as "churn-
ing." For an English translation of *Mura no ie* see Nakano Shigeharu, *The House in the
Village*, trans. Brett De Bary, in *Three Works by Nakano Shigeharu*, Cornell University East
Asia papers, no. 21 (Ithaca: Cornell China-Japan Program, 1979), pp. 19–73.

Hirano Ken called for a sequel to *Muragimo* that would depict the life of the literary
intellectual spanning the transition from Taishō to Shōwa. Hirano, "Hito to bungaku," p.
503. Ōe Kenzaburō determined that this was the best work about a boy in a Japanese village
ever produced. He called the book a novel about "homecoming." Ōe Kenzaburō, "Nashi
no hana no bunshō," in *Nakano Shigeharu kenkyū*, ed. Hirano Ken (Chikuma shobō,

Most scholars have emphasized the parallels between Nakano's child-hood and the experiences of Ryōhei, the hero of the work,[8] but it will never be known to what extent the novel does in fact replicate a stage in Nakano's personal history. Nakano called it "an account of the author's childhood" that explained "how one boy child born in a village in a cer-tain region, to a certain class becomes a person, from the first grade into the first year of junior high school."[9] He protested that placing the child's experiences in the foreground allowed for only intermittent glimpses of larger historical events, but at the same time he acknowledged that he had wanted to touch on the legacy of Tokugawa history for the Meiji period; he confirmed that this was his personal version of the local history, which he had heard from his grandmother. He had merely reproduced the sto-ries of the peasant uprising, of his grandfather's time in the Fukui prison, of the farmer's request for the return of land after the Meiji Restoration, and of his grandfather's trip to the Supreme Court as a village represen-tative, without inquiring as to the relationship of these stories to real events.

Nakano's discussion of his work rests on a conceit of simplicity—a conceit not to be trusted. For Nakano Shigeharu was a man concerned with the rewriting of history and highly aware of the power of language to produce altered visions. If one reads the record closely, Nakano's care-fully chosen words provide clues to a method of interpreting the novel as a mediated form of history that is not autobiography. For example, at the very end of the second introduction to *Pear Flowers*, the author explains that the version of the transition to Meiji history learned at home from his grandmother's folktales remained inchoate in his mind because there was no clarification at school. He had, of course, been made to listen to the Imperial Rescript on Education and to study ethics texts through ele-mentary school and into the junior high years, but the Confucian lan-guage of obedience to imperial authority had not been proclaimed in such a noisy fashion during his childhood as during the shift into the Shōwa era.[10] Again, in terms similar to his recollection of the war literature writ-

---

1960), p. 299. Another critic termed the work a rural almanac for the late Meiji era. See Hotta Yoshie, "Ryōhei to Shigeharu," in ibid., pp. 288, 289, 291.

[8] See, for example, Kimura Hideo, *Nakano Shigeharuron: shi to hyōron* (Ōfūsha, 1979), pp. 252–55, and Mitsuta Ikuo, *Nakano Shigeharuron* (Yagi shoten, 1981), pp. 3–35.

[9] Nakano, "*Nakano Shigeharū zenshu* dai gokan sakusha atogaki," *NSZ* 22:88.

[10] Ibid., p. 395. Nakano's analysis of the increasing intensity of the dogma propagated by the state is borne out by Carol Gluck's discussion of the 1890 Imperial Rescript on Educa-tion as an ambiguous, "ornate" text, which "acquired an interpretive apparatus that by 1940 included 595 book-length commentaries, hundreds of Ministry of Education direc-tives and teachers' guides, and countless evocations in print and oratory." Carol Gluck, *Japan's Modern Myths: Ideology in the Late Meiji Period* (Princeton: Princeton University Press, 1985), p. 127.

ten for children, the author directs the reader's attention to the problem of the Taishō–Shōwa transition, hinting (intentionally or otherwise) that the book might encompass more than Meiji memories. A second clue appears in a brief afterward to the first edition of *Pear Flowers* in book form. There the author requests that his readers adopt a method as they read his book. Taking a proprietary stance toward the place of his childhood and adopting the traditional, Tokugawa domainal designation, he explains that the village dialect and customs of his homeland, Echizen, have rarely appeared in Japanese literature. He notes that he has been successful in bringing them to the fore, and he concludes by directing his readers to a method: "It must be said that I love the words of literature as a carpenter loves his chisel and his plane. I am asking that people read this by following the language."[11]

By following Nakano's request, the reader who engages in a close reading of *Pear Flowers* will find that the young hero, Ryōhei, is quite aware that people wield language in different ways and comprehends the world around him by deciphering words and their uses. In many ways, *Pear Flowers* is about this child's consciousness of the social production and contestation of languages in late Meiji Japan. In this work, Nakano articulates, through a child's inner voice, one of his own central political concerns during his participation in the Culture Movement of the Taishō years. The book can thus be read not only as a reproduction of Meiji history, but also as a complex reworking of Nakano Shigeharu's Taishō biography. Although no critic has hitherto read *Pear Flowers* as a product of the era missing from the series of autobiographical novels, this story, which takes place in the years between the Russo-Japanese War and First World War, is about the issues raised by Nakano in the 1920s in verse and prose manifestos written during the era for which there is no autobiographical record.

The Shōwa novel set in the Meiji era refers to the Taishō years, for reasons that correspond to the stages of Nakano Shigeharu's Marxist manifestos of the 1920s. First, *Pear Flowers* unravels a discovery of history through the child's interpretation of the momentous political and cultural shifts of late Meiji. Second, it provides a commentary on the reproduction and commodification of culture as it documents the entrance into village life of the nationwide print culture that had been both a platform and a target for Nakano's work during the second half of the 1920s. Third, while the work centers on the problem of the social constitution and contestation of language, it also contains the story of the silencing of speech, the final theme of Nakano's changing song during the Taishō years. In sum, this is a postwar reworking of the prewar consciousness of

---

[11] Nakano, "*Nashi no hana* ni tsuite," NSZ 22:71.

one revolutionary youth, seen through the eyes of the child making sense of a history made available to him in the printed and spoken words of late Meiji Japan.

The opening pages of *Pear Flowers* follow a young boy returning from errands in town. En route to his village he stops to compare three faces staring out at him from advertisement boards. The child compares the face of the man with the moustache and the white complexion who wears a triangular hat and sells Jintan (sen-sen) with the large, bald, bearded face in metal-rimmed glasses advertising University Eye Medicine, and the face of the Dunlop Tire man. He knows all of them well and has his own views as to their comparative worth:

> The three signs were all over the place. They weren't always together, but Ryōhei had learned these three by heart. He thought that of the three the Dunlop Tire one could be a Westerner. It was only that Ryōhei had never seen a Westerner. But he thought it was a Westerner. Ryōhei knew "Sen-sen." He also knew "University Eye Medicine." He'd seen this medicine in a narrow box. But he didn't know about "Dunlop Tires." There was a picture of an automobile on it, so he thought it had to do with automobiles, but he wasn't positive. Dunlop Tire. Ryōhei liked this "Dunlop." He tried saying "Dunlop" out loud. It felt good. Out of the three people, he decided this guy was the most important.[12]

The issues of commodity culture and the shaping of language are raised at the outset, but the little boy and the advertisements he studies are soon placed in a setting that gives the book the markings of autobiography. The setting is the coast of the Japan Sea; the time, the years following Japan's victory in the Russo-Japanese War when Nakano entered grade school. Ryōhei, like the author, is being raised by grandparents while his father rises in the ranks of the civil service at the time of the Japanese consolidation of control over Korea. It is not clear to what extent the rich detailing of the child's subjective experience is a product of fantasy or memory or a mixture of both, but the author has chosen to focus on Ryōhei's experience of the process of change. Not only does he dwell on the child's sense of time, he also chooses to map Ryōhei's experience of the markers of Meiji history more than his retrospective accounts of the work would indicate. The author works through the logic of the child: Ryōhei knows that his grandfather was born in the eleventh year of Tempō but has no idea when this year was; his grandfather is probably older because he is bigger; his grandmother should be younger, but she is missing every one of her teeth (p. 194).[13] The narrator has not yet learned

---

[12] Nakano, *Nashi no hana*, p. 7.
[13] The Tempō reign was from 1830 to 1844.

to structure his experience of change, but the student of Japanese history can follow the account of the five-year time span easily, because *Pear Flowers* refers to the nodal events of the closing years of the Meiji reign. The expansion of empire, the execution of Kōtoku Shūsui, and the passing of the Emperor are embedded in the narrative, as Meiji history enters the village through the eyes of a child giving meaning to his immediate surroundings.

Ryōhei experiences the steady Japanese incursion into Korea after the victory at Port Arthur as a familiar mystery. He knows that neighbors talk about "going to be farmers" there, and that Korea is the destination for the letters addressed to his parents that he writes for his grandfather. The assassination of Itō Hirobumi is also a mystery. When the principal gathers the entire school to explain what has happened to the "Number One Politician in the Orient," it sounds like an old-time story to Ryōhei, except for the fact that the principal, as if by magic, produces a newspaper to illustrate the authoritative source of the "terrible big event" that has occurred (p. 151). Ryōhei remains baffled, but at the same time, because of his father's work, he is personally associated with the event to a greater degree than the other students. Nakano provides a child's version of the ritual and the violence surrounding the Japanese imperial expansion of the early twentieth century, as he rephrases the principal's account of the assassination of the elder statesman who had dominated Japanese domestic and foreign affairs since the Meiji Restoration. The last moments of the architect of the emperor-centered constitution, who maneuvered Japanese policy toward Korea in both the Sino- and Russo-Japanese wars, secured Korean acceptance of protectorate status in 1905, and extended total control over Korean domestic politics for his government, are recounted by the son of an employee of the Japanese colonial government. Ryōhei understands most of the words, but since the principal has not explained why the Korean assassin aimed the pistol, the story is simply an interesting tale that is at the same time "strange and weird." In contrast, Ryōhei recognizes the annexation of Korea the following year to be a big event when he reads about it in the newspaper: "Now, Korea seemed to have become Japan." For Ryōhei, the language of the newspaper account is as difficult to understand as the principal's story of Itō's assassination by a Korean nationalist, but he is fascinated by the strange and wonderful photographs accompanying the text. He carefully compares the leader of Japan and the person called His Majesty Lee, who appears alongside the Emperor, and concludes that while the Korean royalty has a beard and is dressed like the Emperor, he cannot compare with his Japanese counterpart, who has both dignity and wisdom (pp. 154, 171–72).

The sensationalized execution of Kōtoku Shūsui and his anarcho-socialist comrades, an event engineered to confirm both the threat of "dangerous thought" and the state's ability to maintain control over internal enemies, also reaches Ryōhei in pictorial form:

> When he opened the magazine there were a number of photos of people lined up. There was also a photograph of a woman. When he read about them he found out it was a story about a trial, but there were characters he couldn't read without their phonetic readings provided so he wasn't too clear what it was about. But they seemed to have been condemned to death. Condemned to death meant they would be killed at the trial he thought. They had tried to kill the Emperor so they were going to be killed ------. (p. 234)[14]

The identities of Kōtoku and the anarchist woman Kanno Suga are foreign to Ryōhei, who cannot pronounce the names or the addresses listed with the pictures until, with a start, he sees Fukui, his own prefecture, listed in the address of one defendant. National history has been brought close to home. The following year it enters Ryōhei's life with much greater definition, with the death of the Emperor. Ryōhei's response to the final marker of Meiji history, the ritualized mourning for the Emperor in July 1912, is consistent with his other attempts to interpret the politics of the adult world. An official proclamation has called the schoolchildren back from summer recess, and within only a few days all of the grammar school students know the word *ryōan*, or national mourning. Again, Ryōhei understands only up to a point. The "prayer" seems different from the everyday family prayer to the Buddha, and the boy decides that somehow the worship must be analogous to his prayer to the guardian deity of tooth cavities, but the adults appear to be taking the replacement of one emperor by another much too seriously. Both the newspapers and the adults respond as though "the heavens and the earth had grown pitch dark," when this was something "that just plain happened in every family" (pp. 272–73).

To the child, the end of the era has meaning insofar as it impinges on his own perceived needs; he has no sense of belonging to a national community. Since his grandmother's death and the return of his parents and younger sisters to Korea, he has been enjoying the company of his grandfather, and the stir made by the grown-ups has ended this idyll. His grandfather awakens him so that they can bow in prayer, facing Tokyo, at the moment the funeral procession is to leave the palace. The Meiji Restora-

---

[14] Kanno Suga was executed for treason with Kōtoku and ten others in January 1911. Twelve others charged with treason were sentenced to life imprisonment, and two of the twenty-six convicted after a secret trial received lighter sentences in an event that has been compared with the Dreyfuss and Sacco-Vanzetti trials. See H. D. Harootunian, "The Problem of Taishō," in *Japan in Crisis*, ed. Bernard S. Silberman and H. D. Harootunian (Princeton: Princeton University Press, 1974), pp. 23–24.

tion has ended, and according to his grandfather they should be grateful because, whatever one said, one had to admit that everything had changed totally since the "Augustrestoration." The child who deduces that his grandfather's slurred word refers to the Meiji Restoration cannot know that the term *goisshin* (which can be translated as either "august renewal" or "august renovation") was the popular term for the changes demanded during the final years of feudal rule. Moreover, he cannot know that it was also the word mobilized by the new revolutionary leadership, which ruled by wielding the institution of the Emperor, the most powerful political symbol of continuity in the Japanese tradition, as it began its project of consolidating centralized rule.[15] It is not merely the terminology of the moment that baffles Ryōhei; he does not understand his grandfather's experience of the end of the era because he has no clear images of the beginning and thus no sense of transformation. The history of the Meiji Restoration has only come to him in impressionistic narration by his grandmother. Pieced together, these stories about peasant revolt and official and state retribution form a family folklore that is also a village history of mythic quality.

Ryōhei plays with his grandmother's version of the transition from Tokugawa to Meiji history, but recent history, comprising the various national crises of his own lifetime relayed in publications and pronouncements, merely intrigues him. In *Pear Flowers*, only the visit to the village of the Crown Prince, son of the Meiji Emperor, pushes Ryōhei into an emotional involvement beyond his usual analytical response to events. This is the second imperial visit to Ryōhei's area. A proclamation had first gone out in 1888, and the entire village had gone to worship the Emperor the year before the constitution was issued. The date is inscribed in the memories of Ryōhei's grandparents because of the fire that had burned down much of the village when it was left vacant by the worshippers. The Emperor had been included in the village oral history because he had given money to each of the one hundred affected households. Now, one generation later, his son has been sent for the villagers to greet, yet Ryōhei's grandmother is not interested. In contrast, Ryōhei joins in the preparations with great alacrity, for his curiosity has been whetted by class-

[15] Nakano puts the word *goisshin* into the phonetic *katakana*, reproducing the sound of the word as Ryōhei would hear it. The phrasing of "the august renewal of all things" in the Edict of Restoration issued by the new Meiji government in 1868 made use of the concept of "imperial renewal" called for by antiloyalist activists who had called for centralized rule by the Emperor. At the same time the bureaucratic term appropriated folk belief as it implied the millenarian urge for "world renewal" expressed during the explosive peasant uprisings of the 1860s. The peasant's ideal of "renewing the world" was combined with the honorific prefix to imply that the revolution of a coalition of feudal leaders and court nobles had been wrought by the new Emperor. For a discussion of this dual aspect of the term *goisshin* see Tōyama Shigeki, *Meiji ishin to gendai* (Iwanami shinsho, 1968), pp. 14–15.

room stories of the imperial grandchildren, who are so virtuous that they waste not even pencil stubs (pp. 120–22).

On the day of the event Ryōhei still has no idea what it means to go see and greet the Crown Prince, but he listens eagerly to the principal's announcement of the visitor's itinerary and notes how the flag has been raised in front of the school, far from the route. In town, police patrol on bicycle, and when Ryōhei hears a warning against worshipping the Crown Prince from the second floor he understands: "It seemed you could worship anywhere, but it had to be from a place that was lower than the rickshaw" (pp. 121, 131–34, 139). The teacher then alerts the children as to the configuration of the procession. The Crown Prince will come in a rickshaw, and his rickshaw will be the third from the front, after the police automobile and the police official's bicycle. When he leaves the castle tower there will be three pistol shots, and two minutes later the police car will come by. Ryōhei hears the shots, begins to worry that he will miss seeing the Crown Prince, and in an anticlimactic rush recognizes his fear to be well-founded. He makes note of the dissatisfaction of his classmates, remarking that "it was different from saying they had not seen him. But it was also different from saying they had." He is impressed by those who have the courage to admit they had not seen the visitor and unmoved by the teacher's exhortations to study hard because theirs is one of the few elementary schools in Japan to have the privilege of seeing the face of the Crown Prince. Later the news coverage of the annexation of Korea confirms his suspicion. He had indeed not seen the man with the "dumbish" face in the army uniform; he had missed the Crown Prince (pp. 144–46, 172–73).

This fictional account of the relationship of the Japanese people to the imperial symbol in Meiji Japan as viewed through the eyes of a child is corroborated in the memoirs of the leading socialist thinker, Yamakawa Hitoshi. Yamakawa recalls how in the Okayama countryside of his childhood, where villagers would form festive processions to attend a viewing, it was said that anyone who saw the Emperor would be blinded, and that a boy given the chance to pray to the Emperor would rise in the world. In spite of such concerns, the Emperor had gone by so fast that most had prayed to the imperial carriage. Yamakawa's conclusion, that because of this he has neither gone blind nor succeeded in life, is lighter and more direct than Nakano's allusion to an elusive being with a "dumbish face." But a more significant difference is Nakano's focus on the Crown Prince rather than on the Meiji Emperor, who visited Yamakawa's home in 1885, during one of his more than one hundred "imperial excursions" in an era of imperial visibility. Nakano points to the second Japanese monarch following the Meiji Restoration, the Taishō Emperor, who would travel through the countryside in a closed sedan outfitted with made-to-order arm-rests, constructed to give the appearance that the unengaged leader was in fact greeting his subjects in active salute en route from To-kyo to his seaside retreat.[16]

The scene in *Pear Flowers* representing the absent presence of the Em-peror is about the preparation for transition to a new imperial reign. Moreover, it is also about a central irony of Taishō political history, the truth that while the ideology and structures constructed to buttress the position of the Emperor were firmly in place by the time of the demise of the first Emperor, his successor could not in any way actively support the system. Yet while *Pear Flowers* alludes to Taishō history, to conclude that Nakano's account of a Meiji boyhood was merely a history of the follow-ing era in disguise would be to deny its focus on a child's experience of historical transition. For not only does the work give the reader a sense of late Meiji politics, it is also a history of the end of storytelling in Japanese history.

According to Walter Benjamin, before the modern era, the storyteller repeated the experience of others for the members of an audience who would interpret the oral chronicles, thereby enriching their imaginations. In contrast, the newspaper debases experience by replacing it with infor-mation accompanied by deadening explication.[17] Nakano's novel raises this issue because Ryōhei's discovery of history is mediated by the Meiji press. *Pear Flowers* is about the insertion of the newspaper and the mass magazine into village experience. The second stage of Nakano Shigeha-ru's changing song of the 1920s, his concern for the reproduction of cul-ture, is thereby worked out in its pages.

At first print culture and oral tradition coexist in *Pear Flowers*. When Ryōhei is learning to read borrowed newspapers, two storytellers visit his village. He listens to his elders recall recent history in a jumpy narrative that leaps from the present into the past and from the global to the village in particular: "first there was talk about the annexation of Korea, and that became talk about the Russo-Japanese War and then that turned into discussion about the soldier's physical examination." He is not sure whether he is listening to truth or myth, to facts or lies, when the host's son's failure to pass the conscription physical is attributed to the large size of his nostrils, but because he knows about the war he is able to follow the gist of the convoluted story, told by the storytellers, of a young

---

[16] Yamakawa Hitoshi, *Aru bonjin no kiroku* (Asahi shimbunsha, 1927), pp. 125–26. Tsurumi Shunsuke characterizes the Taishō era as a reign of an incompetent Emperor who is incapable of making any determinations. Tsurumi, "Taishōki no bunka," pp. 291–92.

[17] Walter Benjamin, "The Storyteller: Reflections on the Works of Nikolai Leskov," in *Illuminations*, ed. Hannah Arendt, trans. Harry Zohn (New York: Schocken Books, 1969), pp. 83–84.

Japanese soldier who falls in love with the daughter of a Russian general (pp. 184-87). By the time of the execution of Kōtoku Shūsui, Ryōhei is deciphering contemporary history in print form, but when the Emperor dies, Ryōhei finds out that the citizens of Tokyo and Osaka have heard the news from special editions of the newspaper that have not reached his village. In Ryōhei's community the communications of Benjamin's artisanal teller of history who works outside of historical categories are ending, although they have not been fully replaced by the reportage of the press.

Ryōhei's experience in *Pear Flowers* is an account of a revolutionary explosion of information and its absorption by a populace of literate consumers one generation after the Meiji Restoration. During the first decade of Meiji rule, when the government recognized that the creation of a national newspaper audience could aid its task of creating a nation of citizens, the newspaper had provided a public forum for community events as villagers gathered to listen to Shinto priests, Buddhist monks, and local officials read and explain the news. A number of daily papers entered the village at government behest and expense, and the press had played an important role in generating political consciousness for and against the new government in the opening decades of Meiji. By the end of the Russo-Japanese War, not only was the newspaper responsible for political polemic and popularization of policy, it was also used to generate profits. The press had been established as part of big business (p. 167).[18]

Taking advantage of new print technology, the newspaper producers competed to reach the broadest audience. By 1905, the extra or special edition was one of many gimmicks employed to package the paper in order to cater to private interests. The newspaper-sponsored competition was another gimmick. With the active encouragement of the press, consumers vied for success in this most public version of the Meiji ideology of getting ahead (*risshin shusse*) and gained a place in a new pantheon of national figures by virtue of such feats as guessing the mileage of railroad tracks. Readers joined running, swimming, and beauty contests and studied the results of movie star popularity contests.[19]

[18] Regarding the history of the public consumption of the newspaper, see Yamamoto Taketoshi, *Shimbun to minshū* (Kinokuniya shoten, 1973), pp. 46–48. The publication of newspapers, which were often shared among villagers, more than doubled between 1904 and the end of the Russo-Japanese War.

[19] Sixteen-year-old Suehiro Hiroko, the winner of the first beauty contest in Japan, was one of the celebrities created by the media. She made headlines at the same time as the two rickshaw runners who gained acclaim for running twelve hours nonstop, but scandal accompanied fame as Miss Suehiro was dismissed from the Peer's school and the *Yorozuchōhō* berated its competitor for encouraging human beings to run from four in the morning until four in the afternoon. For an account of the contests sponsored by the press and the scandal

The looks as well as the content of the newspaper changed as the imagery of advertisements began to dominate the printed page. Advertisements had first appeared in the early years of the Meiji era, and by the turn of the century page-sized ads, diamond-shaped ads, ads purposefully produced upside down, and ads printed sideways were all calculated to attract the reader. By the end of the Russo-Japanese War the advertising news had become an integral part of the paper, as ads for patent medicine like sen-sen and for cosmetics had taken over.[20] The newspaper was a commodity used to sell other commodities in an increasingly capitalist culture.[21]

While the Taishō era, especially its closing years in the late 1920s, has been cited in the history books as the decadent interlude of middle-class consumption, Nakano Shigeharu's writing points to the fact that even before early Taishō, an entire nation was being urged to consume. Ryōhei encounters this phenomenon when his grandfather asks him to monitor the newspaper for photographs of the Emperor because such parts of the newsprint are not for outhouse use. While he finds few photographs, in the course of his search he detects a pattern on the pages. For example, below the theater article is a "story" about Misono powder accompanied by a photograph of a person who appears to be an actor. No matter how many times he reads this, the boy cannot understand the language of this text (p. 169).

Nakano's account of late Meiji culture also refers to the proliferation of magazines. By the end of the first decade of Meiji, over 180 magazines had made their national debut, in formats organized for specialized audiences. For example, Ryōhei's window to the world, *Shōnen sekai*, was a sell-out commanding three printings when it first appeared in book-

involving Suehiro, see Haruhara Akihiko, *Nihon shimbun tsūshi* (Gendai jaanarizumu shuppankai, 1969), pp. 122–24.

[20] On the history of newspaper advertising in Japan see Haruhara, *Nihon shimbun tsūshi*, pp. 43–44, 65–66, 91, and 98–101; Ono Hideo, *Nihon shimbun hattatsu shi* (Osaka: Mainichi shinbunsha, 1922), pp. 340–48; Yamamoto Fumio, *Nihon shimbun shi* (Kokusai shuppan kabushikigaisha, 1948), pp. 241–43; and Yamamoto Taketoshi, *Kōkoku no shakai shi* (Hōsei daigaku shuppan kyoku, 1984). The Jintan Company, the corporation singled out by Nakano in *Pear Flowers*, was in the lead in the production of posters advertising its product. On the advertising innovations of this company, see Yamamoto, *Kōkoku no shakai shi*, pp. 52, 55, 60–61, 195–98.

[21] When half of the special morning edition of the *Jiji shimpō* advertisement commemorating the Emperor's birthday on November 3, 1899, was covered with advertisements, the Emperor of Japan was but one of many items being sold to the Japanese public in the daily newspaper. The fact that Dentsū, the first advertising agency in Japan, was established in 1901, little more than a year after the last political support to the constitutional monarchy had been put into place, confirms this transition from the era of consolidation of a national public to the demand for private priorities encouraged during the Taishō reign. Haruhara, *Nihon shimbun tsūshi*, pp. 91, 98.

stores nationwide in 1897. Along with *Chūgaku sekai* (Junior high world), which appeared the following year, it was to entertain and educate Japanese boys into the Shōwa era. In the pages of another mass-produced magazine, *Taiyō*, Ryōhei comes across the trial of Kōtoku Shū-sui, but he is most influenced by *Shōnen sekai* and *Nihon shōnen*. In *Pear Flowers*, when Ryōhei discovers a new language written by a poet who illustrates his verse in these magazines, Nakano provides a fictional rendering of his reminiscences about his earliest reading habits. Ryōhei does not understand much of the vocabulary, but he adopts it as his own, re-reading passages, reciting them aloud, and memorizing parts by heart with the same intensity he has expended on analyzing pictures. Another author introduces Ryōhei to the world outside the village, in a feature combining fairy tales with childhood reminiscences, and travel articles written from Germany. It is this author who provides a story about the "darkie boy" who is tricked into eating his own mother. Ryōhei attempts to interpret the morality in the story through an analysis of the illustration. Yet his determination, based on a close reading of picture and text, that a Western boy has tricked the African child does not alleviate his disgust with this unnecessary cruelty (pp. 239–42, 299).[22]

The hero of *Pear Flowers* reads with religious zeal, absorbing all facets of the printed world allowed into his corner of Japan. Reading is a pleasure that the child pursues with speed, breadth, and passion, underlining passages as he moves forward. He takes special interest in the red pages of advertisements for additional books. Ryōhei reads advertisements and illustrations as avidly as he devours such varied writings as Buddhist hymns and the *Illustrated Bulletin of the Russo-Japanese War*. When he finds a pretty picture of two students in a field under a sky of billowy clouds, he is more interested in how the artist has created a picture composed of a myriad of tiny lines than in the story represented by the image. When he is struck by the beauty of a picture entitled "Pear Flowers" in *Nihon shōnen*, the youthful connoisseur realizes that pictures can make him look at the world differently. It is a reproduction of an oil painting, it is beautiful, and until that moment he had never once considered pear flowers to be a thing of beauty. But upon testing his first impression he finds it confirmed: "The pear flowers were in bloom. And they were really beautiful. It was just as the picture said" (pp. 298–99, 302, 333).

In addition to the newspaper photograph and the magazine illustration, Ryōhei has access to the moving picture. In *Pear Flowers*, Nakano uses the peasant martyr, Sakura Sōgorō, to talk about the power of the

---

[22] "Darkie boy" is the translation for the Japanese racist epithet *kuronbō*. The poet is Arimoto Hōsui (1886–1976), who published poems monthly in *Nihon shōnen*. Nakano also refers to the illustrator Takehisa Yumeji (1884–1934).

cinema and to problematize the continual reinterpretation of culture as it is reproduced. The association by Ryōhei's neighbors of Kanno Suga, the convicted anarchist companion of Kōtoku Shūsui, with Sōgorō is a clear illustration of Anne Walthall's history of the appropriation and reproduction of the Sōgorō myth for varying political ends. Ryōhei's elders have appropriated the image of Sōgorō as class hero, sacrificing himself for peasants, and Kanno is equated with Sōgorō.[23] Thus a traditional figure is used to challenge the ruling of the state against its critics. Culture has been reproduced in order to make a political statement, but for Ryōhei the power of the symbol of Sōgorō also derives from the technical aspect of reproduction of Sōgorō as screen idol, for Ryōhei recalls the hero from the movies. When his elders mention the martyr, Ryōhei remembers how he had loved the way Sakura Sōgorō, outfitted with a short sword, a cape, and the straw sandals of a peasant, moved toward him on screen: "That same Sōgorō started bobbing along when he came walking this way. Each time he put a foot forward, his head, all of it from the shoulders upward, went bobbing up and down. Why did it get so high and then go down so low, he wondered" (p. 237).

Ryōhei has never seen anyone walk like that, and he cannot decide whether or not he is witnessing a fiction. His version of Sōgorō provides a noteworthy twist to Walthall's conclusion that the worship of peasant martyrs in postwar Japan has been a means of maintaining a sense of local community and identity against the onslaught of a hegemonizing mass culture. Here mass culture dominates local custom, for Ryōhei is concerned not with Sōgorō's moral stance but with the new body language of film gestures. This is but one of the many languages intersecting in *Pear Flowers*, which has been acclaimed for its incorporation of local dialect but has not been studied for its multiplicity of speech-types, or for the hero's response to contesting dialogues, the subject of the third stage of Nakano's changing song.[24]

In Ryōhei's village, the constantly shifting lines between languages demarcate a fragmented rural geography, for Ryōhei's home is not a *kyō-dōtai*, the organic community suspended in time, celebrated by Japanese scholars of an unchanging rural tradition. One single line does not separate the traditional from the modern. Instead, within the village the adult is distanced from the child, the soldier from the civilian, the landlord from the tenant, the father from the son, girls from boys, and men from women. Teaching is not talking, nor is it the same to pray as to mourn or to swear as to sing. The spatial dividing lines extend far beyond the village

[23] Anne Walthall, "Japanese *Gimin*: Peasant Martyrs in Popular Memory," *American Historical Review* 91, 5 (December 1986): 1076–1102.

[24] For responses to Nakano's use of dialect as opposed to language, see Kimura, *Nakano Shigeharuron: shi to hyōron*, p. 273, and Hotta, "Ryōhei to Shigeharu," pp. 288–89.

confines, but within the village boundaries languages define households, separate schoolyard from schoolroom, and isolate rich homes from poor families. Ryōhei also hears alien dialects—the village is not the town, the town not the city; Tokyo is different from Osaka. There is an almost unfathomable national language of politics, there is the talk from the past, and finally, there is the language brought in from abroad. *Pear Flowers*, most often read as yet another example of the ubiquitous I-novel, is in fact a sustained illustration of Bakhtin's theory of the relationship of language to state, society, and the novel:

> The internal stratification of any single national language into social dialects, characteristic group behavior, professional jargons, generic languages, languages of generations and age groups, tendentious languages, languages of the authorities, of various circles, and of passing fashions, languages that serve the specific sociopolitical purposes of the day, even of the hour (each day has its own slogan, its own vocabulary, its own emphases)—this internal stratification present in every language at any given moment of its historical existence is the indispensable prerequisite for the novel as a genre.[25]

Ryōhei accepts the varied languages contained within the Meiji village as natural; they are given. Only at the very end of the book, when he leaves home and begins to study English, is his innocence challenged (pp. 384–85).

A multiplicity of languages is classified and annotated by the child participant-observer. In one representative passage of analysis he examines the use of the term *washi*, one of the many ways to say "I," after a transfer student from the big castle-town of Kanazawa, a white-faced boy in a print kimono, is interrogated in the schoolyard for the ostensible crime of saying the word. Ryōhei responds by mentally cataloguing those entitled to use *"washi,"* as he intuits how language can mark power. The list excludes children and farmers and includes the town doctor, the priest who is an officer returned from the Russo-Japanese War, and "most probably" the local chief of police (pp. 68–70).

In a variation on the same theme of regional variation and its political implications, the boy rejects the following passage in his reader because it does not conform to his experience:

> Happy New Year's time has come around.
> The boys raise high their octopuses and play.
> The girls have their shuttlecock at play.
> It is a peaceful New Year's Day.

(p. 58)

[25] M. M. Bakhtin, *The Dialogic Imagination*, ed. Michael Holquist, trans. Caryl Emerson and Michael Holquist (Austin: University of Texas Press, 1981), pp. 262–63.

Ryōhei does not recognize that *tako* is a homonym for both octopus and kite in Japanese, but his interpretation of the text is sophisticated. He senses that a cultural hegemony is being exercised, and he refuses to respond to this attempt to impose Tokyo culture on a village that is too snow-bound for even kite flying and too poor for the girls to own either fine kimonos or battledore racquets. Ryōhei does not read these differences as a sign of inequity but rather sees the textbook story as an attempt to impose urban ideals on village life. At the same time he strains to classify the differences among cities, sensing that while all cities band together in their attitudes toward the village, Tokyo is a very different place from the provincial city of Maruoka (pp. 58–59, 65–66).

Although Ryōhei does make distinctions, his education has not prepared him to negotiate the class nature of language. When he enters junior high school in a nearby city, he is overwhelmed. Not only do the children of large merchants and officials who now surround him in the classroom speak a different language, they also know what dictionaries to buy to expand their knowledge and therefore their power. In addition to learning their version of Japanese, Ryōhei is faced with the task of mastering English. Language becomes a source of anxiety for him. In the village he had been able to demystify foreign ways of speaking, and he had guessed at verbal and pictorial meanings. His study of English is accompanied by no such aural or visual guideposts, resulting in overwhelming, inexplicable terror that can barely be articulated. This constant anxiety spoils his experience of beauty, and when he returns home for a visit, the pear flowers have lost their lure. He cannot remember how they ever could have appeared beautiful. By then one new word in his repertoire is *heiki*, "it doesn't matter." The wonder of childhood is gone (pp. 354, 372–73).

The novel thus closes by illustrating the denial of dialogue, the fourth and final theme of Nakano Shigeharu's Taishō song. As will be shown, the denial of language was not total during the early 1930s, for Nakano refused to stop writing even after he had been jailed. This determination to wield language in order to protest the abuse of power is illustrated by a rebellion in *Pear Flowers* that takes place in Ryōhei's elementary school classroom. When the teacher leaves the classroom one student climbs onto the dais in the front of the room to mimic the instructor's call to order, another begins to recite a popular tongue-twisting word-game, and, inspired by its rhythms, the children are soon chanting a chain of terms, each of which begins with the last syllable of the previous word, and the sum of which shames the Russian naval commander felled at the Battle of Port Arthur.[26] In one of the few moments of the novel that re-

---

[26] The words of the ditty are *tanuki/kintama/fundoshi/shimeta/tanuki*, which translates as badger/balls/loincloth/knotted/badger. Ibid., pp. 255–56.

cord Ryōhei's voice, he challenges his classmates to string all of the syllables together at break-neck speed so as to form one long word without repeating parts. The children are impressed when no one can match his dexterity, and the hero receives an ovation; this is Ryōhei's moment of glory. When, upon discovering the mutiny, the teacher retaliates by designating each of the day's classes as a "reading period" because the students have not exhibited respect and refers to them as "pigs and cats not deserving of an education," Ryōhei again takes action. Employing the emphasis of irony, he rubs out the designation for the different class periods on the board hanging in front of the classroom and puts the teacher's punishment into words by writing "reading period" in each of the six spaces allotted to different subjects (pp. 257–58). He has resisted the censorship of the children's song by advertising it, just as the adult Nakano continued to publish indirect indictments of state policy in the 1930s after he and his colleagues in the Proletarian Literature Movement had been disciplined into silence through censorship and imprisonment.

While the four stages of Nakano Shigeharu's Taishō consciousness can be found in *Pear Flowers*, to conclude that this account of a Meiji boyhood is merely a history of a Taishō youth in disguise would be to ignore the artifacts of Meiji culture presented within the work—the Jintan sign, the advertisement for cosmetics, the newspaper photographs celebrating the conquest of Korea, the emerging legends contributing to a local history of the Meiji Restoration articulated in rural dialect, the boys' magazine with its own myths and new national heroes, and the textbooks and dictionaries to teach the Meiji schoolchild foreign words and the Japanese language. Nonetheless, the historical issues raised by an examination of these artifacts—the central place of the cultural commodity in the consciousness of the Japanese citizen, the presentation of empire in the pictures in the press, the creation of historical narrative in an era dominated by the media, and the use of language to articulate and to change history—were Nakano Shigeharu's intellectual and political concerns during the Taishō era, the period almost untouched in his overtly autobiographical writings. In this sense *Pear Flowers* was Nakano's contribution to the intense self-examination by Japanese intellectuals who during the late 1940s and 1950s attempted to integrate their prewar revolutionary legacy with the wartime failure of Marxist thinkers who had dominated the intellectual world of the late 1920s and 1930s. It was, in this sense, the sequel to *Churning* that the postwar intellectuals had sought, which does not preclude yet another interpretation of *Pear Flowers* as a product of its moment of production—as a commentary on the end of the postwar era and the beginning of a reconstituted culture of consumerism accompanying the economic growth of the 1960s and early 1970s.

There is no easy answer as to why Nakano chose to avoid direct reference to his youth, and no empirical proof that his aim in writing *Pear Flowers* was to discuss Taishō culture in its Meiji form. What is undeniable is that to break the silences imposed on it and on the populace at large during the war, and to rethink a cultural politics, the Japanese literary left had to understand its own prewar history. Central to that history was the revolutionary fervor of Taishō culture. Nakano's Taishō critique of culture is available in his writings from that era, if not in any memoirs, and will be reconstructed in the chapters that follow. His Taishō biography, pieced together through limited pieces of memoir and through the reminiscences of his contemporaries, comprises the remainder of this chapter.

TAISHŌ IMAGES

In an essay written in 1936, Nakano Shigeharu looked back on his high school years as a time of feverish intellectual activity when he had read all of the contemporary Japanese authors he could find, and consumed *Crime and Punishment* in one day-long sitting, before moving on to *The Brothers Karamazov*. In this brief memoir he touched on his study of the traditional thirty-one-syllable form of poetry, with the introductory aside, "And also I came to know *tanka*."[27] Forty years later, in the afterword to his collected poetry and prewar fiction, he would elaborate on his early relationship to Japanese poetry. He then recalled how in the spring of 1919 he had been drawn "from a world containing only folktales" into the world he would inhabit until 1924, a world containing modern Japanese poetry, the modern tanka, contemporary fiction, a certain type of modern criticism, and foreign literature. In addition to Murō Saisei, the local poet laureate who would become his teacher, and Satō Haruo, he listed such modern Japanese literary figures as Hagiwara Sakutarō, Takamura Kōtarō, Shimazaki Tōson, Kikuchi Kan, Akutagawa Ryūnosuke, and Tanizaki Junichirō as influences. Nakano downplayed the influence of the premodern Japanese heritage, stating merely that he had also read "quite a lot of Japanese works from the past."[28] The life of the literary youth who published his first work in his high school literary magazine thus appears similar in both accounts, but the second account is different. It reveals that Taishō politics had also been present in everyday high school life in the Fourth Higher School in Kanazawa, which Nakano attended from September 1919 to the spring of 1924. In the 1976 essay he recalls meeting people involved in famine relief efforts for postrevolutionary Russia, remembers the formation of a social issue

[27] Nakano, "Waga bungakuteki jiden," *NSZ* 22:9–10 [Shinchō 8/36].
[28] Nakano, "Chosha ushirogaki: seiriteki yōshōnenki to bungakuteki shōseinenki," *NSZ* 1:488.

study group, and mentions having been confronted with a series of deaths. Here the cultural and the political are merged in the notation of the suicide of Taishō writer Arishima Takeo, the massacre of Koreans after the Kantō earthquake in 1923, and the murder of the anarchist Ōsugi along with his family. Nakano's contention is that he was not especially aware of the social currents surrounding him, because he had been a passive, unfocused adolescent.

This, of course, is the image of the young hero of A Farewell to Song, a work written in 1939, which, like the 1930s version of Nakano's memories of high school, emphasizes culture at the expense of politics. The main character, Yasukichi, like Nakano, is forced to repeat two years of classes. The work also echoes Nakano's participation in cultural activities as documented in the nenpu. Yasukichi is a member of the school literary arts magazine and a participant in a local poetry group, but the hypocrisy of the would-be artists in the poetry-writing circle forces him to leave the world of the traditional Japanese poem. He bids a "farewell to song," setting off for university life in the big city because he is convinced that in Tokyo culture he will not find the snares of tradition. In sum, Yasukichi is portrayed as a loner. He maintains a self-conscious distance from his colleagues at school and in the poetry-writing collective.

A Farewell to Song has been widely treated as a roman à clef about a self-conscious adolescent with pretensions to poetry,[29] but the reader has recourse to other contrasting images from histories and memoirs. Nakano's references (in fiction and memoir) to the literary discussions in dormitory and classroom barely begin to capture the atmosphere of the all-encompassing culture of the elite higher school in which, by the turn of the century, the privileged Japanese adolescent had created a highly ritualized subculture, but the historian Don Roden provides an evocative overview of these new traditions: "Custom dictated the way a student must talk (in a manly, forceful tone), the way he dressed (in a worn-out, slightly tattered school uniform), the way he slept (in a mildewy bedroll that never saw the light of day), the way he studied after midnight (only by candlelight), the way he walked down the street (with a pronounced swagger), even the way he relieved himself in his bedroom without traipsing down to the appropriate ground-floor facilities (by simply opening the window)."[30] Roden's history of student culture gives context to Nakano's five years in the Kanazawa higher school as a time when investigation of cultural and political issues came into vogue. Scattered additional sparse images also serve to place him in this culture.

[29] See, for example, Kimura Hideo, Nakano Shigeharu: shi to hyōron, p. 237, and Hirano Ken, "Hito to bungaku," p. 503.

[30] Donald Roden, Schooldays in Imperial Japan (Berkeley: University of California Press, 1980), p. 111.

One former classmate recalls Nakano's love of the German language when the other literary youths were devouring Russian and French literature in translation. Nakano was a member but also a pensive loner who separated himself from the youths who drank chilled wine out of thick glasses at a hole-in-the-wall bar in Kanazawa following afternoons out rowing. The youth was fond of boating, but instead of joining in the antics of his companions, he would row with all of his might "and then sat staring at the water and the sky." He would also stand silently at the edge of the baseball field to observe the students at play. His recurrent absence from the classroom, and therefore from the group, is also remembered. Moriyama Kei offers the image of Nakano Shigeharu dashing into the Cafe Brazil. The young Nakano entered the popular student haunt in the old castle-town of Kanazawa decked out in a brand new blazer, his red neck-tie flowing, a white rose in his lapel. The dandyism could elicit such a vivid memory undoubtedly because it was in stark contrast to Nakano's usual grimy mien. Although it was an integral part of higher school culture to appear unkempt, accounts of contemporaries suggest that Nakano may have developed the style into an art. This is in any case the image retained by Nakano's mentor, Murō Saisei, who recalls his astonishment upon discovering that the author of such fine poetry could be the young man in old clothing made shiny with grit who planned to live until the age of seventy, and to be able by then to write a good lyric poem. In Murō's account, as in the other brief pieces, Taishō political history remains in the background, yet it is certain that by the time of the earthquake of 1923, when Murō returned to Kanazawa and met Nakano, the youth from the farm village, who had adopted the affectations of the insular high school subculture, was determined to be a successful writer.[31]

The next stage of Nakano Shigeharu's education is also represented in fictional form. In 1940, one year after *A Farewell to Song* had left the hero anticipating Tokyo life, *City Walks* provided a narrative about bewilderment with the customs of Tokyo. *Churning*, the much longer work about the college years of the same character, was published in serialized form in 1954, almost fifteen years after *City Walks*. It is the site of Nakano's fullest self-portrait of his years as a university student activist in Tokyo from the spring of 1924 until his graduation in March 1927. He is again, as in *A Farewell to Song*, a marginal member of a student community, but now it is within the context of the politically charged atmosphere of the Shinjinkai (New Man Society) of Tokyo Imperial University, whose student members were committed to the study of the Marxist classics, consumed by the need for austere reforms in their personal lives,

---

[31] See Moriyama Kei, "Hattan: gakusei jidai no Nakano Shigeharu san ni kansuru danpen," *Shin Nihon bungaku* 388 (December 1979): 36. Murō's reminiscence includes his remonstrance to the aspiring poet: "the prettiest thing about you has got to be that face." Murō Saisei, "Shiyū no koto," in *Nakano Shigeharu kenkyū*, ed. Hirano Ken, pp. 432, 434.

and dedicated to the goal of a proletarian revolution in postearthquake Tokyo.

In the Shinjinkai drinking was forbidden and all humor shunned, as the students cultivated an intensely self-conscious dedication to the political struggle marked by night-long debate and self-criticism sessions. The all-male Fourth Higher School subculture had provided a form of relationship not available in the family setting left behind in the towns and villages of Meiji and early Taishō Japan, but the student activists of the Shinjinkai willingly replicated aspects of the social structure they wished to destroy. These young men advocated the male bonding encouraged by an educational system that excluded women from the elite schools and reproduced aspects of the patriarchal family system emerging from the Meiji settlement. These "new men" hired house mothers to serve the prescribed Meiji role of the "wise mother" dedicated to the education of an enlightened male citizenry by managing their group houses. They also enlisted radical young women colleagues in the student movement to act as "housekeepers." These women, who were useful covers for underground activity, also performed the menial tasks of everyday life. When the young men were ready to leave the shelter of the Shinjinkai house, to commit to a genuine long-term relationship with the opposite sex, more often than not they turned to the state-sanctioned institution of the arranged marriage.[32] In *Churning*, Nakano's hero is an outsider imprisoned within this male society, forced to drink on the sly, behind closed doors. Yasukichi's colleagues in the Shinjinkai communal house adore the Communists and hate the socialists, but he does not know the difference and cannot begin to define either term. His housemates discipline themselves with self-criticism and treat any artistic sensibility with contempt; political organizing is their sole concern. Like Ryōhei, Yasukichi attempts to decipher the language surrounding him, a language that includes such mysterious terms as "hegemony" and "kadett," the latter a term not available in his pocket dictionary. Isolated and defensive, the young writer who divides his time between socially significant study groups and work on the arts magazine he helps to publish responds to his alienation with a defensive cynicism.[33]

According to the *nenpu*, Nakano Shigeharu entered Tokyo Imperial

[32] Henry DeWitt Smith II, *Japan's First Student Radicals* (Cambridge: Harvard University Press, 1972), pp. 176–79, 182–84. The mother of Hayashi Fusao, the proletarian writer who was Nakano's entré into the organization, worked as a house mother for one of the Shinjinkai group houses. Ishidō Kiyotomo, "Shinjinkai jidai no Nakano Shigeharu," *Shin Nihon bungaku* 388 (December 1979): 42–43. For a fairly detailed treatment of the still controversial housekeeper system employed by the Japanese Communist Party into the 1930s, see Murakami Nobuhiko, *Nihon no fujin mondai* (Iwanami shoten, 1981), pp. 154–58.

[33] For a representative illustration of Yasukichi's bewilderment at the new language and his ensuing cynicism, see Nakano, *Muragimo*, pp. 131–39.

University in April 1924. He helped to edit all four issues of *Razō* between January and April 1925, when Murō introduced him to Hagiwara Sakutarō. During the summer of 1925 Nakano joined the Shinjinkai, and in October he helped to organize the Shakai Bungei Kenkyūkai (Social Arts Study Group). By January 1926 he had joined others from the Shinjinkai in active support for the strike undertaken by Kyōdō printers, and in February he was a key organizer of the Marukusushugi Geijutsu Kenkyūkai (Marxist Arts Study Group) at the university. In April 1926 the young activist helped launch *Roba*, the second of a series of journals that would benefit from his creative and editorial work over the next several years. The establishment of *Razō* and *Roba* placed Nakano within a modern Japanese cultural tradition of production of the *dōjin zasshi* (magazine of like-minded people), whereby ten or more writers would pool funds to pay for the printing of the journal and would jointly write, edit, and organize its distribution.[34] The political and cultural activity detailed in the official biographical chronology thus correlates with the environment sketched in *Churning*. But there are some glaring contradictions between the image of Yasukichi and the portrayal of the student activist Nakano Shigeharu by his contemporaries in the political and literary movements of the mid-1920s. These portrayals bear close examination because they contrast so sharply with the figure of Yasukichi in his incarnations as a provincial high school student in *A Farewell to Song* and *City Walks*, and as a would-be activist in *Churning*.

Kamei Katsuichirō, who was active in both the Shinjinkai and the prewar Culture Movement, recalls his first acquaintance with Nakano. It was the summer of 1927, by which time Nakano was leading a busy existence within the student society. Kamei came upon Nakano for the first time at a Shinjinkai dormitory during one of the innumerable political discussions. Repelled by what appeared to be Nakano's lack of personal hygiene and yet attracted at the same time by a "fresh, vulgar atmosphere," he observed the interaction between the long-haired youth clad in a loose loin-cloth and six opponents debating the conditions of the farmer. The insecurity sensed by Kamei is consistent with the image of Yasukichi in *Churning*, but the determination of the young man with the sharply defined jaw who opened his mouth sideways in order to talk in a

---

[34] Nakano published twenty-one free-verse poems, four essays, and a three-part translation of Hans Christian Anderson's autobiography in the four issues of *Razō*. *Roba* was actively supported by such luminaries as Akutagawa Ryūnosuke, Hagiwara Sakutarō, and Nakano's mentor, Murō Saisei. The first issue contained two poems by Nakano along with a translation of Heine. Nakano would continue to publish free verse, literary criticism, and translations in every issue during his last year at the university and in the Shinjinkai. His work appeared in every issue of *Roba* except the final issue. From April 1926 through February 1928, twenty-four poems, four essays, and six translations appeared.

quiet buzz was quite different. Nakano would occasionally turn in Ka-mei's direction "as though to gaze at the green leaves outside the win-dow," and in the words of Kamei, there was always "a brightness in those wide-open eyes; something like a form of panic. It was an insecure gaze like he both did and did not have confidence." Kamei goes on to describe the young man's behavior at a meeting of the Marxist Arts Study Group, which had gathered to debate whether Goethe was greater than the pro-letarian writers. He remembers both Nakano's emphatic declaration, "What's so great about Goethe!" and the same "panic-like look in his eyes" at that moment. According to Kamei's interpretation, Nakano did not deny his assertion, but he was conscious of his own lie. Nakano chose to lie for political purposes, but at the same time he was one of those rare people forced to blush at such cynicism.[35] In *Churning*, Nakano would deny any such act of bad faith by picturing himself as an observer of stu-dent politics who was attracted to the sounds of revolutionary words and yet at the same time unable to engage in dialogue with his contemporar-ies. Such representation is also called into question by the account of Nakano's participation in the Shinjinkai offered by his colleague in that organization, Ishidō Kiyotomo, who warns the reader that *Churning* should not be read as historical documentation of the student movement between 1925 and 1927.

According to Ishidō, Nakano tampered with timing, places, and names. Moreover, political history has been censored, for Nakano does not men-tion the major campus battle over student opposition to military educa-tion, which was led by the Communists who had displaced the liberals as the dominant force in campus politics after the earthquake in 1923.[36] Nakano's colleague of half a century allows for this omission from *Churning*, hypothesizing that Nakano may not have known of the event. It is possible (but not likely) that Nakano was not informed of the student struggle, for according to the *nenpu* he did not move to a Shinjinkai dor-mitory until January of the following year. Ishidō also defends Nakano's absence from the sessions of the Social Arts Study Group devoted to Bukharin's theory of historical materialism, Lenin's *State and Revolution*, and Deborin's analysis of Lenin, allowing that the interests of this new

[35] Kamei Katsuichirō, "Nakano Shigeharu," in *Nakano Shigeharu kenkyū*, ed. Hirano Ken, pp. 455–56.

[36] Ishidō's careful reading of *Muragimo* rebuts any treatment of the novel as a mere re-flection of political history, by showing how dates are misquoted, dormitory sites conflated, and some names quoted while others have been changed. Ishidō, "Shinjinkai jidai no Na-kano Shigeharu," pp. 40–45. In his autobiography, Ishidō places Nakano at the center of student activism, citing Nakano's overwhelming victory in the election for student represen-tative. Ishidō Kiyotomo, *Waga itan no Shōwa shi* (Keisō shobō, 1986), p. 70.

man undoubtedly lay in the sphere of socialist literature and not political theory.[37]

What is crucial for the purposes of reclaiming Nakano is not Ishidō's documentation of Nakano's omissions, but his characterization of Nakano as a highly political student activist. According to Ishidō, Nakano won an overwhelming victory in an election for student representatives and had an uncanny grasp of Marxist thought. The illustration given by Ishidō to show how Nakano's responses to political texts were characterized by a depth lacking in his contemporaries hinges on Nakano's sensitivity to language and on Ishidō's retranslation of an incident recorded in *Churning*. In the fiction, a group is reading a German edition of *State and Revolution* and is translating Lenin's contention that insurrection must be *kunst*. Their dictionary has given them three options for the term, and all have taken for granted the term "technique" over the first synonym, "method." Ishidō, who participated in that debate, recalls that only Nakano chose the third option, "art," to illuminate Lenin's ideal.[38] Nakano was not the dumb-struck bystander portrayed as Yasukichi. Contrary to all of Nakano's accounts of his youth, he did have an understanding of Marxism and a commitment to political action.

Sata Ineko, who was Nakano's protégé in the proletarian literature movement, places Nakano in a setting apart from the campus activity described by Kamei and Ishidō as she describes emotional ties and activity that contrast sharply with Yasukichi's diffidence: "When I recall the Nakano Shigeharu of the *Roba* era, what always comes into view is this image of him walking from these stone gateways into the private walkway. Dressed in slacks and clogs, broad shouldered, he carries a package in both hands. Without raising his face, in one determined line, carrying his parcel he approaches me with his hurried, busy gait."[39] Sata's image is of a friend come to share rice cakes from his home village with the newlywed Sata and her husband, Kubokawa Tsurujirō, a fellow left-wing writer, and a high school classmate of Nakano. She remembers Nakano's blunt exclamation that in the Shinjinkai dormitory no one was about to sit around a hearth to enjoy a homemade treat, and her acceptance of the explanation that the "Marxist" practice of the politicized students did

[37] Ishidō, "Shinjinkai jidai no Nakano Shigeharu," p. 41.

[38] Ishidō places Nakano's theoretical insights in the context of the low level of expertise attained by most Shinjinkai members at this time. Even Nakano was no match for the right-wing constitutional scholar Uesugi Shinkichi. Rather than going down in defeat and humiliation, Uesugi won a much publicized debate with no effort and chastised the group of higher school graduates, under the leadership of Nakano Shigeharu, to "go home and at least read your *Capital*." Ibid., p. 43.

[39] Sata Ineko, *Natsu no shiori* (Shinchōsha, 1983), p. 78.

not allow for the frivolity of such socializing.[40] At the end of 1926 when Sata cooked the *mochi* for herself, her husband, and her husband's colleague from Fourth Higher School days, she knew the Tokyo University activist as a member of a community of young literary bohemians. Her memoirs indicate that Nakano's visit was not merely an escape from the doctrinaire atmosphere of the Shinjinkai. Instead, the young man was affirming bonds with the young couple and his own links with a consciously reconstructed Japanese culture by eating the regional delicacy with a family of friends. Here and elsewhere, Sata's recollections of the man who first encouraged her to become a writer offer exceptional images from the intertwined lives of a close group of young people. The public pronouncements and activities of the decade-long Culture Movement of revolutionary intellectuals have been duly catalogued in the history books, but Sata's history provides a new view of the creation of community among men and women who challenged the mores of late Taishō Japan in the pages of their magazines, on the stage of the revolutionary theater, and in private rituals celebrated during the second half of the 1920s.

Sata's recollections illustrate how the practices of the cultural revolutionaries who also became Nakano's close allies during his last year at the university countered the male prerogatives and the social division of labor legalized in the "Book of Relatives" of the family-centered Meiji Civil Code of 1898. According to the state, social organization in Japan was to be based on the family group or "house" and not on the "individual unit" as in the West. Marriage, the "act by which houses are formed and relatives are called into being," was contingent on permission of family and state: a member of a house needed the consent of the household head in order to marry, along with an official imprimatur. The code emphasized more than once that such union was not official until a government registrar had been notified. The husband was to choose the place of residence for the newlyweds. Within the new family unit, parental power was to be delegated to the head of the household, for the benefit of the child, the public, and the state, and "for the interest of the parent." Thus, within the household two complementary roles were clearly demarcated. The husband was responsible for the "safety and happiness" of his wife, children, and relatives. The interests and tasks relegated to the wife's domain included "the purchase of food, coal, firewood, charcoal, oil, etc.; the making of clothes; the payment of house rent," and other tasks related to clothing, food, and dwelling.[41]

[40] Ibid., p. 80.

[41] See J. E. De Becker, trans., *Annotated Civil Code of Japan*, 4 vols. (London: Butterworth 1910), 2:1, 29, 36–39, 47, 56, 66–67. For discussions of the Civil Code see the Japanese classic on the historical transformation of the family, Kawashima Takeyoshi, *Nihon shakai no kazokuteki kōzō* (Nihon hyōronsha, 1950). See also Sharon Sievers, *Flowers in*

Sata and Kubokawa had broken these rules when, after a brief romance, they had moved into a room vacated by Kubokawa's roommate following an impromptu beer fest subsidized by the mother of another member of the *Roba* collective. When Nakano and the revolutionary actress Hara Masano followed suit four years later, they flaunted both law and custom by adopting the most formal language to announce, by postcard, that two members of their community had granted permission for the nuptials to take place. This appropriation of tradition through the use of honorific language, along with Nakano's acceptance of his bride-to-be's prenuptial negotiation that she would marry him only on the condition that she could continue her work as an actress, should undoubtedly be read as a contestatory slap at official ideology. Yet it was not merely a negative gesture, for the rephrasing of traditional practice in a radically new context, like the partaking of rice-cakes with a family of friends, expressed Nakano's respect for kinship bonds based on shared politics and work in the Culture Movement.[42] The young writer found a place for tradition in his everyday life, a tradition that he modified in practice when he, Sata, Kubokawa, and other *Roba* associates played the premodern card game *hanafuda*: no money changed hands; play was an end in itself. And when Sata's first child was born, Nakano took on an avuncular role by choosing the name of the newest community member, and by presenting the proud parents with a bright red baby quilt—a colorful luxury that would have been considered decadent in the colorless halls of the Shinjinkai. He was rejoicing as a member of an extended family of revolutionary artists.[43]

According to the *nenpu*, one year after his graduation from the university, and from his place in the Shinjinkai, Nakano was part of the residential collective of the Japan Proletarian Arts League and an editor of its journal, *Puroretaria geijutsu*. Sata brings this history to life by providing an image of Nakano's new community, wherein wives addressed husbands with loud familiarity, shunning any use of honorifics. Instead of submitting to any patriarchal authority, they publicly shared the workplace in the league's divisions of literature, theater, music, and art.[44] She

Salt: The Beginnings of Feminist Consciousness in Modern Japan (Stanford: Stanford University Press, 1983), pp. 110–12; and Watanabe Yozo, "The Family and the Law: The Individualistic Premise and Modern Japanese Family Law," in *Law in Japan: The Legal Order in a Changing Society*, ed. Arthur Taylor von Mehren (Cambridge: Harvard University Press, 1963), p. 365.

[42] According to Hara Izumi, Nakano kept his part of the bargain. Interview with Hara Izumi, Tokyo, October 30, 1982. For Sata's account of wedding practices, see Sata, *Natsu no shiori*, pp. 81, 97.

[43] Ibid., p. 95.

[44] Ibid., pp. 85–86.

contributes an image of Nakano from this period: he is singing the Internationale with great gusto, as part of an impromptu chorus.

Sata's memoirs fit into the *nenpu* chronology. One way of reading this chronology is to conclude that after leaving the Shinjinkai, the student society that emphasized political activism, in the spring of 1927, Nakano entered a community that placed primacy on cultural affairs. In other words, the Proletarian Arts League house replaced the Shinjinkai dormitory as the center of Nakano's activism. Alternatively, one can agree with most scholarship on Nakano, which emphasizes how during the 1920s the political writer vacillated between politics and culture. Such an approach presumes Nakano's ambivalence by drawing a line: before graduation the *Roba* writer had organized a strike for the Shinjinkai; after graduation the political organizer of the Proletarian Arts League wrote poetry. On one side of the line, the memoirs of Kamei and Ishidō contradict the portrait presented in *Churning* of a young artist isolated within a community of student activists by giving Nakano a central role in the formulation of political ideals. On the other side, according to Sata's memoirs, Nakano interacts with others in the formulation of a new community dedicated to the production and reformulation of culture. Her account emphasizes the cultural sphere over the realm of politics inhabited by the students debating Lenin's revolutionary strategy. But her image of Nakano's visit also renders politics and culture inseparable because it combines the three columns of everyday life, literary production, and political activism. The portrait of the young political organizer bringing delicacies, sent to him by his family, to his comrades who are challenging established forms of family life serves to highlight the simultaneity of Nakano's political and cultural revolutionary ideals. The social conformity of the Shinjinkai, which was pervaded by questions of political theory and strategy, stood in stark contrast to the practices of the *Roba* community members, who concerned themselves with the creation of new cultural forms, but Nakano did not experience the societies of the students and writers as mutually exclusive arenas.

Nakano's resolution of the supposed tension between political and cultural spheres is not recounted in his autobiographical writings but is evident in his essay "A Fragment on Takuboku." Nakano presented this revisionist account of Ishikawa Takuboku's socialism twice. The essay appeared in the seventh issue of *Roba* in November 1926, but according to the *nenpu*, it had first been offered as a public statement at a Shinjinkai conference on campus earlier that year. In other words, "A Fragment Concerning Takuboku," a text synthesizing questions of political action and cultural practice, crossed the imaginary line between the two supposed spheres of politics and culture. Two different audiences were given the same message as Nakano made his stand both as a student-activist and as a cultural revolutionary.[45]

Nakano's message, in its written form, pretended to offer only "one fragment," but in fact it offered a totalizing vision, because it placed Takuboku within the line of Meiji poets "moving back and forth within Nakano's consciousness."[46] According to Nakano, Kitamura Tōkoku, Hasegawa Futabatei, Kunikida Doppo, and Ishikawa Takuboku shared a characteristic that separated them from other Meiji poets. Rather than aiming to make a completed art, they had worked toward an examination of life in its totality. Nakano gave three reasons for choosing to focus on Takuboku at a time when Nakano and his contemporaries were living "amidst contradiction, unrest, and upheaval." First, Takuboku's life was lived in closest proximity to the present era. Moreover, he had therefore left behind strong views on life and social organization for Nakano's generation to consider. Finally, his many followers were misinterpreting his social thought. Nakano's goal was to reclaim this revolutionary poet through examination of his thought, for Takuboku's poetry could not be understood in the absence of an exploration of his ideas (pp. 3–4). To that end, Nakano charted three succeeding images of Ishikawa Takuboku. In his first stage Takuboku had been a romantic lyric poet. He had dedicated himself to the explication of the relationships among art, life, and social structures during the second stage of his career. During the final stage of his career, Takuboku had transformed himself into a socialist critic dedicated to the explication of the relationships between art and life and art and social structures. To confirm Takuboku's self-definition as socialist, Nakano quotes from a letter written by Takuboku in 1911, at the time of Kōtoku Shūsui's execution, in which Takuboku tells how he had become a "Social Revolutionist" and had "quietly" turned to a "socialistic" way of thinking when he realized that social and economic structures and the family system could not be left in place (pp. 7–8).[47]

Nowhere in this essay on Takuboku did Nakano interject his own experience, but *Roba*'s readers knew that Nakano, too, had turned away from the production of lyric poetry. During the first half of 1925 they had read more than twenty poems about the loneliness of an isolated country boy in the big city in the pages of *Razō*. There had then been one year of silence after the final issue of the magazine in May 1925, and when Nakano's voice reappeared, in *Roba*, like Takuboku in his second phase, he too had begun to explore the relationship between art and social structures. The scathing social commentary in the poems published in *Roba* between its inception in the spring of 1926 and November, when the Ta-

[45] For the reference to the talk on Takuboku, see *Nenpu*, NSZ 28:271. Nakano's essay on Takuboku first appeared in *Roba*, no. 11 (November 1926): 42–52.

[46] Nakano, "Takuboku ni kansuru danpen," NSZ 16:3 [*Roba* 11/26].

[47] The words "Social Revolutionist" and "socialist" are in English in the original.

kuboku essay appeared, had provided ample testimony to Nakano's new way of thinking. Nakano, too, had quietly turned to a revolutionary politics. The connection between Takuboku and Nakano would not have been a tenuous one for the audience listening to the talk at the university as well. They knew him as the leader of a faction of Marxist students in the Shinjinkai dedicated to an exploration of other relationships between Marxism and art. If the readers and listeners had any doubts as to Nakano's agenda, a second letter by Takuboku quoted in Nakano's essay served to further clarify Nakano's thoughts. In this letter, written in August 1911, Takuboku had explained the goal of a certain magazine. The journal was to be more than a literary magazine; it was also to provide the impetus for "a fundamental critique by youth of current social structures, economic structures, political structures, and so forth" (p. 8). This was another statement of Nakano's position that the political and cultural spheres were inseparable. Politics and culture were mutually informing and reinforcing.

Nakano Shigeharu's essay on Ishikawa Takuboku reconciles the tension between politics and art cited by so many readers of Nakano. It also combines the seemingly contradictory images provided by Kamei and Ishidō, on the one hand, and by Sata, on the other, by illustrating the simultaneity of Nakano's everyday life, literary production, and political activism during the years when Nakano was a college student, a member of a literary magazine, and a Marxist political activist. However, one contradiction does emerge from the memoirs of Nakano's three contemporaries, a contradiction created by a significant silence. In all three biographical fragments, Nakano Shigeharu is a Marxist, but aside from Ishidō's reference to Nakano's facility with the language of Marxism, nowhere do his contemporaries discuss how or why this claim is merited.

Nakano himself admitted to a silence, if not to this particular absence. He said that his so-called autobiographical trilogy was fictional and "not documentation." While it was based on his years at the Fourth Higher School and at Tokyo Imperial University between 1919 and 1927, it fictionalized his experience because of the exigencies of form, time, and politics. He had always intended to write fictional accounts about the student days of one individual, but even serious intentions of recording his own experiences could not withstand the loss of detail to the passing of time, nor the censorship imposed on writing during the war, when the first two novels were written. He did not mention the presence of self-censorship, but this factor was undoubtedly at work when Nakano decided, in 1954, to depict his hero in *Churning* as an apolitical cynic, an image at odds with the accounts of Kamei, Ishidō, and Sata.[48] It must also have been at

---

[48] Nakano, "Chosha ushorogaki: hitotsu no kōtōgakkōki to hitotsu no daigakuki," *NSZ* 5:407–13.

work when Nakano wrote one of his only accounts of his entrance into the revolutionary life of Taishō Japan:

> Around 1925, 1926, and 1927, at the time I was a university student, Japanese society as a whole was rocking. I didn't know the extent of the depths of this motion, nor the amplitude of its vibrations, but even so it reverberated even to me. Some university students, girls and boys, attempted to enter into life with some workers. The actions of the workers, the philosophy of the workers, offered us an image, on the one hand, of the road to social and political revolution and, on the other hand, of revolutionary art—the art of the working class. Right there, I, who had thought that I would make literature my work, came to enter the proletarian art movement. What had been nurtured during my increased closeness to Murō Saisei—if one can say that something had been nurtured—this appeared to some extent at this time. During that process, I believe, these poems were born.[49]

The above fragment of history appeared in 1956, as an afterword to the fourth publication of Nakano's collected poetry. It was followed by Nakano's statement that this "something" appeared in the form of poetry during a brief period of time; he had only written poetry for a while before beginning to express himself in prose form. This history does not mention another silence, between the two bursts of poetry—the silence between the last issue of *Razō*, in May 1925, and the first issue of *Roba*, in April 1926, which contained Nakano's first political statements in print, in the form of poetry. This silence corresponds to a blank space in the *nenpu*'s column for literary production, from Nakano's entrance into the Shinjinkai to the Kyōdō Printers' strike and the organization of the Marxist Arts Society. Thus, while Nakano's reference to the "rocking" of society bears resemblance to his description in 1926 of life amidst "contradiction, unrest, and upheaval," it can only be conjectured that during the year of silence when there was no poetry, when in fact the writer produced only one short story, he was studying the ideas of Marx, for Nakano left no record of why or when he became a Marxist other than this polemical lip service to the dedication of the Japanese working class. There is, in other words, no list of treatises or reference to a canon enshrining Marx's truths. Even in Nakano's essays on politics and art, Marx is almost never mentioned. But if Nakano Shigeharu did not leave an authorized explanation as to the exact route to his adoption of Marxism, he did leave a record of the transitions in a Marxist analysis of Taishō culture and politics. These stages are not those that appear in the codified histories of the Proletarian Literature Movement. Instead they are avail-

[49] Nakano, "Iwanami bunkōban, *Nakano Shigeharu shishū* atogaki," *NSZ* 22:201 [1956].

able amidst the contradictions, unrest, and upheaval announced in his essays, stories, and letters, and they are most clearly evident in his poetry.

Nakano stated that without an examination of the thought of Ishikawa Takuboku, including its transitions, his poetry could not be read as the product of a socialist. A similar statement can be made about Nakano himself: Without an examination of the thought of Nakano Shigeharu, including its transitions, his poetry cannot be read as the poetry of a Marxist. The following chapters provide the first investigation of Nakano Shigeharu's dialogue with Marx; they search out the ways in which Nakano quoted Marx without citing him. They also consider the way in which he moved beyond Marx in his analysis of Taishō culture. None of the images of Nakano's Taishō years evoked by the reminiscences of his peers mentions his concern with nonrevolutionary culture. But unlike his discovery of Marxism, or the actual details of his childhood, Nakano's critique of Taishō culture is available in his writing. As will be shown below, his Meiji memories of the pictures in print culture and the power of the newspaper were central themes comprising his explication of contemporary society during the second half of the 1920s. To begin to reclaim this revolutionary as a Marxist, we must consider his manifestos on art as politics in relation to other Marxist manifestos.

CHAPTER TWO

A World Split in Two

NAKANO SHIGEHARU'S MARXIST MANIFESTOS

Since the 1930s Nakano Shigeharu has been captive within the canonized history of the Japanese revolutionary Culture Movement, which has, in turn, been grafted onto the history of Japanese Marxism, a history almost always written as a series of debates over organizational strategy. Nakano's position as leader of the Proletarian Literature Movement was assured when he appeared in the multivolume *Nihon shihonshugi hattatsu shi kōza* (Lectures on the development of Japanese capitalism).[1] He was there positioned within a rubric set in an essay by Yamada Seizaburō entitled "History of the Culture Movement,"[2] in one of the series of bound pamphlets that would provide a conceptual vocabulary for Japanese history, economics, political economy, and culture. Yamada's schema, which was to be recapitulated in almost every history of proletarian literature that would appear in English or Japanese, was essentially a chronology of factions and their journals. In Yamada's account, and in the histories that have followed, literature is eclipsed by institutional structure in a narrative situating the origin of proletarian literature in 1923, with the appearance of the journal *Tanemakuhito* (The sower). According to this narrative, *Tanemakuhito* was followed, after the earthquake of 1923, by its successor *Bungei sensen* (Literary arts front). The histories then attribute the split in the movement in 1926 to dissent within the Nihon Puroretaria Geijutsu Remmei (Japan Proletarian Arts League, or JPAL), resulting in the appearance of the Rōnō Geijutsuka Remmei (Labor-Farmer-Artists League, or WPAL), in 1927. The histories then record the merger of the Zenei Geijutsuka Dōmei (Vanguard Artists League, or VAL) with JPAL in 1928 to form the Nihon Musansha Geijutsu Remmei (All-Japan Federation of Proletarian Arts, NAPF). According to this uniform narrative of institutional structures, in 1932 NAPF was replaced by the Nihon Puroretaria Bunka Remmei (Japan Proletarian Culture Federation, KOPF), which disbanded in 1934, as the movement dissolved.[3]

---

[1] Noro Eitarō, gen ed., *Nihon shihonshugi hattatsu shi kōza*, 7 vols. (Iwanami shoten, 1932–33).

[2] Yamada Seizaburō, "Puroretaria bunka undō shi," in "Bunka undō shi," *Nihon shihonshugi hattatsu shi kōza*, vol. 3, ed. Noro Eitarō (Iwanami shoten, 1932–33).

[3] The most representative version of this history is presented in the nine-volume *Nihon*

In these literary histories, Nakano first appears as a member of the Marxist Arts Study Group who remains in the Japan Proletarian Arts League after a factional dispute with the group forming the Labor-Farmer-Artists League. Along with several other rebels, the almost unknown young adherent of the theorist Fukumoto Kazuo takes over the movement to lead it in a self-consciously Marxist direction. The members of these two factions then spar in the pages of their respective journals, *Puroretaria geijutsu* and *Bungei sensen*. According to these accounts, Nakano was central to the process whereby revolutionary writers passively molded their literature to meet the demands of political strategies. He would, in other words, encourage the subservience of art to politics.

There is a truth to the above narrative, just as there is historical basis for the stage-theory approach to most histories of Marxist thought,[4] for Marxism was incorporated into Japanese intellectual life in stages. The process began with the import of Marxism as an admixture undifferentiated from strains of syndicalism during the early years of Taishō. A second stage, of intense study of the works of Marx and Engels, followed. By the mid-1920s, intellectuals had completed the process of importation, translation, and study of European Marxist writings, which had begun after the First World War, and were eager to apply them within their own work. This led to the third stage, when an explosion of indigenous scholarly and literary writing on Japanese society and history informed by Marxism was published during the second half of the 1920s and the early 1930s. In the histories of Japanese Marxist thought and literature, the influence of the young theoretician Fukumoto Kazuo is always emphasized, and this aspect of the history of Japanese Marxism is also most significant. In 1924, the year of the completion of the translations of all three volumes of *Capital* and less than a decade before the appearance of

---

puroretaria bungaku taikei (History of Japanese proletarian literature) (Sanichi shobō, 1954–55), which codified the literature of the movement for a postwar audience. The introductory volume chronicled "The Womb and Birth of Proletarian Literature," volume 1 was about the "Era of the Movement to the Fore," and volume 2 traced the "Era of the Establishment of the Movement." In the next three volumes the movement flowered, to be followed by volumes 6 and 7 on the "Era of Oppression and Dissolution." The last book was on the "Era of Apostasy and Resistance." In this series the chronological demarcations corresponded to the establishment of organizations, so that the linear narrative developed within the explanatory essays accompanying each volume of reprinted novellas, essays, and poems reads as a series of reorganizations of acronyms.

For the most comprehensive English-language reproduction of the schema and of the standard arguments see George Tyson Shea, *Leftwing Literature in Japan* (Hōsei University Press, 1964). Iwamoto Yoshio provides a modified version in "Aspects of the Proletarian Literature Movement," in *Japan in Crisis*, ed. Silberman and Harootunian, pp. 156–82.

[4] For a representative narrative of Japanese Marxism as a series of stages of debates, see Koyama Hirotake, *Nihon marukusushugi shi* (Aoki shoten, 1956).

the complete works of Marx and Engels in Japanese translation, Fukumoto Kazuo, the young scholar recently returned from Germany, did
rock the Japanese intellectual world with his interpretations of the
thought of Lenin in the new journal *Marukusushugi* (Marxism). Moreover, his debate with socialist theoretician Yamakawa Hitoshi, which is
always summarzied in the accounts of Fukumoto's influence, was one of
many disputes over organizational strategy within the Japanese revolu
tionary left. But Fukumoto, like Nakano, has been diminished by such
histories, for "Fukumotoism" was not merely a strategy for political actions. Fukumoto's pronouncements about change embodied a theory of
social structure and social change. His essays, like Nakano's earliest revolutionary writings, were not merely calls to revolutionary organization.
Like Marx's *Communist Manifesto*, they were also an analysis of the
process of historical transformation of a world split in two. Both Fukumoto's essays and Nakano's writings belong within the history of Japanese Marxist theory that set forth visions of social revolution and transformation, a history beginning with the Japanese translation of the
Communist Manifesto.

When Kōtoku Shūsui and the Meiji socialist leader Sakai Toshihiko
translated the Samuel Moore English-language edition of Marx's classic
in 1906, they could render the preface into their own language with little
difficulty, for Marx's account of the response of the Communists of Western Europe to the fear tactics of the leaders who had cried out that "a
Spectre is haunting Europe" could be translated into the terminology of
the political reportage of foreign events. Marx's opening chapter, beginning with the universalist proclamation, "The history of all hitherto existing society is the history of class struggles," was more problematic. Kōtoku and Sakai chose to express this idea in terms applicable to their own
society, although there were no words in Japanese for either "bourgeois"
or "proletarian," as they explained in a footnote following the first chapter of the translation appearing in the anarcho-socialist *Heimin shimbun*
(Commoner's newspaper) of November 13, 1904. After deliberation, the
authors chose the word "gentleman" (*shinshi*), with its contemporary
connotations of the vulgar self-interests of those populating the upper
reaches of society. The term "commoner" (*heimin*) was selected as the
translation for "proletarian," which, the authors noted, could also have
been translated as "laborer." A follow-up article on December 11 elaborated on the choice of "gentleman" over other common terms for the rich
and powerful, including the Japanese word for "capitalist." The article
claimed that according to contemporary usage the term *shinshi* stood for
a way of life and was therefore the most appropriate translation: "the
original meaning has faded completely, and it merely means those who
have money, wear fine clothing, live in a grand house, indulge in lives of

luxury, frequent houses of assignation, have country houses, ride in car-
riages, keep a mistress on the side, or accept bribes, gamble, and take the
heads off others."⁵ Sakai was content to change class to "clique" and to
define the bourgeoisie as a "clique of gentlemen" (*shinshibatsu*), a com-
posite of various cliques of regional, academic, political, and financial
powers standing in opposition to the poverty-stricken commoners, who
were not given subclassifications like the bourgeois clique.

As the historian Matsuzawa Hiroaki, one of the few scholars to discuss
Marxist thought outside of the standard institutional framework, has
noted, the understanding of class exhibited by Kōtoku and Sakai in their
translation of the *Communist Manifesto* illustrated the Meiji socialist's
inability to place within a social whole social relationships that are at
the same time economic. Rather than seeing the reproduction of society
through the reproduction of such relationships, these thinkers focused on
the anticipated dissolution of the social order. Thus, because the two
members of the second generation of Meiji journalist socialists could not
grasp the historically constituted economic and social interrelationship of
class, the original intent of the *Communist Manifesto* was misrepre-
sented. Kōtoku and Sakai fractured the bourgeois class into a series of
privatized relationships, working against Marx's definition that the bourgeoisie "cannot exist without constantly revolutionizing the instruments
of production, and thereby the relations of production, and with them the
whole relation of society."⁶

In contrast, by the 1920s, the Japanese Marxists of Nakano Shigeharu's generation who had access to the complete works of Marx and Engels and commentaries on the works of Marx would come to terms with
the historical determinants of class. The writings of this generation of
Marxists would reflect the recognition that the bourgeois could not be
defined by his clothing or house, nor could the proletariat be termed
"poor," for such generalizations did not distinguish between feudalism
and the capitalist mode of production. Working from Marx's premise
that "capitalism is merely one historically specific form in which the
means of production and labour power are combined to reproduce the
material conditions of life,"⁷ these Marxists would affirm Marx's presumption that neither the bourgeoisie nor the proletariat could exist outside this system dedicated to the production of capital, and that neither
class could exist without the other.⁸

⁵ *Heimin shimbun*, December 11, 1904.
⁶ Matsuzawa Hiroaki, *Nihon shakaishugi no shisō* (Chikuma shobō, 1973), pp. 9–23,
40–42; Marx, *Manifesto of the Communist Party*, in *The Marx-Engels Reader*, ed. Robert
C. Tucker, 2d ed. (New York: W.W. Norton, 1978), p. 476.
⁷ Marx, *Communist Manifesto*, p. 478.
⁸ The quotation is taken from the definition of "non-capitalist means of production,"

By the late 1920s the eager Japanese intellectual could find translations of Marxist theory appearing almost simultaneously with the European original. In fact, the quantity and quality of Marxist texts encompassing works on theory and revolutionary strategy equaled that of Germany. This refinement had come about in a process that can only be remapped by denying the usual boundaries placed between revolutionary arts journals, such as the ones edited by Nakano, and Marxist publications devoted to the analysis of social theory and political developments. For example, the literary magazine *Bungei sensen*, the first journal of the Proletarian Culture Movement to publish Nakano's views, appeared in June 1924, two months after the inauguration of the influential Communist journal *Marukusushugi*, which was dedicated to introducing Marxist theory. Such lines can be traced between revolutionary politics and revolutionary culture, thus associating writers, readers, and organizations that have been segregated in separate historiographies, and thereby placing social science and cultural commentary within one variegated Marxist discourse on history, society, and revolutionary transformation.

By the spring of 1924, when Nakano entered Tokyo Imperial University, a broad range of journals had begun to educate the committed Marxist intellectual. Although Nakano did not publish in the Marxist magazines *Social Thought*, *Labor-Farmer*, *Fairy Tale Movement*, and *Proletarian Science*, which were to appear during the following decade, he undoubtedly read at least some of their articles. Marxist analysis was available not only in left-wing publications, but also in the so-called bourgeois press, which competed to publish the works of Marxist literary and social critics and writers. By 1930, for example, 23 percent of the articles in *Chūō kōron*, the leading magazine aimed at an apolitical mass audience, were written by Communist and non-Communist writers on the revolutionary left, including Nakano Shigeharu. During the second half of the 1920s Nakano would publish in many of the journals of the Communist-oriented literary left and the mainstream press, while at the same time attacking his colleagues in the literary arena both for writing empty polemic in revolutionary journals and for collusion with the vulgar stan-

provided by John Weeks in *A Dictionary of Marxist Thought*, ed. Tom Bottomore et al. (Cambridge: Harvard University Press, 1983), p. 353.

An excellent index to the translations of Marx and Engels into Japanese, which includes a breakdown of the number of monographs, newspaper articles, and anthologies translated per year between 1904 and 1973, is Marukusu-Engerusu Shoshi Henshū Iinkai, ed., *Marukusu-Engerusu hōyaku bunken mokuroku* (Kyokutō shoten, Nauka, Ōtsuki shoten, 1973). A good source for the chronology of translations and commentaries is Tōyama Shigeki, Yamazaki Shōichi, and Oi Tadashi, eds., *Kindai Nihon shisō shi*, vol. 1: *Kindai nihon shisō shi nenpyō* (Aoki shoten, 1957).

dards of the bourgeois press.[9] Nakano's writings from the 1920s and early 1930s belong within the Marxist dialogue among Japanese thinkers in the arts and social sciences relating their own experience to the historical tenets proclaimed in European works. They are also a response to European Marxists. What was the appeal of Marxism to this Japanese writer? As a writer turned revolutionary, how did Nakano Shigeharu view the process and prospects of cultural revolution? Of what importance to Nakano was Marx's theory? Finally, what was Nakano's relationship to Fukumoto Kazuo, who has so often been cited as the cause of Nakano's turn to Marxism? The beginnings of answers emerge through an analysis of the manifestos issued by Nakano as he began his work as a revolutionary in the mid-1920s.

Nakano left no account as to why he turned to Marxism, but in an afterword to his early short stories and poetry, written for the 1976 republication of his complete works, he retraced his move from a poetic, anarchist stance into revolutionary cultural politics by offering his response to the work songs included in Hosoi Wakizō's documentary account of the life of the woman textile worker, *Jokō aishi* (The sad history of the woman factory hand). He recalled that he had read the work when he was a university student and had been immediately, intensely moved by the work, as were his colleagues. Yet none of the intellectuals in his circle had discussed the songs, nor had they made any attempt to treat the work theoretically or to analyze the author's preface. As part of his remembrance, Nakano quoted several stanzas from the "changed song" of the mill girls who attached words from their own lives to folk melodies.[10]

Nakano's reference to the need to understand both the production of these songs and their reproduction in Hosoi's documentary history is oblique, but it appears that he identified with these songs when he began to formulate his own opinions about the creation of a revolutionary culture. These early ideas were worked out in a series of manifestos privileging the consciousness of contending, interrelating classes. These were simply worded essays about the place of art in society and the meaning of culture in history. They were characterized by a respect for emotion, for historical specificity, and for simplicity.

---

[9] Regarding the presence of "proletarian" works in the so-called bourgeois press, see Jay Rubin, *Injurious to Public Morals: Writers and the Meiji State* (Seattle: University of Washington Press, 1984), p. 247, and Kurihara Yukio, *Puroretaria bungaku to sono jidai* (Heibonsha, 1971), pp. 134–35. Koyama Hirotake notes that by 1932 Marxist historians were engaged in debate. According to Koyama's interpretation, the mass media was but a substitute for an effective organizational structure, and intellectuals on the left were mere pawns of organized journalism, deluded into thinking that the class struggle could take place in legal theoretical activity and scholarly study. Koyama, *Nihon marukusushugi shi*, pp. 74–77.

[10] Nakano, "Chosha ushirogaki," *NSZ* 1:490 [*Nakano Shigeharu zenshū* 1976].

Nakano's first manifesto, written in 1926, a year after the appearance of *The Sad History of the Woman Factory Hand*, was about changing verse. In "Shi ni kansuru ni san no danpen" (Two or three fragments on poetry) Nakano asked two questions: "What is a lyric poem?" and "What constitutes proletarian poetry?"[11] There were no ready answers, for when Nakano wrote these questions the Marxist canon contained no clear guidelines to the production or interpretation of poetry, because there was no Marxist theory regarding the relation of Marxism to verse. The closest protocol available was Mayakovsky's mechanistic admonition that poetry was "a manufacture," and that the verse-maker could perfect his craft armed with a good notebook, a knowledge of theoretical economics, and "the realities of everyday life," although it is not clear whether Nakano had access to this work.[12] In the absence of theory and Japanese poetry that could describe and change Japanese class consciousness, Nakano was seeking his own method as poet.

To present his criteria for lyricism, in "Two or Three Fragments on Poetry," Nakano contrasted a hypothetical love poem with the four stanzas of praise to "the adamantine incarnation of all the greatness and vigor of the proletarian" and to Communist Party "warriors and martyrs" comprising the preface to *The ABC of Communism*.[13] The love poem, he explained, expresses man's yearning for one woman and is infused with intense expression of emotion. Its error lies in the individualistic, self-righteous, despairing stance of its author. In contrast, the verses of the preface written by Bukharin and Preobrazhensky were group-oriented, hopeful, and bright. Their language was clear and distinct, and as a result, the preface penetrated directly to the heart. These principles of consciousness of class, optimism, and clarity were the axioms informing Nakano's prewar cultural criticism. His concern with emotion was also to resound throughout the direct, simple language of his theoretical writings as he continued to employ colloquial language to develop both his theory and poetry. For example, simplicity was his admitted aim as an artist, two years later, after he had become one of the most respected leaders of the Proletarian Literature Movement. In a characteristic statement that glossed over the complexity and intensity of his intellectual and political mission he began an essay entitled "Soboku to iu koto" (On simplicity) with the following confession:

> All in all I think that in this whole world simplicity's the best thing there is. This thing's got to be the most beautiful and the finest. This thing is what moves me.

[11] Nakano, "Shi ni kansuru danpen," *NSZ* 9:3–10 [*Roba* 6/26; 1/27]. The original version included the qualifier "two or three" in the title.

[12] Vladimir Mayakovsky, *How Verses Are Made*, trans. G. M. Hyde (London: Jonathan Cape, 1970), p. 56.

[13] Nakano, "Shi ni kansuru danpen," pp. 3–4.

If only I could just grasp this—I think that all year long. If I should have to do some sort of artistic work, all in all this thing is what I aim at. Of course usually I just aim.[14]

Nakano's first manifesto, an indictment of his compatriots for failing to move forward with history, also revealed that his search for a method relied on a stage theory of history and a notion of Japanese historical specificity. He employed Hegelian imagery in "Two or Three Fragments on Poetry" to refer to a rising spirit that demanded a new poetic form for a newly rising art: "The new worldview, new concept, the newly rising, powerful, lively spirit in the end transcends the limits of the understanding of the old spirit" (p. 561).

There is a notion of dialectical historical flux relating feeling to form in Nakano's contention that this new spirit cannot sleep with the old in the manifesto of 1926 which placed the poet in relation to the material world. Nakano was moving toward a materialism, but his belief that art emerges from the experience of production had not yet emerged in his fragments on poetry. The most rigorous aspect of the essay was Nakano's schema of four schools of Japanese poetry, each of which was lyrical, each non-proletarian and bereft of detail. These schools were the "fantasy poems group," the "reminiscence school," the "shouting school," and the "cacophony school." Nakano phrased his literary criticism in a poetic short-hand that would characterize his prewar cultural criticism. His sympathy toward the cacophony school, for example, was limited to the following words: "It is street neck bloody prostitute bombs revolution filth, bang, crash, shriek, scream, etc. It is just an unbearable feeling and total black nothingness" (p. 6).

While Nakano was most sympathetic to the cacophony approach, even this school could not produce conceptual, proletarian poetry, which had to be almost scientific in its empiricism. Nakano demanded a specificity that could come to terms with materiality, for facts were "things":

All must be tested. All must be chosen in most meticulous detail and the most minute discovery must not be dealt with carelessly. This is because they are related to facts and facts—in other words things themselves—and things only can provide knowledge of the truth. (p. 8)

In defense of his concern, Nakano quoted Poincaré's explication of what happens when the degrees of a telescope sighting are altered even by only a few units. Shifting the emphasis from the position of Sakai Toshihiko, who had sought to explicate the meanings of the word "gentleman" in his Japanese-language *Communist Manifesto*, Nakano placed his sight on the proletariat by criticizing a college student who had extracted from the

[14] Nakano, "Soboku to iu koto," *NSZ* 9:169 [*Shinchō* 10/28].

word "proletarian" only "the 'stench' of poverty." The student guilty of generalization had not been capable of grasping the everyday, material experience of the proletariat in a living, vital manner (p. 560).

In "Fragments on Poetry," Nakano established the poem as a political tool for the class struggle and began to outline a method. Yet, after the war, looking back on his poetry, Nakano would not refer to his early theory. He would claim that as a young poet he had been a disciple of Murō Saisei, who along with Hagiwara Sakutarō was one of the leading Taishō poets to work in a colloquial language. Nakano would second Hagiwara's determination that none before Murō had "truly grasped the nostalgic rhythm of words and brought them to life within our emotions."[15] Hagiwara Sakutarō had praised Murō for his use of the "simple, familial daily talk" deeply beloved by the Japanese people. According to Nakano's postwar memoirs, it is this focus on the quotidian that had stunned Nakano when he first encountered Murō's *Ai no shishū* (Collection of love poems): "It wasn't anything great. It wasn't a great passionate anything that flared forth. It was a regular nothing within everyday life, but I understood that nothing, as though experiencing it for the first time."[16] In reviewing his history as a poet, Nakano chose to remember his love of simplicity while remaining silent about his attempt to reconcile poetry and dialectical materialism, but his early essays remain as testimony to this effort. When in the fall of 1926 Nakano chose to elaborate on "Fragments on Poetry," he chose to write about Hagiwara and not about Murō, in an essay entitled "*Kyōdō bōkeishi* ni arawareta fundo" (Anger appearing in *Poems of scenes of the homeland*),[17] as he continued his exploration of the dialectic relationship of feeling to Japanese poetic form.

In this second manifesto on revolutionary culture, Nakano credited Hagiwara for recognizing that the old forms had been sung out, and for thereby taking the discovery of his school of poetry, which had succeeded in destroying the old forms and creating new ones, one step further. Until that time there had been almost no poetry of anger, but thanks to Hagiwara, rage had finally made an appearance. Other Japanese poets had either hidden their experience of new emotions or had not been capable of feeling, but Hagiwara experienced and expressed new sensations and produced new creations based on the destruction of the past. Good poets like Hagiwara were capable of beginning from a liberation of emotions arising within specific historic conditions; Hagiwara's freeing of feelings—

---

[15] Nakano, "Shijin to shite no Murō Saisei," *NSZ* 17:388 [*Nihon shijin zenshū* (Shinchōsha, 1976)]. The original title of this essay was "Murō Saisei. Hito to sakuhin."

[16] Nakano, "Wasureenu shomotsu," *NSZ* 17:423 [Kokubun Ichitarō, ed., *Wasureenu shomotsu* (Meiji tosho shuppan, 1959)].

[17] Nakano, "*Kyōdō bōkeishi* ni arawareta fundo," *NSZ* 19:173–83 [*Roba* 10/26].

and of verse—arose from his ability to come up against the change in social conditions with the full force of his being. Nakano qualified his highest of praise with the caveat that Hagiwara's work was ultimately petit bourgeois, but that this did not mean that Marxist intellectuals had all the answers, as he made clear in a third manifesto.[18]

In this third manifesto, "Hitotsu no genshō" (One phenomenon),[19] which appeared in the September 1926 issue of the *Teikoku daigaku shimbun*, the young critic referred to the powerful new role of the left-wing writer in the mass media. The Japanese literary world was witnessing a "social scientific examination of the literary arts and a materialist examination of spiritual culture in the broadest sense, arising out of a social necessity." Nakano distinguished among three types of "Marxist" writers: thinkers who rejected a materialist historical analysis, those who affirmed it, and those agonized artists who, in a "dishevelled, chaotic state," had turned to socialism. Nakano was sympathetic to the cause of these writers, who were "in motion." Because they were progressive "they [were] people anxious to grasp onto something firm," but they lacked a method because the mere refutation of bourgeois ideology would not suffice.[20] Nakano's "Geijutsu ni kansuru hashirigakiteki oboegaki" (Notes on art written on the run),[21] his fourth essay as manifesto and his most Marxist in method, published in the October 1927 issue of *Proletarian Arts*, would provide an answer to their dilemma.

In "Notes on Art Written on the Run," Nakano emerges as a Marxist analyzing social formations and the relationships within and between them. While a reading of the first three manifestos serves to answer the query regarding Nakano's view of the process of cultural revolution, this essay also responds to the question on the appeal of Marx to Nakano. Speaking for a righteous "we," he continues his attack on the would-be Marxist literary critics whose efforts appear to be aimed more at attaining breakfast or a cigarette than at a theory for art. Continuing the process, begun in "One Phenomenon," of separating out true Marxists from false, he scoffs at the theory of those who are merely passing: "Their words change with yesterday and today and within each statement is contained a contradiction." The only theoretical base of these charlatans is the declaration of their "one secure eternal truth"—"I am a Marxist" (p. 69).

In this essay Nakano never does analyze what it means to be a Marxist, but he offers an alternative to a series of quotations, ostensibly from his erstwhile Marxist colleagues. He then explains why the maxims relating

[18] Ibid., pp. 174–75, 183.
[19] Nakano, "Hitotsu no genshō," NSZ 9:11–13 [*Teikoku daigaku shimbun* 9/13/26].
[20] Ibid., p. 11.
[21] Nakano, "Geijutsu ni kansuru hashirigakiteki oboegaki," NSZ 9:68–78 [*Puroretaria geijutsu* 10/27].

state to society, superstructure to forms of property, law to modes of production, the mediating role of the state to the political domination of one class by another, and the resultant responsibility of the proletariat to conquer bourgeois democracy are not relevant, by listing an alternative set of questions. Rather than focusing on the state's relationship to society, his four questions (p. 70) encircle the dialectical relationship of contemporary history to class consciousness: What relevant aspects of history are reacting back upon their own causes? How are these facets of history brought into being? How are social relationships positioned and the conditions of daily life conditioned? What is the "consciousness" determined by history—the consciousness that gives content to art—and what is its specific historical character? The concern for historical specificity voiced in the first two questions is a rewording of the requirement for concreteness and detail established in the earlier manifestos. The third and fourth queries indicate the appeal of Marx to Nakano. In other essays and in poems and short fiction he would elaborate on the placement and motion of social relationships in capitalist society introduced in Marx's *Communist Manifesto* and detailed in *Capital*.

Marx's focus on the pairing of the two interdependent figures of the bourgeois and the proletarian was a reworking of Hegel's master-slave relationship in the *Phenomenology of Mind*. In Hegel's formulation, the master holds the bondsman in slavery, enabling him to enjoy the object of his desire, which to the bondsman is an object of the application of his labor. At first it appears that the master is independent. But through the act of labor the essential nature of lordship and bondage is revealed, as the bondsman emerges as a truly independent entity, existing for itself and not the other. The master merely negates the object through his desire, but by shaping or objectifying the object, the bondsman realizes that he exists for himself. He has chosen the option of labor for the master in order to survive, as an alternative to death, but it is through this very work that he gains autonomy.[22]

In the *Communist Manifesto*, Marx replaced Hegel's individual actors by classes in his elaboration of history as the history of class struggle. Marx's focus was on the present, on the splitting of society into the two great classes, the bourgeoisie and proletariat. Here again, the process of labor provided the basis for a liberation of the enslaved because it revealed the bondage for what it was. The bourgeoisie could not exist "without constantly revolutionizing the instruments of production," and it was this inevitable "revolutionizing of production" that distinguished the bourgeois era from the preceding epochs as "all fixed, fast-frozen re-

[22] G.W.F. Hegel, *The Phenomenology of Mind* (New York: Harper & Row, 1967), p. 239.

lations, with their train of prejudices and opinions" were swept away. According to Marx, the emergence of class consciousness is inevitable during this stage of history: "All that is solid melts into air, all that is holy is profaned, and man is at last compelled to face with sober senses, his real conditions of life, and his relations with his kind."[23] In *Capital*, Marx expanded his social analysis, explicating how during the process of capitalist production this capitalist relation was constantly reproduced, "on the one side the capitalist, on the other the wage-laborer."[24] The apocalyptic, telescoped vision of revolution in *The Communist Manifesto* was replaced in *Capital* by sustained economic analysis emphasizing the genesis and the reproduction of the relationships within capitalism.

When Nakano chose to apply Marx's theory to a series of specific pairs of relationships within contemporary Japanese society in "Notes on Art Written on the Run," his scenario was closer to the revolutionary situation of the *Manifesto* than to the sociological prose of *Capital*. In this manifesto he offered eight brief tableaus of "intimate" (*shitashii*) situations. In each, a different form of state power responded to an attempt by one group to end its oppression. The actions, linked in one continuous litany in the original text, are spaced here in order to delineate clearly the actors who were later to appear in Nakano's poetry in an extension of the following angry recital of conditions of struggle:

—the factory representative body, in session to oppose enormous wage decreases and massive job firings, was smashed to smithereens by state officials
—farmers waiting for a meeting, opposing the "do not enter" signs posted far and wide by the big landlords, were tied with rope and dragged to the district courthouse
—the tenant who submitted a petition of grievance for rent decrease to the bad landlord who consecutively has been raising the rent was promptly served with eviction notice
—the factory girl who had gone to request just a short rest because the child in her womb had begun to move was stripped naked in the cold and hit with water from a hose
—the Korean speaking his own language in his home, because it was his language, was pulled out and in the name of vagrancy put in custody for a period longer than delimited by law
—the Levellers Association member standing and talking was arrested because the person to whom he was speaking was a worker
—the wagetaker who went to pick up his accumulated salary was, in reverse, legally taken away

[23] Marx, *Communist Manifesto*, p. 476.
[24] Karl Marx, *Capital*, vol. 1: *A Critical Analysis of Capitalist Production*, ed. Frederick Engels (New York: International Publishers, 1967), p. 578.

—the student who began to think of things honestly was expelled for his honesty.[25]

Nakano is more concerned with the determinants of revolution than with the reproduction of social relationships; his "bondsmen" are unsuccessful in attaining independence, but their consciousness of their enslavement allows them to protest. The two sides of the revolutionary battle have been established and the "we"—the workers, peasants, small shopkeepers, women, colonized, special *burakumin*, students, and soldiers raising their voices to request the "bread, a place to sleep, innocent chitchat, and learning"—are moving toward revolt. Their calls become outcries, but the whip wielded by the imperialist bourgeois landowners to whom all capitalists, landowners, and large families are subordinated, will not permit such protest. Their outcries have therefore been transformed into a crescendo of lamentation by all oppressed peoples forming the "yeast" of bourgeois revolution. At the forefront of this three-stage process of "outcries–lamentations–struggle" is the working class, which is on the verge of exploding into demonstrations and massive destructive riots against the despotism of state authority. Nakano attributes this revolutionary upsurge to the close ties between the rapid natural growth of the labor movement and "our Marxism" (pp. 72–73).

Nakano elaborates on the contemporary Japanese versions of the master-slave relationship in order to answer his third and fourth questions about the reality of Japanese social relationships and the determinants of contemporary consciousness. The contemporary Japanese social existence, he concludes, is one of oppressed peoples squelched by despotic might. The role of consciousness is to raise the cries to lamentations (without sparing the flow of blood), and the distinct historic characteristic of consciousness, which must be reflected, grasped, and depicted by art, is its opposition to despotism during this current stage of imperialism. In answering his fourth question, on consciousness, he responds to the historical question of Nakano's views on the process and prospects of cultural revolution. In the polemic of this manifesto, art is capable "of sewing together a million hearts belonging to all oppressed people with one thread of red blood" (p. 74).

In answer to the second question regarding the importance of Marx's theory for Nakano, it can be concluded that Nakano has reformulated Marx's dichotomy of bourgeois oppressor against oppressed proletariat. The art of the working class is the art of all oppressed peoples, revealing

---

[25] Nakano, "Oboegaki," *NSZ* 9:72. The Levellers Association refers to the Suiheisha, the nationwide organization formed in 1922 to emancipate the outcastes or *burakumin* members of the citizenry. The term "factory girl" has been coined herein, to refer to the Japanese term for female mill worker, *jokō*.

all shameful aspects of Japanese society. Art will have political significance only when it is capable of grasping the tendency of the proletariat
that is moving toward revolution, for it will then be able to act upon the
historically inevitable causes of this revolutionary change and thus make
revolution. Nakano is not direct, but in his emphasis on consciousness
he is hinting at a theory of reciprocal causality relating economic and
ideological factors or Marxist base and superstructure. His major concern is not the articulation of a theory of ideology, but a method of producing revolutionary art that will not fall prey to any formulaic approaches advocated by the "quack doctors" who attempt to delimit
suitable topics. Rejecting the thesis of one colleague on the literary left
who has called for the depiction of "love, death, the market, the dance
hall," or in other words the details of the everyday life of the young Japanese intellectual (because workers will be bored by reading the all too
familiar details of factory life), Nakano demands an overview of social
reality that does not isolate elements but considers them together, within
the totality of social relationships in Japan. Here he reiterates his concern
for specificity in a call for a realism: "To depict the whip as whip, torment
as torment, shameful aspects as shameful, must be our method of depiction" (pp. 73–75).

The manifesto "Notes on Art," which demands the representation of a
history of protesting voices and escalating actions within literature, is one
rewording of Marx's *Communist Manifesto*, and as such it illustrates the
influence of Marx on the Japanese writer. Because Nakano emphasizes
the varied groups comprising the category of oppressed people en route
to revolution, with this manifesto, Japanese Marxism might appear to
have come full cycle back to the translation of Kōtoku and Sakai equating
the bourgeoisie with all types of privileged groups and associating the
proletariat with the poor, but Nakano is much more specific than Kōtoku
and Sakai. He gives the worker a vanguard position in this essay, just as
his later works would emphasize the need to capture the specificity of all
aspects of the worker's existence. The historical narrative of Marx's
Communist Manifesto can thus be associated with the ideology of the
young activist, but inasmuch as Nakano has been labeled a "Fukumoto-
ist" in almost all of the histories of Japanese Marxist literature, and the
theory of Fukumoto Kazuo predominates in the history of Japanese
Marxist thought in the mid-1920s, when Nakano's manifestos first appeared, the manifestos of these two thinkers should also be compared.
Just as the foregoing discussion has removed Nakano's early ideas from
a schema emphasizing organizational strategy and factions within a political movement and placed them instead in a series of "manifestos" in
order to emphasize his approach to the analysis of society, so must Fukumoto Kazuo be reclaimed as a theorist whose contribution to Japanese

Marxism extended beyond the realpolitik of consolidating a vanguard political party in order to make communist revolution. The rest of this chapter, through a brief examination of one aspect of Fukumoto's theory, will show that while Fukumoto was the spokesman for Lenin's theory of political action, his theory also mediated the Marxist manifestos of Nakano Shigeharu and the thought of Georg Lukács, the Western Marxist theorist of consciousness.

CHANGING FUKUMOTO CHANGING LUKÁCS

The standard treatments of "Fukumotoism," in histories of both Marxism and the Proletarian Literature Movement, have placed the thought of Fukumoto Kazuo in the context of his debate with Yamakawa Hitoshi over the structure of a mass-based left political movement.[26] According to these narratives, Yamakawa advocated a new politics for the socialist and labor movements based on the demands of the masses. This "change of direction" was to link the masses to an anticapitalist ideology. In opposition to Yamakawa's indictment that the movement had been all theory and no action, Fukumoto responded by advocating the formation of one nationwide proletarian party. His prerequisite for the achievement of this goal, theoretical purification or struggle, has come to be equated with his quotation from Lenin: "bevor man sich vereinigt, muss man sich reinlich scheiden—'Was tun?' " (before one unites, one must be cleanly separated—"what is to be done?"). In other words, thought must be purged of all non-Marxist aspects.[27]

[26] For a summary of the Fukumoto-Yamakawa debate that cites the essays comprising the argument, see Matsumoto Kenichi, ed., *Gendai ronsō jiten: shisō to bungaku* (Ryūdō shuppan, 1980), pp. 24–29. Japanese historians have summarized "Fukumotoism" as a theory concerned with organization, exemplified by Fukumoto's quotation of Lenin's dictum that before uniting, one must be separated. This is taken to mean that Fukumoto demanded theoretical clarification and unification within a Marxist revolutionary leadership before revolutionary organization could proceed. The actual content or logic of the actual theory that was to be purified and consolidated is not examined. See for example Koyama, *Nihon marukusushugi shi*, pp. 23–33, and Hariu Kiyoto, "Shakaishugi no tetsugaku no jūyō to tenkai no shosō," in *Nihon kindai tetsugaku shi*, ed. Miyakawa Tōru and Arakawa Ikuo (Yūhikaku, 1976), pp. 149–200. For an English-language version of the debate centered on Fukumoto's "division before unity" principle of organizing, see Germaine A. Hoston, *Marxism and the Crisis of Development in Prewar Japan* (Princeton: Princeton University Press, 1986), pp. 49–57.

[27] For a discussion of Yamakawa's essay, see the editor's afterword in Takabatake Michitoshi, ed. *Yamakawa Hitoshi shu* (Chikuma shobō, 1976), pp. 483–87. According to Takabatake, in this essay "Yamakawa reflected on the fact that until that point the proletarian movement had been a movement of 'political denial' by a minority. It was a manifesto proclaiming that in order to move forward in the struggle against bourgeois politics [political resistance] it was necessary to stand atop the real demands of the masses and to move fore-

In the histories, the content of Fukumoto's Marxism is not examined. It is implied that Fukumoto, like the Lenin of *What Is to Be Done?*, aimed at the organization of a vanguard party in order to make revolution, and that Nakano also advocated such organization and was therefore willing to place politics before art. Rarely has a connection been made between Fukumoto's Marxism and the Marxism of the intellectuals who, along with Nakano, chose literary production as a means of making revolution. Kurihara Yukio's reading of Fukumoto Kazuo provides one such mediation. According to Kurihara, Fukumoto was a theorist who contributed a totalizing thought to Japanese Marxism. The key work for understanding Fukumoto's Marxism is thus not his "change of direction" essay, but "Ōshū ni okeru musansha kaikyū seitō soshiki mondai no rekishiteki hatten" (The historical development of the problem of the proletarian class party organization in Europe), an essay serialized in the April–June 1925 issues of *Marukusushugi*, soon after the young scholar's return from study in France and Germany the previous September. In Kurihara's view, this essay opened a new era in Japanese Marxism. For the first time, a Japanese Marxist had condensed Marxism in its totality, by uniting the concepts of theory and praxis, by providing a role for the intellectual, by broadening the scope of the class struggle beyond the dichotomy of capitalism and worker to one of all oppressed peoples, and by viewing the proletarian political struggle as a totality without distinguishing between ideological and political battle.[28] In other words, the sense of the socioeconomic whole missing from Sakai's *Communist Manifesto* was to be found in Fukumoto's dialectical and materialist theory, not in his political strategy.

Working from Fukumoto's own admission that *History and Class Consciousness* by Georg Lukács, and in particular its last essay, "Towards a Methodology of the Problem of Organization," was the source for Fukumoto's conclusions in "The Historical Development of the Problem of the Proletarian Class Party Organization in Europe," Kurihara claims that "one cannot escape the feeling that this essay as a whole is an echo of the conclusions of *History and Class Consciousness* stripped of the theoretical process." So convinced is Kurihara that Lukács is the overwhelming influence on Fukumoto's theory, he is willing to surmise that if Fukumoto had stayed in Europe for an additional year, or if he had had access to the denunciations of Lukács and Korsch emerging from the fifth Comintern Congress, "this thing called 'Fukumotoism' might not have

ward 'into the masses.'" For the original essay, see ibid., pp. 71–81. For Fukumoto's essay see Fukumoto Kazuo [pen-name Hōjō Kazuo], "'Hōkō tenkan' wa ikanaru shokatei wo toruka," *Marukusushugi* 18 (October 1925): 18. Fukumoto's translations and the secondary sources omit Lenin's interrogatory conclusion.

[28] Kurihara Yukio, *Puroretaria bungaku*, pp. 30–35, 38.

existed."[29] Whether or not Fukumoto Kazuo had *History and Class Consciousness* and Karl Korsch's classic, *Marxism and Philosophy*, hidden in his pocket upon his return to Japan from Germany cannot be determined now. Yet while it is rarely cited in the works on Japanese Marxism, *History and Class Consciousness* (first published in Berlin in 1923) was available in Japan by the following year. Undoubtedly it was circulated from pocket to pocket within the circle of a new generation of Marxists (including Nakano's good friend, Ishidō Kiyotomo, who to this day owns his 1924 edition of the classic). There is no conclusive evidence that Fukumoto read Lukács, nor that Nakano studied Fukumoto or Lukács, just as there are few direct citations of Marx by Nakano.[30] But the reader willing to make connections based on interpretations of texts written by Lukács, Fukumoto, and Nakano during the mid-1920s will see that the thought of Lukács gave Nakano a way of viewing society and history that would render his approach to his poetry Marxist, and enable him to establish himself as a revolutionary writer. This is the approach of Kurihara, who has concluded that Nakano Shigeharu grasped the "essence of Marxism" via Fukumotoism. The argument herein builds on Kurihara's thesis that Nakano Shigeharu "grasped the essence of Marxism" via Fukumotism to conclude that Fukumoto's theory gave Nakano a way of

[29] Kurihara surmises that Fukumoto had no opportunity to hear reports of the attacks on Lukács and Korsch by Zinoviev and Bukharin or to read the published critiques before he published his essay. Ibid., pp. 34–35.

[30] Miyakawa Tōru's approach to Fukumotoism, based on the premise that the works by Lukács and Korsch were "hidden in Fukumoto's pocket" and used as a manual upon which he based his writings, agrees with Kurihara's thesis. According to Miyakawa, Fukumoto's contribution to the history of Japanese Marxism was his direct import and translation of the thought of these two philosophers. While totally derivative, Fukumoto's approach to Marxism liberated it from the constraints imposed both by Meiji and early Taishō Marxists and by non-Marxist academicians who had insisted on confining its application to the realm of social science. Miyakawa contends that Fukumoto's philosophic world-view challenged this political-economism and created the demand among a new generation for a theory to counter the apolitical "humanism" of the early Taishō years. Miyakawa Tōru, *Miki Kiyoshi* (Tokyo daigaku shuppankai, 1970), pp. 60–63.

None of the Japanese-language secondary works alludes to a translation of *History and Class Consciousness*, although the 1927 translation of the chapter "Toward a Methodology of the Problem of Organization" by Kobayashi Yoshio is cited in Kunimatsu Kōji et al., eds., *Rukaachi kenkyū* (Hakusuisha, 1969), p. v. Ishidō Kiyotomo recalls a Shinjinkai dormitory discussion session devoted to "Toward a Methodology of the Problem of Organization." According to Ishidō's memoirs, works by Korsch and Lukács were imported in great numbers at the time when Nakano was active in the Shinjinkai. The early writings by Marx that were available to the young Japanese Marxists were from the *German-French Annals*, *The Holy Family*, and *The Poverty of Philosophy*. Ishidō sees the influence of these works on Fukumoto (and not on either Yamakawa Hitoshi or Kawakami Hajime), an influence mediated by Lukács and Korsch. Ishidō, *Waga itan no Shōwa shi*, pp. 71, 77, 80, 139. I am grateful to Ishidō Kiyotomo for sharing his copy of *History and Class Consciousness*, which was distributed by Kokusai shobō in 1924.

viewing society and history that would render Marxist his approach to his poetry, placing him in the position of revolutionary writer. This is to say that Fukumoto's essay points back to *History and Class Consciousness*, especially to the essay entitled "Class Consciousness," and informs Nakano's early manifestos valorizing proletarian consciousness, the centrality of social relationships as a category of art, and the value of the artist's adherence to historic specificity. A reading of Fukumoto's essay "The Historical Development of the Problem of the Proletarian Class Party Organization in Europe" (hereafter referred to as "Historical Development") alongside several essays from *History and Class Consciousness* confirms Kurihara's hypothesis that Nakano Shigeharu, the young poet, did indeed turn to Marxism because of Fukumoto Kazuo, and not because "Fukumotoism" articulated a theory of power politics. This is central to the project of reclaiming Nakano as a Marxist, because to understand Nakano's "Fukumotoism" as grounded in the formulations of Fukumoto and Lukács in regard to class consciousness is to attribute to Nakano Shigeharu a philosophy of history.

It cannot be concluded uncategorically that Nakano Shigeharu read *History and Class Consciousness* in the mid-1920s, yet there is little doubt but that Fukumoto Kazuo's theory of consciousness, set forth in *Marukusushugi*, made familiar the theory of consciousness set forth by Lukács. As stated above, Nakano left no detailed record as to why he turned to the production of revolutionary art, nor did he leave a reading list to confirm that he followed the words of Fukumoto in *Marukusushugi*. Nonetheless, his commitment to the production of poetry, stories, translations, and essays, and to lectures on poetry and art as a member of the Proletarian Literature Movement attests to a faith in the ability of art to make revolution through the alteration of consciousness. This attitude is confirmed in his impressionistic memory of the impact of the newly emerging factory folk songs, leading to his urge to participate in the production of new forms of art like the changed songs, but it is also evident in Nakano's famous debate with the theorist Kurahara Korehito over the popularization of art. Without repeating the volleys exchanged by the two revolutionary literary critics, it should be emphasized that the central and original thrust of Nakano's argument in the debate over how to create art for the masses was his emphasis on the need to listen to the responses of the working class to their oppression. The role of literature was to clarify this response, because consciousness could not be manipulated from outside, and only elaboration of the working class experience of hunger and anger could encourage revolutionary action.[31] There is strong internal evidence to indicate that Fukumoto's writing in *Maruku-*

[31] See Miriam Silverberg, "Changing Song: The Marxist Poetry of Nakano Shigeharu," Ph.D. diss., University of Chicago, 1984, pp. 68–90.

sushugi, emerging from tenets in *History and Class Consciousness*, led Nakano to this theory of revolutionary consciousness, a theory first made evident by the scenarios set forth in "Notes on Art."

In his "Historical Development" manifesto on European working class organization, published in the April 1925 issue of *Marukusushugi*, Fukumoto established that only the working class, conscious of its impoverishment and alienation, could abolish class society, because of its special historical position. Quoting from the German, he contended that only the proletarian could view society in its totality. He concluded that society would be changed via a praxis resulting from the proletariat's growing consciousness from within its revolutionary struggle.[32] Fukumoto cited Marx's eleventh thesis on Feuerbach, on the goal of philosophy: consciousness must not merely reflect but must change the world. Through the class struggle the working class could become a class for itself, and not for capital. It could be a class for itself (*für sich*), not of itself (*an sich*). Moreover, there was a reciprocity to this process: without sufficient consciousness there could be no complete class struggle, and without the struggle, no full consciousness. According to Fukumoto, the revolution would take place in a three-stage process. A revolution in consciousness would be followed by a political revolution, to be completed by the economic revolution, but the battle for consciousness was predominant, for within each stage a struggle in consciousness was to be followed by economic and then political struggle. Class consciousness was clearly the determinant of decisive political action.[33]

In this passage Fukumoto attributed the notion of the unique role of the proletariat to Marx, but he was echoing Lukács. In "Class Consciousness" Lukács prophesized in italicized emphasis that "when the final economic crisis of capitalism develops, *the fate of the revolution (and with it the fate of mankind) will depend on the ideological maturity of the proletariat, i.e. on its class consciousness.*" Lukács explained how this grasp of evolutionary change could be transformed into a revolutionary weapon on the part of the proletariat, which would serve the unique function of saving all classes. Changed consciousness alone would not suffice, but it could be the source of liberating actions.[34]

In another essay within the same volume, "Reification and the Consciousness of the Proletariat," the European Marxist defined class con-

[32] Fukumoto Kazuo [Hōjō Kazuo], "Ōshu ni okeru musansha kaikyū seitō soshiki mondai no rekishiteki hatten I," *Marukusushugi* 12 (April 1925): 44. The German word *totalitäts-betrachutung* was translated *zentaisei*, or totality.

[33] Fukumoto [Hōjō Kazuo], "Oshu ni okeru rekishiteki hatten II," *Marukusushugi* 13 (May 1925): 7–10, 13–14.

[34] Georg Lukács, *History and Class Consciousness: Studies in Marxist Dialectics*, trans. Rodney Livingston (Cambridge: MIT Press, 1968), p. 70.

sciousness and gave the prerequisites for the emergence of proletarian class consciousness. Class consciousness was the rational reaction imputed to a particular position within the process of production, and the worker could "only become conscious of his existence in society when he became aware of himself as a commodity" (p. 168). In conclusion, the author related economics and political transformation to consciousness, as would Fukumoto in his treatise. Lukács ended with an admonition valuing the role of consciousness (as a component of praxis) by repeating that the objective economic revolution could only "give the proletariat the opportunity and the necessity to change society," and that any transformation could only be the result "of the 'free' action of the proletariat itself" (p. 209).

The valorization of specificity as applied to the everyday life of the worker is the second theme linking the thought of Lukács, Fukumoto, and Nakano. According to Fukumoto's social theory in the article in *Marukusushugi*, the conditions of contemporary society were concentrated in their most extreme form within the life conditions of the proletariat. It was crucial for the proletariat to gain awareness of their position; the proletariat was to find its goal and its historic actions in its own living conditions. For Fukumoto, this notion of life conditions formed part of a dialectic. Self-awareness of the proletariat of its conditions was simultaneously an awareness of the whole, and this self-consciousness (*jiko ninshiki*) was simultaneously the subject and object of knowledge. Theory and revolutionary praxis could be unified if the proletariat would only recognize that through self-knowledge it could move to change itself and thus society.

Here, too, *History and Class Consciousness* could easily have been Fukumoto's source. Lukács had emphasized the importance of detail when he allowed that both the proletariat and the bourgeoisie experienced the reification of "every aspect of its life." The issue at hand was how to make the proletariat aware of how these parts fit into a historically constructed social whole: "The historical knowledge of the proletariat begins with knowledge of the present, with the self-knowledge of its own social situation and with the elucidation of its necessity (i.e., its genesis)" (p. 159). In sum, Lukács showed man in capitalist society confronting a society that he himself had made. Through an awareness that he moved in a self-created world, subject and object could be unified, and the proletariat need no longer be at the mercy of natural laws. For Lukács, unity of thought and action could only be achieved by the comprehension by the proletariat of a new "we" as the conscious subject of history.

The focus on the relationship of such a "we" to history and to the bourgeoisie, along with the emphases on consciousness and on specificity, is the third aspect to Fukumoto's changing of Lukács. He reworked Hegel's

master-bondsman relationship, as had both Lukács and Marx before Lukács. Quoting from the collected works of Marx and Engels, Fukumoto
placed wage labor and capital in opposition. These two forms of the
world of private property and their positions were to be examined, not
separately, but as aspects of the whole. From there he could introduce
Marx's notion of how alienation is experienced differently by the two
classes: the bourgeoisie sees its own strength; the powerlessness of the
proletariat is a source of the realization of the inhumanity of the relationship and of the system of production, and consequently, of revolutionary
consciousness and action. The one class is conservative; the other destructive.[35]

In the schema set forth by Lukács, the bourgeoisie and the proletariat
were the components necessary to provide the only vantage point from
which to understand the organization of contemporary society.[36] He cited
Marx's formulation, from the third volume of *Capital*, of the differing
experiences of alienation by classes related within capitalism—the prop-
erty-owning class, which feels at home in its self-alienation, and the proletariat, which "feels itself destroyed by this alienation and sees in it its
own impotence and the reality of an inhuman existence."[37] Lukács provided the focus for Nakano's emphasis on social pairings in "Notes on
Art Written on the Run." According to the terms of "Class Consciousness," the only way to understand any stage of history was to view the
whole in terms of relationships: "The real nature of socio-historical institutions is that they consist of *relations between men*." This liberated the
student of history from a formalism that treated the social institutions of
history as fossilized objects, products of the "eternal laws of nature." Lukács explained that when analyzing capitalist society, one had to realize
that, according to Marx, capital was not a thing but a social relationship
between persons mediated through things. Marx's *Poverty of Philosophy*
was the source for the correction that "these definite social relations are
just as much the product of men as linen, flax, etc." In the bourgeois
schema all human relationships had taken on the abstract forms of the
elements of natural science and of the laws of nature. Thus, the bourgeois
historian mistakenly focused on relations between individuals, when the
true categories revealed by Marx were the relationship between worker
and capitalist, and between tenant and landlord. To "eliminate these relations" was to "abolish the whole of society." In the words of Lukács,
"history contains nothing that does not lead back ultimately to men and
the relations between men."[38]

---

[35] Fukumoto, "Ōshu ni okeru rekishiteki hatten I," pp. 40–41.
[36] Lukács, *History and Class Consciousness*, p. 59.
[37] Ibid., p. 149.
[38] Ibid., pp. 49–50, 131, 186.

Whether Nakano Shigeharu actually read *History and Class Consciousness*, or whether he merely read Lukács through Fukumoto's translations in the pages of *Marukusushugi*, is not crucial for this reclaiming of the consciousness of Nakano. A reassessment of Nakano's relationship to Fukumoto is important. The histories have emphasized how Fukumoto's politics gave Nakano a model for the organization of the revolutionary writer. What is posited here is that Marxism provided a view of the world and of historical agency that would give him the impetus to embrace poetry as his revolutionary work. Just as Nakano's self-portrait of an intellectually muddled observer-participant of student politics in *Churning* must be called into question by memoirs of contemporaries who recall a very different persona, so must his portrayal of Yasukichi's relationship to a certain Marxist theoretician who makes an appearance in *Churning* be challenged. Many years after the battles of the 1920s, Nakano Shigeharu referred to Fukumoto Kazuo as "A bore—a total bore,"[39] but Fukumoto's place in the writer's life was sufficiently important for Nakano to devote a segment of *Churning* to an encounter with Fukumoto. The Fukumoto character appears in the context of a political shift in student activism following the Peace Preservation Law of 1925. Political activity has been sharply curtailed, and as a result, the youths have turned their enthusiasms toward philosophical concerns. Yasukichi views their concern with the methodology of dialectical materialism as historically necessary but ultimately passive activity. Nakano barely disguises the allusion to Fukumoto's debate with Yamakawa Hitoshi in the pages of *Marukusushugi*: Yasukichi has read the writing of "Iwasaki" in "Studies in Marxism" and cannot understand how his colleagues in the student movement can treat the essays like the Bible. Nonetheless, he is intrigued by the titles—"We Must Start from Mr. Yamada's Treatise on Change of Direction" and "The Resolution Following Cannot Be Without the Division Before It"—and by a style of thinking illustrated in the phrase "the question as to how a thing must become is already answered within the knowledge as to how the thing is at the present."[40] Yasukichi attends Iwasaki's campus lecture, which is a major campus event, and there encounters a bearded, dark-complexioned man thirty-five or thirty-six years of age, dressed in striped slacks and speaking on methodology. Yasukichi understands none of the talk, suspects that the other students surrounding him may also be at a loss, and determines that he may side with the faction of students who treat the thinker as a pedant, in contrast to those who have designated him their leader, yet he is impressed by

---

[39] Shirai Yoshimi, "Nakano Shigeharu ni okeru inazuma tetsugaku," *NSZ, Geppō* 22, vol. 10 (January 1979): 2.

[40] Nakano, *Muragimo, NSZ* 5:224–25.

Iwasaki's surprisingly plain demeanor. The man has the simplicity of a farmer, and when Yasukichi leaves the room with the sounds of German ringing in his ears, he feels like he has made the distinction between dialectical materialism and the materialist grasp of history. But ultimately he feels defrauded, and he lashes out in private: "philosophy—methodology—the thought that he was basically a pantheist raised its head in rebellion." In private rebellion, he recollects village folk practices, protesting that "this is my philosophy."[41] What is important for the reader of this postwar novel seeking clues to Nakano's Taishō experience is not the autobiographical detail of childhood or student experience that may have been inserted into a narrative that admittedly depoliticizes the fictionalized character of the young Nakano. The significant element is that in Nakano's remembrance, Fukumoto Kazuo appears as a theorist of historical materialism, rather than as a strategist of party organization.

Nakano Shigeharu refused to leave behind any account of his discovery of Marxism, yet the reader of Nakano's earliest Taishō manifestos begins to hear a Marxist voicing of theoretical and political concerns. The reader can reimagine a Marxist vision of society rooted in concern for relationship, detail, and the consciousness of both. This voice sings out even louder in Nakano's poetry. His poems, like his earliest theoretical essays, can also be read as a series of manifestos, for if the poems written in Tokyo during the second half of the 1920s were even more distant from the actual words of Marx and his European descendants than Nakano's early, theoretical manifestos, they were also the actual working out of Marxian concepts applied to Nakano's own society and culture—a culture in which a young man in Western clothing and wooden clogs could leave his study of European political theory and revolutions to huddle over a brazier with colleagues and celebrate family through the simple act of cooking. Kurihara Yukio has concluded that the Marxism grasped by Nakano and mediated by Fukumoto Kazuo was transformed into a Marxism bearing no relationship to Fukumotoism.[42] The chapters to follow are a variation on this thesis. They will discuss how the Marxism in Nakano Shigeharu's writing, because of his concerns with the work of the writer and with the specific experience of the commodification of late Taishō capitalist culture, which was being increasingly strangulated by the state, went far beyond the conceptualization of consciousness found in Lukács or Fukumoto. Instead, they were to resonate with the thought of other, contemporary non-Japanese Marxists. One unresolved issue for the young Japanese poet turned Marxist was the place of the intellectual revolutionary. According to both Fukumoto and Lukács, only the op-

[41] Ibid., pp. 224–27.
[42] Kurihara, *Puroretaria bungaku*, p. 41.

pressed proletariat could attain the self-awareness that was a prerequisite for the creation of art capable of grasping and transforming everyday life. Nakano's manifesto, "Notes on Art Written on the Run," follows from this premise, but his self-delegated role as revolutionary artist inserted an element into the scenario that Nakano would have to come to terms with in his version of the specificity of Japanese society in the closing years of the Taishō era. While Nakano moved beyond Lukács to wield a theory of the historical transformation of culture more analogous to the ideas of Antonio Gramsci and Walter Benjamin, it cannot be overemphasized that Nakano discovered history in the words of Marx. To reclaim his discovery of history, we must turn to the first stage of his changing song.

CHAPTER THREE

Song I: The Discovery of History

PLACING HISTORY INTO POETRY

In *Literature and Revolution*, Trotsky noted that the years of revolution had been years of almost total "poetic silence" because "the nightingale of poetry, like the bird of wisdom, the owl, is heard only after the sun is set."[1] Revolutionary literature was to await the end of the current transitional era, but in the meantime poetry was changing: "Language, changed and complicated by urban conditions, gives the poet a new verbal material, and suggests or facilitates new word combinations for the poetic formulations of new thoughts or of new feelings, which strive to break through the dark shell of the subconscious."[2]

This was not a Marxist theory for poetry, nor could Nakano have read Trotsky's thesis in 1925 when he was turning to a revolutionary cultural politics. Yet this theorizing, along with Trotsky's statement that a rearrangement of classes in society "shakes up individuality, establishes the perception of the fundamental problems of lyric poetry from a new angle, and so saves art from eternal repetition"[3] encapsulates Nakano Shigeharu's experience as a Japanese poet working in a new social order and highly conscious of his cultural heritage. Nakano never theorized about his poetic explorations of the experiences of the city-dweller of Taishō era Tokyo, but his poetry preceding and following his turn to Marxism, like his earliest manifestos on literature, shared Trotsky's determination that a proletarian poetry required a technique, transcending mere description of working conditions. Like Nakano, Trotsky sought a new form for poetry, a new language, a "changed song." The emergence of Nakano's allegiance to Marxism and to a Marxist poetry can be found in the early manifestos, but it appears most forcefully in his poetry, as does his own independent formulation of a notion of the production of poetry as revolutionary praxis. What a reading of Nakano's earliest manifestos in poem form, produced during 1925 and 1926, can demonstrate is that he

---

[1] Leon Trotsky, *Literature and Revolution*, trans. Rose Strunsky (New York: International Publishers, 1925), p. 19.

[2] Ibid., p. 167.

[3] Ibid., p. 12.

was able to place a Marxist poetry into Japanese history because his historicizing of nature allowed him to experience the city in history.

In "Danpenteki yosō" (Fragmentary forecasts),[4] an overview of the literary world written for the mainstream *Bungei shunjū* in January 1928, Nakano called for a "way of seeing things," a *mono no mikata* that could distinguish his work from two wrong-headed approaches. The author gave short shrift to the writers representing the first approach—writers such as Tanizaki Junichirō, who could not see the movement of things and did not even attempt to do so. Socialist writers were guilty of an idealism: "For them always in the beginning there is the word." Only by having what Nakano termed "the eyes of a Marxist" could one engage in a third alternative allowing the writer to give life to art. This third, Marxist view was historicist—"Only when things are seen in their historical form are they for the first time seen accurately." To grasp the process of history was to be in command of a complexity not available in a university history textbook, and although all of the rich aspects of history, such as the history of medicine and the ways of viewing art, could not be reclaimed, the process of historical change had to be understood.[5] Most central to Marx's notion of history, and to Nakano's, is the placement of man as historical subject who creates history through praxis, or revolutionary action that alters his environment. This change had to be brought about not only by revolution, but also by labor, which in Hegel, Marx, and Nakano is linked with consciousness and placed within nature. In this sense, Nakano belongs within the line of "Western Marxists" who, according to the definition of Russell Jacoby, were "committed to a Hegelian core of Marxism, the idea of humanity producing itself through its own praxis."[6] Nakano's historical transformation from apolitical lyrical poet to Hegelian, Marxist lyrical poet concerned with subjectivity, consciousness, and revolutionary praxis is inscribed most sharply in his poems on the seashore.

The poet had grown to love the coast of the Japan Sea as a youth, and he would continue to imagine it as his vision of society and of history took form. "Shiranami" (White waves),[7] one of his earliest poems, was

---

[4] Nakano, "Danpenteki yosō," *NSZ* 9:113–16 [*Bungei shunjū* 1/28].

[5] Ibid., pp. 113–14.

[6] Russell Jacoby, *Dialectic of Defeat: Contours of Western Marxism* (Cambridge: Cambridge University Press, 1981), p. 46. Jacoby contrasts "scientific" with Western Marxism. According to his dichotomy, the so-called Scientific Marxists, who triumphed in the Soviet Union, claimed that dialectics could be applied uniformly to society and to nature.

[7] Nakano, "Shiranami," *NSZ* 1:493–94 [*Razō* 1/25]. All translations are from *NSZ*, vol. 1, which has reproductions of Nakano's poems in their original form, but the original place of publication and date of first appearance will also be listed in the footnotes.

the first of these explorations in verse form, written within a year of Nakano's move to Tokyo in the spring of 1924.

WHITE WAVES

What is here is a desolate, narrow shore line
The undulatings swell far out to sea
And meeting they approach
And on this shore
Raising lonely voice
They fall, in autumn guise
That echoes deep
Redounds sadly on mountains closing in on water's edge
Even the sturdy train is wont to hesitate
Spray surrounds the windowpane like fog
Ahh—the land of Echigo; the beach of Oyashirazu Ichifuri
In the rest between crashing whitecaps
Does not this heart, on my journey, assume a chill damp

Nature overwhelms the narrator, as the waves control the poet's emotions. In addition, history is obliterated, as Nakano invokes the premodern term for the Niigata Prefecture area, the country of Echigo, thus adopting a mythic tone associated with folklore. There is a sense of suffocation as the notion of the mountains closing in serves to magnify the sounds of the waves, through the echo. Space is also overpowered by time as Nakano uses the term "rest" or time off (*hima*) to denote the physicality of the sea water, which has subsided in between the oncoming waves. The young student commuting through his homeland is free only to observe and to be captured by an omnipotent nature, and the melancholy affect of the poem is heightened by the name of the beach, as the literal translation of the word "Oyashirazu" is "not knowing ones parents," another indicator of divorce from time.

One month later, in February 1925, "Suihen wo saru" (Leaving the water's edge)[8] intensified this theme of domination by nature. In this poem the water actively commands the poet to leave, thereby silencing him. Again, nature is endowed with voice and emotion, and the poet's response is rendered passive and despondent:

LEAVING THE WATER'S EDGE

I shall leave this quiet water's edge
Even the water loathes me today
As the heart of the water is well behaved
It won't tell me so

[8] Nakano, "Suihen wo saru," *NSZ* 1:497 [*Razō* 2/25].

Except if I head away in that direction
The water will no doubt begin to sing its own quiet song
I shall leave this quiet water's edge
The water appears to invite me to do just so

Although nature is in command, the lyrics expressing its power are soft and tentative. The decision to leave is based on ambivalent feelings expressed in the term "I shall leave" (*sarimashō*), which indicates a future act, but it is said without declaratory impact in a tone consonant with the poet's speculation that the water will begin to sing (*utaihajimerudeshō*). The personification of nature as poet is secondary to the problem of the poet-narrator's stance in responding to nature's dictate. He is neither within nature nor totally apart from it and instead stands beside it, ever ready to respond to its rhythms.

In "Nami" (Waves),[9] published in May of the same year, both the poet and society are totally overwhelmed in a landscape where "neither man nor dog exists." Here the reproduction of the rhythm of the waves implied in the first of the sea poems, "White Waves," is developed to its extreme. Neither time nor spatial or geographic differentiation is possible within the cyclical tableau painted by Nakano. Man is outside of nature, and nature is outside of time:

WAVES

There are neither persons nor dogs and there are only waves
The waves are white ones and without pause they are falling away
The waves come running then are quietly falling away
The waves again come running then are quietly falling away
Neither persons nor dogs there
Where the waves fall away the wind comes up without break
The wind contains the fragrance of the seashore and is wet with spray
The waves from morning on are falling away
Even after evening they are still falling away
The waves fall away on this seashore
This shore continues onto that shore beyond
And also it continues all the way to the north
All the way to the south—it also continues
In the north there are also homelands,
Toward the south there are also homelands
And there are beaches
The waves there too are falling away
Continuing from here on they are falling away
Even there the waves come running then are quietly falling away

[9] Nakano, "Nami," *NSZ* 1:503–504 [*Razō* 5/25].

The waves fall away from morning   [stanza break]
The waves fall away from their tops downward
Even after evening they are still falling away
The wind is blowing
Neither persons nor dogs there

The setting of "White Waves" has been extended, so that the beach of Oyashirazu and the homeland of Echigo merge into one continuous shore line where time is of so little consequence that even morning cannot be distinguished from evening.

The young poet has begun his project of changing poetry, through the production of a changed song or *kaeuta*. He has introduced in the three poems a new form by which to express traditional concerns, like the Meiji poets, to whom he has given credit. The disciplined meter of the Japanese poem, restricted by the rule of five- and seven-syllable units, has been replaced by Nakano's sometimes unwieldy phrasings, which gain their strength through repetition of word endings, words, and entire lines. Yet he has maintained the haiku poet's stance toward nature as an entity for the poet to observe as he records his emotions. Like many poems written by his Japanese predecessors, Nakano's verses are tinged with a sad recognition of a transience that the poet cannot control.

Nakano's conception of nature in the above poems adheres to Feuerbach's formulations which Marx attacked in *The German Ideology*.[10] Marx clarified his own position as antithetical to Feuerbach's separation of man from nature and placement of nature before human history. In the words of Marx, Feuerbach could not see that "the sensuous world around him is not a thing given direct for all eternity." Marx elaborates: the sensuous world is a "historical product" of "the activity of a whole succession of generations, each standing on the shoulders of the preceding one, developing its industry and its intercourse, and modifying its social system according to the changed needs."[11] The Marxist philosopher Ernst Bloch shows how Marx's third thesis on Feuerbach, which concludes with the theoretical pronouncement that "the coincidence of the changing of circumstances and of human activity or self-transformation can be grasped and rationally understood only as *revolutionary practice*," is developed in the first volume of *Capital*, where man is posited in relation to the external world and to nature. In Marx's dialectic, human activity and consciousness are placed within nature, as "transformative praxis" or activity, which in turn determines consciousness.[12]

[10] Karl Marx and Frederick Engels, *The German Ideology* (Moscow: Progress Publishers, 1976), p. 46.

[11] Ibid., p. 45.

[12] Ernst Bloch, *On Karl Marx* (New York: Herder & Herder, 1971), pp. 55, 72.

Nakano Shigeharu adopts this dialectic in "Kitami no kaigan" (The beach at Kitami),[13] his first poem to look at things from a Marxist perspective. This poem, positing man within nature and nature within a progressive history, appeared one year after "Waves," as one of the first of twenty-three poems that would be published in the journal *Roba* over the following two years. This text, like most of the *Roba* poems, did not call for revolutionary activity overtly as did later poems that challenged Japanese society from the pages of the Communist-backed *Puroretaria shimbun* and the journals of the revolutionary Culture Movement during the second half of 1927 and the opening months of 1928. Nonetheless, "The Beach at Kitami" is a Marxist manifesto developing in verse form both a theory of social change and a critique of contemporary Japanese society. It can be surmised that in 1926, when Nakano wrote "The Beach at Kitami," the young Shinjinkai member was still in the process of formulating his own version of Marxism as it applied to Japan. Yet the vagueness of the social analysis in the poem cannot be attributed solely to his lack of familiarity with Marxist theory, for the poem also spoke of the historical reality: the actors in class conflict were still emerging within late Taishō culture. Nakano implied that just as the shadowy scavenger on the beach receives increasingly sharp definition during the course of the verses, so the lines of class conflict were being drawn more and more dramatically in escalating labor union strife and in tenancy struggles coming out of the history retold in the poem:

THE BEACH AT KITAMI

The seashore is buried in gases
The beach is soaked wet
Along that beach moves the black shadow of a man
The black shadow of a man holds a hand-net
The black shadow of a man raises the hand-net seeking out a meager catch
Who is this black shadow of a man
Where did the black shadow of a man come from I wonder?

The catch it seems must always be meager
The hamlet it would seem quite cold
Not much to talk about between wife and child
And will his catch be sold then

[13] Nakano, "Kitami no kaigan," *NSZ* 1:504–505 [*Roba* 4/26]. Kitagawa Tōru contrasts "The Beach at Kitami" with the seaside motif of "Waves" and treats this poem as the transition into Nakano's *Roba* poems. He concludes that the poem's treatment of the reality of an imagined world that cannot be grasped by a camera's eye expresses a methodological shift resulting from Nakano's encounter with Marxism. The focus here is on Nakano's treatment of the process of history rather than his evocation of a future. Kitagawa Tōru, *Nakano Shigeharu*, Kindai Nihon shijinsen 15 (Chikuma shobō, 1981), pp. 79–83.

In his hand will change remain then
No indeed
He will quietly move up this beach farther and farther to the north
Lowering the hand-net
Wife and child taken along
Animals not taken along

Finally a train may run along here maybe
Large buildings to stand
Black smoke to rise from high chimneys maybe
And lively oiled voices to rise rush up maybe
And then at that time
Where will the black shadow of a man be
Where will his son and daughter be
And will they not take ill
And will there be a doctor
And will they not then die then

Where does the black shadow of a man come from I wonder?
The black shadow of a man is wet

While the labor of fishing from a hand-net is primitive, this action places the shadow of the fisherman firmly within nature as he acts upon it. Nakano rejects what Lukács has termed the bourgeois notion of nature, which would have nature grow organically, in contrast to the artificial constructs of human civilization,[14] for the beach of Kitami is transformed into an industrial site. Nakano focuses on the image of the shadow laboring within nature because he wants to underscore the idea of man as subject within nature, transforming it. Like Lukács he rejects the bourgeois materialism of the eighteenth century wherein man appeared as the product of his social milieu and adopts Marx's notion that "all production is appropriation of nature on the part of an individual within and through a specific form of society." Thus, the lone black shadow who at first appears isolated on the beach and captive to the whims of nature is involved in the appropriation of nature. According to Marx's acerbic attack on Bruno Bauer in *The German Ideology*, even when the sensuous world is reduced to a stick, this presupposes the historic action of the production of the stick.[15] Nakano would not have access to *The German Ideology* until almost a decade later, but Marx developed the vision of man within nature, acting to change it and himself, most fully in the first volume of *Capital* in a passage that, according to Ernst Bloch, was an elaboration of the Third Thesis. Bloch concluded that

[14] Lukács, *History and Class Consciousness*, p. 136.
[15] Ibid., p. 134. Marx, *The German Ideology*, pp. 47–48.

this pronouncement decisively emphasized man's relation to the external world and to nature, but this segment is also decisive in its graphic wording of man in motion:

> [Man] opposes himself to Nature as one of her own forces, setting in motion arms and legs, head and hands, the natural forces of his body, in order to appropriate Nature's productions in a form adapted to his own wants. By thus acting on the external world and changing it, he at the same time changes his own nature.[16]

The black shadow of the man on the Kitami Beach is Nakano Shigeharu's version of the mythic Robinson Crusoe, the object of Marx's scorn in his documentation of bourgeois ideology's denial of the social context for the individual's appropriation of labor. According to Marx, such mythologizing has denied the truth that the individual engages in sensuous activity within nature and that he does so, perforce, in conjunction with other individuals in a nexus of social relationships. This idea appears in *The German Ideology*, where Marx places the individual within history: "the first premise of all human history, of course, is the existence of living human individuals," whose first act is that they produce their own means of subsistence. These individuals "enter into [these] definite social and political relations" and cannot be conceived of independently of social structure or state, which evolve from relations between men as they "actually are, i.e., as they act, produce materially, and hence as they work under definite material limits, presuppositions and conditions independent of their will."[17] Yet political economists like Smith and Ricardo, whom Marx labeled eighteenth-century "Robinsonnades" in his introduction to the *Grundrisse*, had concocted the individual, isolated hunter or fisherman—the "Natural Individual . . . not arising historically but posited by Nature." The ideology of the society of free competition, by freeing the individual from seemingly natural bonds of social obligations arising from earlier eras, had succeeded in obscuring the relationality of worker and employer in the present.[18]

Neither *The German Ideology* nor the *Grundrisse* were available to Japanese students of Marxism, but in *Capital*, the work available to Nakano by 1925, Marx provided the most complete critique of the bourgeois writer's vision of Robinson Crusoe's self-sufficient labors on his "island bathed in light." Here Marx relied on the mythic hero to contrast his autonomy with the overt, visible, personal dependence of the producer within the system of compulsory labor in medieval Europe, preceding the

[16] Bloch, *Karl Marx*, p. 72.
[17] Marx, *The German Ideology*, pp. 37, 41.
[18] Marx, *Grundrisse*, trans. Martin Nicolaus (New York: Vintage Books, 1973), p. 83.

masking of social relationships within the capitalist system of commodity production and exchange.[19] Lukács was to provide an elaboration on the conceit by incorporating it into his theory of consciousness. He would conclude that bourgeois thought could not accept the historic truth that the subject of historic action was class. Instead, the subject constructed by bourgeois thought was the individual capable of perceiving only fragments of a social totality. The actions and knowledge of this "egoistic bourgeois" who was "isolated artificially by capitalism" were animated by "an individual isolated consciousness à la Robinson Crusoe."[20]

In Nakano's poem the life of the man producing the human shadow can only be inferred from the queries of the narrator in the first verse. He is an autonomous Robinson Crusoe on a desolate beach, until the narrator gives him a history by questioning his origin and conjectures about his social nexus—his family—within a rural, hamlet society. When the shadow moves on, Nakano does not offer any commentary on his consciousness, for it is his *movement*, along with his displacement, that comprise the subject of the remainder of the poem, a commentary on the process of historical change. The first verse has indicated that production is an appropriation of nature; the rest of the poem proceeds to place that appropriation within a social context, and then to determine that the social forms are within a shifting, transformative history of actions. History is a process of development—of both material production and consciousness.

The poet depicts a historical transition made possible by the grafting of urban onto rural, industrial onto agricultural, and modern onto premodern. Japanese capitalism displaces Japanese feudalism, not only through his image of the replacement of shore line by train and buildings, but through his use of language. There is a shift from the contemporary colloquial language of the first stanza into a more archaic rural dialect in the second verse as Nakano surrounds the isolated shadow with family and community; the interrogative verb ending connoting conjecture, *darō*, is substituted by a harder rural ending; *karō*, and a premodern term for emphasis, *sadameshi*, is used to emphasize the degree of coldness in the hamlet. The dearth of material for conversation is also indicated by the *karō* ending the line. Both the phrasing of "not much to talk about" (*hanashi no tane ga sukunakarō*) and the question as to whether the catch will be sold (*ureyōka*) also imply a premodern or precapitalist mode of language and thus of consciousness. Within the same stanza Nakano shifts out of this mode to readopt the modern *darō* ending for conjecture.

[19] Marx, *Capital*, 1:76–77.
[20] Lukács, *History and Class Consciousness*, pp. 135, 165.

The transition to urban industrialization is denoted by the modern colloquial "maybe" (*kamoshirenu*) in the third stanza, and the same tone is maintained for the remainder of the poem.

Nakano evokes the transition to capitalism within Japan by implying a complex process of replacement of one mode of production and of language by another. His image of historical change here is best expressed in his own words, offered five years after the publication of "The Beach at Kitami" as part of an indictment of an evolutionist approach to history. The author rejects the notion that the capitalist side is "on this side of the river, and socialist society on the other side," and that the two need merely be bridged. Instead there is a dialectical movement:

> We must comprehend that capitalist society is born, as the development of the history of class society, and from that very capitalist society the working class is born, and this class fights with capitalism, and topples it. It is there, within the process of the establishment of the dictatorship of the proletariat, that we find the movement of mankind from capitalist society to socialist society.[21]

In 1931, with this passage, Nakano would emphasize that "revolutionary struggle" and not evolutionary notions of "development" or "turning point" were relevant analytic structures for the conceptualization of history, because struggle was the only means to historical transformation. But in 1926, Nakano's sights were aimed at the second part of this conclusion. In other words, he was not rehearsing the struggle of revolution, but discovering the idea of the dialectic of historical change.

In 1926, "The Beach at Kitami" rejected the bourgeois method of history, which would isolate objects, by placing the shadow within the seaside setting on which Nakano superimposes the structures of industrial society. In this seascape the actor is no longer at the water's edge or viewing it from afar, but is within the landscape, acting on it. The poem places objects—the shadow, the beach, the buildings devoted to industrial production—within a system of relations, thus making the concept of change plausible, and thus illustrating Bloch's exegesis of Marx on Feuerbach:

> A little penetration will show that every object in our normal surroundings is by no means a pure *datum*. An object is, rather, the final outcome of antecedent processes of human labor; and even the raw material, quite apart from the fact that it is completely transformed, has been drawn from the forest by labor or hewed out of the rocks, or improved after being extracted from the depths of the earth.[22]

---

[21] Nakano, "Puroretaria geijutsu to wa nanika?" *NSZ* 9:340 [Sōgō puroretaria geijutsu kōza, vol. 1, 5/31].

[22] Bloch, *Karl Marx*, p. 69.

Five years later an article in the popular magazine *Kaizō* would explain Marx's critique of Crusoe to a Japanese audience;[23] but in the poem published in 1926 Nakano provided an illustration without citation. Nakano had not chronicled the rise in consciousness of a new working class, but had attempted through his depiction of the shadow, who is denied labor and possibly life, to express the contradiction resulting from progress. In other words, the shadow was not conscious of his role as actor or of the forces overwhelming him. There was a gap between history and the consciousness of history, as set forth by Lukács:

> As history is essentially dialectical, this view of the way reality changes can be confirmed at every decisive moment of transition. Long before men become conscious of the decline of a particular economic system, and the social and juridical forms associated with it, its contradictions are fully revealed in the objects of its day-to-day actions.[24]

According to Lukács, this gap could be closed through the creation of the subject of the *creator*, and this is what "The Beach at Kitami" accomplished. For while Nakano's subject, the black shadow of a man, is eventually to be replaced by others, he does move in a self-created world, constructed from the materials provided by a historicized nature. Again, Nakano is in agreement with Lukács, who cited Vico's famous dictum that "men have made their own history."[25] The shadow is an actor through his labor just as his capitalist successors on the beach, who speak in "lively, oiled voices" as they build the factories and the trains and profit by them, are actors. "The Beach at Kitami" thus chronicles both misery and progress, but through its focus on transition to industrial society it problematizes the present, placing it within history.

For Lukács, the historical knowledge or consciousness of the proletariat could only begin with knowledge of the present, as it recognized its own social situation. This class could only then move forward in revolutionary action.[26] Nakano's poetry took this theory of historical change in another direction. Most Japanese poetry had effaced history, but this Japanese poet had now shown man to be actor and transformer of nature and society, which opened his poetry to further change via the production of new sorts of verse, or *kaeuta*. These changed songs, in turn, demanded literary and social change, because Nakano had met the requirement set forth by Marx in the *Poverty of Philosophy* as quoted by Lukács: "[But] the moment we present men as the actors and authors of their own his-

---

[23] Ōkuma Nobuyuki, "Marukusu no Robinson monogatari," *Kaizō* (June 1929): 14–31.
[24] Lukács, *History and Class Consciousness*, p. 175.
[25] Ibid., pp. 112, 142.
[26] Ibid., p. 159.

tory, we arrive—by a detour—at the real starting point."[27] By centering man as actor, Nakano could create the "we" that Lukács had termed the subject of history; he could document the history of the "we" that was the subject of history—the "we" whose action was in fact history. And in the poems of Nakano Shigeharu, the "we" or the *wareware* that appeared most vividly as a newly emerging class were the revolutionary intellectuals.[28]

Placing the Intellectual into History

Just as a close, chronological reading of Nakano's verse written from 1925 through 1926 (the era corresponding to his first experience of activism) places Nakano's notion of nature into the history of his thought, so also is there a profound shift in the poet's consciousness of himself as a thinker. During this period he joined the Shinjinkai and the Kyōdō printers' strike and helped initiate the Marxist Arts Study Group, *Roba*, and the Proletarian Arts League. The poems give no details of these events, but they document the process whereby Nakano self-consciously placed himself within Japanese history and in the political arena as a writer creating a group experience. Nakano's project for the prerevolutionary intellectual contrasted sharply with Trotsky's idea that the intellectual in the Soviet postrevolutionary context was to be a bearer of culture who gave form to the experience of the peasant turned proletarian. According to Trotsky, "Our art is the expression of the intellectual, who hesitates between the peasant and proletarian and who is incapable organically of merging either with one or the other, but who gravitates more towards the peasant, because of his intermediary position, and because of his connections. He cannot become a peasant, but he can sing the peasant."[29] Nakano's intellectual is himself a revolutionary actor, and while the figures and the settings in his prewar revolutionary poetry varied, the poet would insist on a recurrent theme: the urgency of his work. The poems would not spell out specific tasks for completion, nor would they offer guidelines for revolution. Rather Nakano would imply that the intellectual works with words, and that this task is inseparable from revolutionary organizing. Art and political action are not distinguished in the making of revolutionary history. Here then is the answer to the question raised by Nakano's choice of revolutionary labor, but unanswered by Fukumoto or Lukács. Nakano resolved that just as the worker faces the

[27] Ibid., p. 160.

[28] Ibid., p. 145. Kitagawa has also commented on the very apparent shift from a focus on the experience of a single individual to the use of the group subject during the *Roba* era. Kitagawa, *Nakano Shigeharu*, p. 129.

[29] Trotsky, *Literature and Revolution*, p. 11.

capitalist, the revolutionary writer confronts his nonrevolutionary counterparts and capitalists in the publishing world. To forge art, specifically poetry, is to wage war. Art becomes inseparable from literature, literary production from labor, and the violence of the mass media from the alienation experienced in the workplace as—to borrow a phrasing from Trotsky—the poet seeks to sing the peasant-worker and the colonized and to sing the intellectual in his changed song. When in January 1925, in the first issue of *Razō*, Nakano placed a Japanese folk hero, Urashimatarō, in the center of a poem by that name[30] (one of his earliest free-verse poems), he initiated the process of inserting the intellectual into history.

In the legend of Urashimatarō, the hero is spirited to a glorious underwater paradise astride a tortoise and returned to earth carrying a treasure chest, which he is admonished to maintain sealed. Upon opening the Pandora's box, he is immediately transformed into an old man, deprived of the eternal youth promised him by a princess. Urashimatarō is akin to Robinson Crusoe—he is alone, outside of history, until he is forced to confront the historical gap between his departure and his reentry into time and society. The story of Rip Van Winkle may provide a better Western analogue to the Japanese folktale, but the central issue for Nakano is that the man, like Crusoe, lacks a sense of history or memory, and therefore possesses no identity.

URASHIMATARŌ

Raining this night
Again at the house just nearby they've begun the phonograph
The little girl does sing "Urashimatarō," raising her piercing voice
Urashima rode on a tortoise . . . . . .
Was the favorite of the princess . . . . . .
Then old white-haired he
You sing too
Then tell me—of whom this song sings

While the last two lines of this poem invite the reader in, to participate in a dialogue with the music and with the poet, "you" would appear to be the narrator himself, seeking to gain some connection with his own surroundings. The poem contains a song—an *uta* within an *uta*, which the narrator cannot transcend. He cannot go beyond hearing the song on the phonograph "again" because the literature of Nakano's poem, the legend of Urashimatarō, the reproduction of the legend in song form, and the present are merged in his use of language, which obliterates a sense of historical change. The chant-like lyrics are in smooth harmony with Nakano's use of the somewhat archaic term *koyoi* for "this night," which

[30] Nakano, "Urashimatarō," *NSZ* 1:403 [*Razō* 1/25].

often appears in love songs. The narrator strives to identify Urashimatarō and, by implication, to place himself in society and history by breaking out of the confinement of his experience as audience for the song, as "again" the phonograph begins to play its song.

In "Tanbo no onna" (Women in the rice fields),[31] the poet is again a passive observer, this time of labor and consequently of a sociality that is denied him. Nonetheless, as in the previous poem, he uses words implying a desire for ongoing conversational exchange, as he opens with the affirmative "it is so" or "Yes" (sōdesu) as though he and the reader are in the middle of a dialogue:

WOMEN IN THE RICE FIELDS

Yes
What tranquil weather
The sky is all clear and a black thrush passes over
And in the rice field stubble sprouts shoot up .
You are all seated there
You are all three chatting on a small straw mat
You are pinning up one another's hair
And turning to me, walking by, you call out to me so fondly

Three gentle women sitting in the rice fields
I want to go over to join in with you
I want to go and sit there
To hear your special talk
But you all there
You all there are women of the quarters and I am but a student
Yes indeed, it is truly tranquil weather
There there is a straightforward footpath   One narrow paddy path in back
    of your own streets
I want to go over there to mix in openly
But nonetheless I must depart

Good-bye women in the rice fields
I will return to you one smile
Now then breathe in much good sunshine
Now then breathe in much clean air
I will leave now
Good-bye   people of the rice fields   You three in the rice fields

This may be a poem about an adolescent ill at ease with his sexuality, intrigued by the allure of the "special talk" of the women who sell their

[31] Nakano, "Tanbo no onna," NSZ 1:496 [Razō 2/25].

bodies in the quarter behind the rice fields.[32] But another reading is possible. According to this interpretation, the placement of the women in the fields renders them farm women, women at rest from rural work. In other words, the rural origins of the prostitutes in the first reading become significant. If the women are taken to be farm laborers, Nakano confronts a contradiction raised in Trotsky's *Literature and Revolution*, the intrinsic distinction between manual, physical labor and the activity of the intellectual. The poem then affirms the labor of the women as superior. Beginning with the assertive "Yes" (*sōdesu*), the poet forcefully describes the work site of the women without the use of the conjecture or doubt that characterized his pre-Marxist seaside poems. The narrator acknowledges that he is separate from the workers and is actively jealous of their "special talk," which implies a life not open to him. Yet the poem is also tinged with nostalgia in its use of the premodern language for weather (*hiyori*), and of the soft, rural adjective *tanto*, quantifying the sunshine. It is as though the narrator recognizes that the farm women will not be isolated from the world for long. The narrow paddy path behind the city is too close to the new urban capitalist world for it not to impinge on the pace of their production; the subjugation of the countryside by the bourgeoisie, set forth in *The Communist Manifesto*, may be implied. In any case, the narrator's identity as an urbanized intellectual—as a "student" of the society instead of a producer within society—and his vantage point from the footpath illustrate Marx's separation of rural from urban in the *Manifesto*. In *The German Ideology* Marx emphasized this division by stating uncategorically that "the most important division of material and mental labor is the separation of town and country."[33] Thus, while this poem can be read as a commentary on the merging of rural with urban labor, it shares with "Urashimatarō," "White Waves," and "Leaving the Water's Edge" an emphasis on the poet's separation from society.

The pain of solitude is most clear in the early poem "Yoru no aisatsu" (Evening greetings).[34] Here the poet creates a comrade to mitigate the isolation in a world reduced to the four walls of the intellectual's room. A shadow reappears here, in changed form:

EVENING GREETINGS

The night's come round again
Old shadow on the wall

[32] This reading provides one exception to the paucity of sexual allusions in Nakano's work. In this context it should be noted that by the time the poem was published in the first edition of Nakano's collected poems, he had taken out an erotic allusion by deleting the line about the women tying up their hair. Cf. Nakano, *Nakano Shigeharu shishū* (Nappu shuppanbu, 1931), pp. 138–40.

[33] Marx, *Communist Manifesto*, p. 477; Marx, *The German Ideology*, p. 72.

[34] Nakano, "Yoru no aisatsu," *NSZ* 1:502 [*Razō* 5/25].

Sad nighttime has again come round
I'll just go out for a while
Over that-a-way for a quick one and then back
Brother there on the wall
You'll be bored I know
Be patient all alone there for a while
I'll be back real fast
And then when I'm back old boy
As always, old boy
You can make me cry and have a good ole time
Because there at your knees
I'll be crying quietly
Well then old boy/brother on the wall/old shadow
I'll be going out for a while
Stretch yourself out busy yourself reading something maybe a magazine

The closeness of the space is reinforced by the use of time in the poem. Time comes "round again" in an endless repetition of a cycle of passive actions: the narrator reads, drinks, and thinks. "Evening Greetings" appeared in May 1925 along with "White Waves." Both signaled the end of one stage in Nakano Shigeharu's thought, for he published no poems between that May and the following April when "The Beach at Kitami" appeared in the first issue of *Roba*. By this time the poems in *Roba* and elsewhere made it very clear that the poet had broken out of the melancholy expressed in "Evening Greetings" and "White Waves" by placing the intellectual within history and thus society, by giving him work.

The break in Nakano's poetry from 1925 until April 1926 indicates that his energies during the hiatus were channeled into a discovery of Marxism.[35] The political activism column of the hypothetical chronology tends to confirm this conjecture, but Nakano left no document from that year other than the short story "Oroka na onna" (A foolish woman),[36] which won him first place in a fiction and photography contest. The story, organized around a conversation between a student and a waitress, was cited for its freshness and restlessness by Murō Saisei, the judge for the short story component of the competition.[37] Murō saw something new and wonderful in the story of a young woman who had planned marriage with a fellow factory worker who then abandoned her for the army, but in no way can the story be said to reflect any study of Marxist theory, or to express the sentiments evident in Nakano's poetry and essays from

[35] Kitagawa Tōru also pinpoints Nakano's turn to Marxism as occurring in 1925, coinciding with a year of silence undoubtedly spent in study. Kitagawa, *Nakano Shigeharu*, pp. 76–79.
[36] Nakano, "Oroka na onna," NSZ 1:157–62 [*Shizuoka shinpō* 1/1/26].
[37] Murō Saisei, cited in "Kaidai," NSZ 1:556.

1926 onward. In the pages of *Roba*, the references of an intense intellectual in motion bristled in a changed poetry animated by a dedication to work. The opening line of "Yoakemae no sayonara" (Farewell before daybreak),[38] which appeared in *Roba* one month after "The Beach at Kitami," stated Nakano's new sense of direction simply and directly, as he declared, "We must to our work":

FAREWELL BEFORE DAYBREAK

We must to our work
For that we must have consultation
But when we consult
Policemen come and beat on eyes and noses
So we changed the second floor
Thinking of the alley and the sneak-out back

Six youths are sleeping here
Below one pair of married couple and one baby sleep
I do not know the past lives of these youths
I only know that they are joined with me
I do not know the couple's name below
I only know they happily lent us the second floor

Daybreak will come presently
I suppose we'll have to move again
Clutching onto satchels
We shall have our detailed meeting
Steady steady we will heft our work
Tomorrow night no doubt we'll sleep on different borrowed bedding

Daybreak will come presently
This four and half mat room here
These diapers hanging on the cord here
This sooty naked light bulb here
The celluloid toys here
Borrowed bedding here
Fleas here
I say good-bye to you
To make the flowers bloom
Our flowers
The flowers of the couple below
The flowers of the baby
To make all those flowers furiously bloom at all one time.

[38] Nakano, "Yoakemae no sayonara," *NSZ* 1:505–506 [*Roba* 5/26].

This is a different farewell from the parting extended to the women in the field or to the shadow on the wall, for the narrator is no longer an idle, aimless observer. He now has tasks to complete, and, most importantly, the intellectual is no longer alone but is now a part of "we"—of the comradeship of the group joined with him. There is also a new use of language, evidenced not only in a new, freer sense of play with words, as in the phrasing "we changed the second floor" (*nikai wo kaeta*), a purposefully awkward term implying the switch from one apartment to another, or in the understatement that the policeman will "beat on eyes and nose." The use of the sympathetic, child's term of respect for the authority of the police officer in this phrase, *omawari ga kite me ya hana wo tataku*, along with the euphemism for revolution—"making flowers bloom"— may be explained away as avoidance of government censorship, but more likely it is Nakano's conscious, Brechtian attempt to force a confrontation with violence by distancing the reader through what seems at first to be inappropriate language.

The poet's sense of time is no longer cyclical. Although the work site will be reproduced on different second floors, and on different bedding, he is now living and working within teleological movement toward revolution. His colleagues appear more anonymous than either the fictional shadow-brother or the three flirtatious women in the fields. They are given neither names nor historical pasts, because joint participation in the class struggle provides sufficient basis for their relationship. In contrast, he does picture the life of the proletarian couple. The listing of diapers, naked light bulb, toys, and old bedding provides the detail demanded by Nakano in his essays on art. The term *sayonara* with short "o" is also a commentary on the worker's life, for this abbreviated form of the formal farewell is the Tokyo worker's use of language. Nonetheless, "Farewell Before Daybreak" does not proceed beyond its affirmation of work to discuss the narrator's labors. Instead, the poem "Hibi" (Days)[39] outlines one version of what forced the pace of the movement of the poet-revolutionary who sought periods of rest in borrowed rooms:

DAYS

Friend's got appendicitis
Almost might be fired
All the guys in the house gone broke
Soon as they see a body say got a cigarette on you
Haven't you say
Have to run errands
Have to read economics

[39] Nakano, "Hibi," *NSZ* 1:508 [*Roba* 7/26].

And got the urge to make 'em cave in
Aritaotomatsu[40] and
Newspapersandbooks and
Diet members and ministers and genrō
Whatever one sees
Only deceptions appear to tease
You push them away, with study/more study
But you can't quite study
You sleep on the train
In one day twenty-four hours you can't get it done

This is verse written by a harried student, but it is not homework that fuels his anxiety; his task is to analyze his own society, preparatory to changing it. He is in the process of transferring the skills learned at Tokyo Imperial University, and in the Shinjinkai group-house alluded to in the poem, to revolutionary work. The tools are the same—they are his papers, his books. And, as expressed with fervor in the poem "Sōji" (Cleaning),[41] most importantly, it is language that he will wield in his struggle as he separates out the newspapers from the books, along with the various political forces that threaten to overwhelm him in one unified image of injustice, so that he may create and present his own categories in his work:

CLEANING

Having useless things around is useless
All of it, without exception I threw into the fire
Varying sorts of paper
Varying sorts of language
Postmarks and
Seals and
Notations of places and people's names
And lip-shaped red paint
Chocolate spit out onto paper and
All burned up without a trace
Anything that tries prying open the cover on the past
That tries repeating and rewinding and lining up the same complaints
Anything that tries thus to shrink the speed of work
All of it leaving nothing I burned completely up
Pouring water on the ashes
Sweeping them all away
I leaped at the continuation of my work

---

[40] The meaning of this apparent slurring of terms, written in *katakana*, is not clear.
[41] Nakano, "Sōji," NSZ 1:509–10 [*Roba* 9/26].

"Cleaning" is a negation of the sentiments expressed in "Urashima-tarō." The narrator is in control of his identity, and of his history. He does not ask for a clarification of subject, because he is the subject, acting through his work and in control of his history, unlike Urashimatarō, who by opening the cover on the past was overwhelmed by the burden of time and thereby immobilized. The poem is also an affirmation of the political over the personal as it indicates that the narrator has hitherto led an aimless existence because he has experimented with various people and varied use of language. His life is now focused. As in "Farewell before Dawn," the term "work" is sufficient to affirm that the intellectual is now a laborer within the revolutionary process.

Nakano Shigeharu has obliterated the distinction between manual and intellectual labor which was so clearly outlined by Marx and affirmed by both Trotsky and Lukács. As discussed above, his early poetry had alluded to the division of labor so castigated by Marx in *The German Ideology* wherein he noted that the "division of labor only becomes truly such from the moment when a division of material and mental labor appears" after which consciousness could "flatter itself that it is something other than consciousness of existing practice."[42] Just as material and mental labor are isolated from each other, enjoyment and labor are mutually exclusive categories of experience, as are production and consumption. Only by negating the division of labor, concludes Marx, can these divisions be obliterated. Trotsky would accept this division of mental and manual labor as the basis for his notion of the "culture-bearing" role of the intellectual, who aims at civilizing the revolutionary proletariat. For Lukács, it was the division of labor that gave the worker sole access to revolutionary consciousness. Through material labor he had unique access to understanding the premise of capitalism, the production and exchange of the commodity: "[For] his work as he experiences it directly possesses the naked and abstract form of the commodity, while in other forms of work this is hidden behind the facade of 'mental labor,' or 'responsibility,' etc."[43]

In contrast to Trotsky and Lukács, in "Cleaning" Nakano makes no distinction between physical and intellectual labor, because by the late 1920s, he had come to recognize that the intellectual in Taishō Japan was enmeshed in a commodity culture, and that the intellectual's writings, produced in newspapers and numerous magazines, were just one other commodity whose use value was disregarded by the capitalist publishers who were purveying a product. Here, too, *The Communist Manifesto* provided guidance, for while Marx had documented the division of labor

---

[42] Marx, *The German Ideology*, p. 50.
[43] Lukács, *History and Class Consciousness*, p. 172.

in *Capital* and other works available in Japan by the middle of the 1920s, the first chapter of his brief history of class struggle had also recognized how intellectuals were denied any real autonomy in the age of bourgeois rule. Marx saw that even the poet had been put to work for capital: "The bourgeoisie has stripped of its halo every occupation hitherto honored and looked up to with reverent awe. It has converted the physician, the lawyer, the priest, the poet, the man of science, into its paid wage-laborers."[44]

Although this analysis may have provided guidance, Nakano came to his conclusion that the intellectual was a producer by placing the intellectual within Japanese history. He historicized the role of the writer within the development of a literary culture of production, of which he was a member. Instead of denouncing the division of intellectual and manual labor, or the declassed situation of the potential culture-bearer, he turned the truth regarding the leveling of intellectual and manual labor noted in the *Communist Manifesto* to his own political ends, affirming that the wage-laborer could produce culture and proclaiming that he, the intellectual, was in fact unschooled. His historic inquiry into the place of the intellectual in history was in many ways premised on presumptions about the production of culture also expressed by his Italian contemporary, Antonio Gramsci.

Nakano had no access to the thirty-three notebooks filled with Gramsci's writings on history and consciousness,[45] for the Italian Marxist began his prison notes in 1929, several years after Nakano had begun to relate the Japanese intellectual to contemporary culture in his prose. But the two men, schooled in the same canon relating politics to culture, a canon containing Marx, Trotsky, and Lukács, asked similar questions in order to relate revolutionary culture to contemporary politics in two different national contexts. A very similar problematic informed their interrogation of culture as a social force as evident in their fundamental agreement as to the transformative power of consciousness. In the language of Gramsci, ideologies " 'organize' human masses, and create the terrain on which men move, acquire consciousness of their position, struggle, etc." (p. 377). In other words, culture has a material force, which can be grasped by all. Unlike Trotsky and Lukács, Gramsci refuses to accept a division of society into those who work with their minds, and those who engage in manual labor as he reveals eloquently when he explains how *homo faber* cannot be separated from *homo sapiens*, because each man is a "philosopher" who "participates in a particular conception of the

[44] Marx, *Communist Manifesto*, p. 476.

[45] See Antonio Gramsci, *Selections from the Prison Notebooks*, ed. and trans. Quintin Hoare and Geoffrey Nowell Smith (New York: International Publishers), 1971.

world" and "brings into being new modes of thought" (p. 9). Gramsci does not altogether deny the division of laborer between thinker and maker: "All men are intellectuals . . . but not all men have in society the function of intellectuals." He elaborates on this significant deviation from Trotsky's conception, with a home-spun illustration—all at some time fry a couple of eggs or sew up a tear in a jacket, but this does not make everyone a cook or a tailor (p. 9). The criterion for gauging whether an individual is an intellectual is not his work viewed in isolation, but rather "the ensemble of the system of relations in which these activities (and therefore the intellectual groups who personify them) have their place within the general complex of social relations" (p. 8). While all men are in a sense intellectuals, Gramsci is highly aware of the "new intellectuals" of the modern world of specialized labor. He wants to know the role of such intellectuals as the journalist and the recipient of technical education in a prerevolutionary state: in what ways do they sustain it? How can they overthrow it (p. 5)?[46] His discussion emphasizing Marx's idea of the intellectual as wage-laborer confirms how these technicians work to reproduce a capitalist social order. In stark contrast to Trotsky's intellectuals, who are to facilitate the formation of new structures, working toward a classless society, Gramsci analyzes the relation of the intellectuals subservient to the state who work to enforce adherence to the ruling group's domination, either by creating consent or via "legal" discipline (p. 12).

Like Antonio Gramsci, Nakano Shigeharu developed a vision of a new intellectual. The new Japanese intellectual of Taishō Japan was the writer who emerged from the elite universities to populate the bureaucracy and the offices of the nation's powerful newspapers and mass magazines, but a place also had to be made for the revolutionary writer, like Nakano, who refused to be hegemonized. The writer working outside of the ideological structures imposed by the state had to be placed in relationship to the worker who would, after all, make the revolution. Gramsci resolved this problem by placing the relationship between intellectual revolutionary and revolutionary worker within the mediating structure of the Communist party. Within the political party, the intellectuals from within the working class could be "welded together" with the traditional intellectuals. The proletariat, within the party, could be trained as political intellectuals. Unlike Trotsky, Gramsci allowed the bourgeois intellectual to join together with the proletarian. During this process he was to gain a legitimate position within the revolutionary movement; in return he was to give his advanced intellectual expertise (p. 4). Nakano's resolution was much more ambiguous, and ultimately, for both objective and subjective

---

[46] This is true for Gramsci's two categories of "organic" and "traditional" intellectual.

reasons, he was unable to relate his image of the revolutionary producer of culture to his vision of a proletarian revolution. Before reviewing how Nakano placed the writer alongside the worker in his version of the history of class struggle, Nakano's placement of the intellectual in Taishō culture, after his discovery of history, must be recalled.

In his essays on art, Nakano defined himself as "amateur," as when he differentiated himself from such denizens of the intellectual world as Marxist philosopher Miki Kiyoshi. He contended that he was willing to leave the interpretation and annotation of problems related to art to scholars like Miki, but that in any case the proletariat would be the ones to change the old world.[47] This blunt, purported anti-intellectualism was Nakano's method of underscoring his conviction that knowledge of social structure or social change that did not lead to political action was but "scholarship" belonging to the owners of property. But no matter how Nakano worked to adopt simple talk in his essays and poetry, he could not deny that he was an intellectual who published his work in nonrevolutionary newspapers and journals, such as the *Tokyo asahi shimbun* and *Shinchō*. Moreover, his essays on art reveal that he identified with the leading Japanese authors of the twentieth century. While he attacked the literary establishment, or *bundan*, because its members "go from newspapers to magazines, first here, then there, spreading links in a chain, sometimes forcing links when they should not connect,"[48] he could not deny that he, too, had a place within these interconnections. When Nakano admonished his colleagues to seek the guidance of Miki Kiyoshi, he wrote as a participant in the production of mass culture. "Let's all knock this off,"[49] his condemnation of the mutual decoration of writers through the use of the honorific suffixes *shi* and *dono*, was an acknowledgment of a comradeship in a shared enterprise.

Nakano's sense of membership in an intellectual community of Japanese producers who are both trapped by and shaping history appears most clearly in "Akutagawa shi no koto nado" (On Akutagawa and other matters).[50] This essay, composed of twenty brief commentaries, is an elegy to the leading modern Japanese writer, Akutagawa Ryūnosuke, a dialogue with Akutagawa's thoughts on art, and an analysis of the place of Taishō culture in the history of modern Japan. The miscellany-like form adopted by such Japanese writers as the fourteenth-century essayist Yoshida Kenkō, who collected his ideas in seemingly spontaneous, random

---

[47] Nakano, "Geijutsu ni seijiteki kachi," p. 281.
[48] Ibid., p. 277.
[49] Ibid., p. 276.
[50] Nakano, "Akutagawa shi no koto nado," *NSZ*: 9:102–12 [*Bungei kōron* 1/28].

fashion, conformed with Nakano's stance of amateur author.[51] However, a reading of Akutagawa's famous essay of the previous spring and summer, "Bungeiteki na, amari ni bungeiteki na" (Literary, altogether too literary),[52] makes it clear that Nakano Shigeharu's miscellany is not merely a formalistic adoption of an indigenous mode of literary expression. It is also an engagement with Akutagawa about the nature of the Japanese literary tradition. Nakano's essay repeats many of Akutagawa's allusions and touches on similar issues as Akutagawa's essay, which ranges over such cultural figures as the Tokugawa playwright Chikamatsu, Flaubert, and Jean Cocteau and addresses such problems as the "call of the wild" in Gauguin, the question of what makes an artist great, and Akutagawa's choice to write like a journalist, "as though he were talking."[53]

Akutagawa Ryūnosuke committed suicide on July 24, 1927, after recording misgivings regarding "an unfocused anxiety over the future." Immediately, his death became a marker in Japanese literary history. Kurihara Yukio, who has termed the suicide "the first page of Shōwa literature" and a premonition of an era of crises and unrest, claims that the Japanese left experienced the suicide not as the demise of a writer but as "the death of the thought of an era." They did not identify with the writer because of the shared perception that had he been a Marxist, he would not have had to kill himself because he would have been able to look to the future.[54] A more ambivalent response from the literary left, which made note of the instant apotheosis of the tortured writer, can be found in the diary of the poet Akita Ujaku: "Akutagawa's death has been announced. The death of feudalism. It can't be seen merely as the death of a bourgeois writer. But it's rather like putting on airs to go on and on about liking him after his death."[55]

Half a year before the suicide, Akutagawa had begun the process of inserting Nakano Shigeharu within the symbolic orchestration of his death, by expressing hope in proletarian literature because it demanded a social consciousness from the writer. In this context he had singled out

[51] See, for example, Donald Keene, *Essays in Idleness: The Tsurezuregusa of Kenkō* (New York: Columbia University Press, 1967).

[52] Akutagawa Ryūnosuke, "Bungeiteki na, amari ni bungeiteki na," *Akutagawa Ryūnosuke zenshū* (Iwanami shoten, 1978), 9:3–80 [*Kaizō* 4/27; 5/27; 6/27; 8/27]. A similar nine-part essay was published elsewhere, simultaneously in two parts. This was "Zoku bungeiteki na, amari ni bungeiteki na," *Akutagawa Ryūnosuke zenshū* 9:81–87 [*Bungei shunjū* 4/27; 7/27].

[53] Akutagawa, "Bungeiteki na, amari ni bungeiteki na," p. 32.

[54] Kurihara, *Puroretaria bungaku to sono jidai*, pp. 19–22.

[55] Akita Ujaku, *Akita Ujaku nikki*, ed. Ozaki Kōji (Miraisha, 1965), 2:25. See also Arima Tatsuo, *The Failure of Freedom: A Portrait of Modern Japanese Intellectuals* (Cambridge: Harvard University Press, 1969), pp. 167–72.

Nakano's poetry as possessing the necessary "poetic spirit" in a "native-born beauty unseen until now."[56] He sealed this pronouncement by inviting Nakano to visit him at his home, one month before his death, thus ensuring the perpetuation of the legend that he had bestowed the mantle of literary successorship upon Nakano. The piece "On Akutagawa and Other Matters" was Nakano's response to the then emerging legend and to the last segment of "Literary, Altogether Too Literary," which expressed Akutagawa's interest in the warriors of the proletariat who had chosen art as a weapon.[57] Nakano's essay is about the work of the writer. By focusing on the writings of specific authors, Nakano takes the reader from Akutagawa's suicide back into Meiji history, and then moves forward to the present state of art and culture in Japan. This narrative, which appeared in the pages of the respected *Bungei kōron* six months after the suicide, provides Nakano's most extensive exposition on the specificity of Japanese cultural history and the role of the intellectual producer who exists within a literary lineage and within the contemporary capitalist system.

Nakano's tribute to Akutagawa opens with the poet's expression of pain at the death of a colleague. He admits that he had not been able to write anything after Akutagawa's suicide, even after committing himself to the submission of an article. Six months later, he has again been asked to write, partly because of Akutagawa's "last testament" granting literary leadership to him. Nakano here rejects the legend, saying he does not understand this final statement. He then places Akutagawa within a much broader context by claiming that he will merely begin with Akutagawa in order to fulfill his obligation to write.[58] In the second segment, entitled "Akutagawa Ryūnosuke," Nakano presents his meeting with Akutagawa in militantly straightforward language stripped of any embellishment that might encourage the mythologizing then in process. Unlike the later versions he would write, which would emphasize the younger man's discomfort and the older writer's monopoly of the conversation, this is a simple story of a brief relationship, depicting a vulnerability in the older writer and countering any great man theorizing:

> I only spoke once with this man of letters who committed suicide. In June of last year he had contacted me through an intermediary, to say he wanted to

[56] Kitagawa, *Nakano Shigeharu*, pp. 152–53.

[57] Akutagawa, "Bungeiteki na, amari ni bungeiteki na," p. 79. Nakano would return to the visit twice, reenacting it both in a short essay written in 1934 and in *Muragimo*. See Nakano, *Chiisai kaisō, NSZ* 19:199–204 [*Bungei shunjū* 11/34] and *Muragimo*, pp. 359–70. These accounts focus on Akutagawa's concern, based on a rumor denied by Nakano, that the young proletarian writer had intended to give up writing for politics. (The process of finding a tension between politics and culture in Nakano's work had begun.)

[58] Nakano, "Akutagawa shi no koto nado," p. 102.

talk with me so I should pick a convenient time and place. And I had errands in Tabata that day (he had heard that from someone—that's why he knew that). And also, since I had no intention of making such a noted person meet me somewhere, I set out myself.

We talked of many matters in fine fashion, for a number of hours. Then he brought out some slips of paper saying, "Look at my poems." They were aphorisms rather than poems. One of them, a verse two lines in length, on the Emperor, was good. As soon as I had looked at them he quickly put them away somewhere. Apparently they will be included in his collected works. I was treated to dinner and went home. (pp. 102–103)

Nakano reports that one of the two or three letters written to him by Akutagawa were interesting, but that he has thrown them away, like any other correspondence, so as not to burden anyone. His account concludes with his low-key commentary on the suicide:

I was walking along a street around seven in the morning when I first knew of his suicide. I bought several newspapers and got on the train but I was aware of heat welling up behind my eyelids. I felt greatly sorry for this man who committed suicide. I still feel that way. (p. 103)

Nakano continues to counter any apotheosis of Akutagawa by stating in a section entitled "Public Opinion" that he is opposed to Akutagawa, but that he is also opposed to the sort of public opinion surrounding the death. The poet wants to protect Akutagawa from this escalating sentiment, and he does so within the following segments by humanizing the Japanese man of letters as he inserts him into modern Japanese literary history alongside Kitamura Tōkoku, Futabatei Shimei, and Kunikida Doppo. Nakano concludes that Tōkoku, whose suicide is being compared with Akutagawa's death, was defeated, along with the others, by Japanese capitalism, which produced a "puny" positivism that can only be vanquished via a militant materialism (p. 104). He establishes that there is a richness in the modern Japanese literary tradition that must only be analyzed within the context of the history of Japanese capitalism. But he does not neglect the question of the production of good literature, and rather than glorifying any rising class or movement, he works toward a method. In the fifth section, entitled "Writing," he repeats one of the premises of his earlier manifestos when he declares that "most likely the most simple writing is the finest writing." Playing on Fukumoto's famous quote from Lenin regarding division preparatory to unification, he seeks out a model for the text that can unite the relations of the various parts of speech, after separating out each of these relations. In other words, a conscious effort must be made to produce new forms of speech. Language is one of the problems confronted by the Proletarian Literature Movement because inappropriate language can make even the simplest of things appear difficult (pp. 104–105). When the author finds simple writing in the Japanese classics and in their traditions, he is tracing his heritage far back beyond Meiji, to the beginnings of Japanese literary tradition, but he continues to counter the deification of specific authors. In his way he reworks Akutagawa's self-effacing view—"Had I not been born, someone most certainly would have produced my writing"[59]—by concluding that the problem of literature is not the issue of authorship, but the problems raised by the writing itself. He is interested in a historic overview that can introduce the progressive nature of the breaks in the history of Japanese literature. For example, no one can criticize Saitō Mokichi, for to do so would be to criticize the poetic form of *tanka*, which Saitō has sharpened and refined into its most modern form. Now the poet can no longer return Japanese poetry to Takashi, Sachio, Shiki, or again to the Manyō verse. Thanks to Saitō, the history of poetry has moved beyond the *tanka*, and there is no turning back.[60]

The author is less kind to other intellectuals who have contributed to the course of modern Japanese history. The ninth section, "The Tokutomi Brothers," is a wry satire on the representation of Meiji history, recited in the form of a tribute to two heroes who have been offered to the public as exemplars. Nakano parodies the accounts of heroic achievement in the Samuel Smiles tales so beloved by Meiji ideologues and further demystifies them by inserting given names alongside sobriquets.

> Roka/Kenjirō and Sohō/Iichirō were a fine example. They literally offered themselves up to Japanese capitalism, and throughout their lives sent shivers down men's spines and made them ill. At Kenjirō's funeral Iichirō gave a speech saying, "We were close as brothers. My brother was able to advance to the top as well as he did, solely due to his own efforts."[61]

Nakano lets the fable speak for itself, but this brief paragraph, written in Nakano's spare, simple style, contains a sharp attack on the complicity of Meiji thinkers who created the ideology of upward advancement or *risshin shusse* that would bolster the creation of the bureaucratic state.[62] It is a critique of the intellectual as both the subject and the creator of

[59] Akutagawa, "Bungeiteki na, amari ni bungeiteki na," p. 82.
[60] Ibid., p. 106. Nakano cites the same figures as Akutagawa when he refers to the poetry of the Meiji writers Nagatsuka Takashi (1879–1915), Itō Sachio (1864–1913), and Masaoka Shiki (1867–1902). Cf. Akutagawa, "Bungeiteki na, amari ni bungeiteki na," pp. 17–18.
[61] Nakano, "Akutagawa shi no koto nado," pp. 106–107. Nakano refers to the journalist and historian Tokutomi Sohō (1863–1957) and the novelist Tokutomi Roka (1868–1927).
[62] See Earl Kinmonth, *The Self-Made Man in Meiji Japanese Thought: From Samurai to Salary Man* (Berkeley: University of California Press, 1981).

mythology. Nakano continues in the same acid vein in the section entitled "History," offering one of his few references to an individual Japanese political leader:

> Tokutomi Iichirō wrote a great history of Japan, incorrectly. I do not know whether this was intentional. Only that the medals hanging from his chest are the very same as those hanging from the chest of General Tanaka. (Stendahl, when he came across folks dangling medals, apparently would wonder with a chill, "How many did he kill for those?") (p. 106)

Nakano's version of the reality rather than the representation of modern Japanese history in the eleventh section, "Bourgeois Democracy," explains the historical context for the appearance of the bogus scholar: "Japanese history has aborted bourgeois democracy." Here is his theory of the rise of the modern Japanese state, which has made no place for a modern citizen:

> All was resignation and admiration. The stalwart heart of the bourgeoisie rising to power was thus aborted. The Japanese constitution became an appointed constitution. . . . To a *citoyen* the people of Japan were unconnected human beings and it is only the proletariat that can bring alive the experience of the *citoyen* within itself. (p. 107)

The proletariat is privileged here, but the writer does not elaborate on its historic mission. Instead he continues to talk about the process of writing. His anti-scholar stance is belied by the breadth of his reference as when in the twelfth segment, "Again on Writing," he refers to Jean Cocteau, Mori Ōgai, and Flaubert, whose works he selects for emulation because they are "covered with fine language" (and also possibly because they have been featured in Akutagawa's essay on the altogether literary). He repeats his criteria, "Fine writing is, again, the most terse writing. And to be most terse means that only that which is necessary is brought forward." The segment ends with a reformulation of Nakano's plea for simplicity: "Good writing does not possess elegance, but rather appears to have been placed there" (pp. 108–109).

In the next segment, Nakano brings Japanese literary history up to the present by setting forth the reasons for the schisms in the Proletarian Literature Movement in polemical prose dotted with names and dates, but he is more concerned with technical questions related to the production of art by the revolutionary artist. Although he lauds the working class laborers who, while living "within an exceedingly narrow conscious life and possessed of an especially narrow artistic life," are capable of responding to poetry and theater in a primitive but accurate fashion, Nakano is in fact more interested in the director's method than in the audience, as when he comments on a recent production of Robin Hood: "I will only say that a fable into which the form of socialism has been pushed cannot be art" (pp. 109–11).

As Nakano approaches the end of his essay, in section 18, "Translation," he analyzes the work that has been central to the livelihood and education of the Japanese intellectual since the Meiji Restoration. He knows the importance of this task of translating Western works of literature and scholarship for the Japanese audience and includes himself within the ranks of Japanese writers who have undertaken the task of translating, for both meaning and money. At the same time he is consistent in his attack on false scholars who do not recognize scholarship to be a political act; the work of translation must also provide a transformation. He acknowledges that translation is difficult, admits that he has produced some false translations, and at the same time affirms the importance of writing and reading even inaccurate translation. It is the scholars "lying high and mighty atop" their inaccurate translations and the university professors who flatter themselves that they can translate works of art who are at fault (pp. 111–12).

For Nakano, translation work can only be part of a process inseparable from reading and writing. And writing, the act of producing literature, through either translations or original creation, is a form of revolutionary production, because it captures and alters the consciousness and thus the actions of the working class as exemplified by the response of a restless, vocal antiwar audience represented in the segment on the theater. The problem is that instead of altering consciousness in such a direction, contemporary Japanese culture under capitalism threatens to engulf art in its system of commodity exchange.

In the last two stanzas of the essay, "Advertisement No. 1" and "Advertisement No. 2," Nakano appears at first to accept this system, which would arbitrarily fix the value of ideas and of cultural artifacts at a certain quantity of cash, thus providing a profit to the seller of the item instead of to its producer. Nonetheless, "Advertisement No. 1" soon goes even beyond a critique of commodity culture as one aspect of capitalism, as Nakano comments on the complexity of the specifically Japanese commodity culture which, because of the work of cultural translation, is able to incorporate foreign works of art. European literature and Asian art objects are jumbled within the marketplace where the intellectual is forced to sell his treasures to survive. Whereas the proletarian sells his labor power, thus creating surplus value for the capitalist, the intellectual supplies cultural objects, created either by himself or by others. Nakano's two advertisements are not an acceptance, but an attempt to unmask this new order of things:

XIX. Advertisement No. 1

I need some change so I want to sell the following two things. You can subtract some from the price. If those interested will write to me I will show the items to you.

Complete Works of Heine (Hoffman und Kampe, ed., published 1861–63, all 20 volumes, 100 yen). Ancient Korean Doll, one. (4,000 yen)

You just can't find the Heine in Japan. Can't even get it in Germany. I just named the ancient Korean doll—it's an earthenware piece. Small. Maillol can't compare. (p. 112)

Nakano has fixed a price on poetry, by pricing the Heine, and the Korean doll is posited within a world market by the comparison to the French object. The two items, so different in quality, in history, in form, and in use have had their differences obliterated, as they are both means to an acquisition of money. These commodities comprise the first part of Marx's formula for the exchange of commodities. They are the first "C" of C-M-C, presented in the first volume of *Capital*, which explains how a commodity is sold so that a producer can purchase an item of equal value. In Marx's words, "The exchange becomes an accomplished fact by two metamorphoses of opposite yet supplementary character—the conversion of the commodity into money, and the re-conversion of the money into a commodity."[63] Nakano will sell these commodities, to make money, which he in turn will spend on an item advertised for in the last stanza of "On Akutagawa and Other Matters":

XX. Advertisement No. 2

Looking for benevolent person to build a bedstead. (Apparently Kaji Wataru wants one also, but he's already got one made of tangerine boxes or something.) One that's sturdy and simple would be good. (p. 112)[64]

The two ads when combined comprise the opportunity for behavior appropriate to a mercantile economy. Nakano, in other words, is interested in spending his money on an item or commodity, for its own use. The sale and consequent purchase do illustrate how, in Marx's terms,

Circulation bursts through all restrictions as to time, place, and individuals, imposed by direct barter, and this it effects by splitting up, into the antithesis of a sale and a purchase, the direct identity that in barter does exist between the alienation of one's own and the acquisition of some other man's product.[65]

[63] Marx, *Capital*, 1:105.
[64] Kaji Wataru was a colleague in the Culture Movement.
[65] Marx, *Capital*, 1:113.

Yet these ads are merely a construct, albeit a powerful construct, attesting to the reified forms culture can take. The advertisements are a product of the poet's imagination, for in reality he lives within a capitalist and not a mercantilist society which bases its economic behavior on Marx's final formula: M-C-M'. As Marx explains in the chapter "The General Formula for Capital," in the earlier circuit C-M-C, "the same piece of money changes its place twice. The seller gets it from the buyer and pays it away to another seller." The circuit, he continues, begins and ends with a commodity, and the satisfaction of wants or "use value" is the end of the transaction. Under the capitalist system, however, it is the commodity and not the money that "changes its place twice." Industrial capital is money that is changed into commodities to be sold and thereby reconverted into more money. Therefore, the leading impetus for this process is not use, but exchange value.[66]

Nakano develops his analysis of Japanese capitalism from a position within the system of commodity circulation, because he views himself as a producer. His labor produces objects, literary texts that are resold via the medium of journals or newspapers, in an unprecedented cultural setting wherein he is able to reproduce and sell his product. Akutagawa also raised the issue of the mass production of art and called himself a journalist,[67] but the important comparison in this reclaiming of Nakano Shigeharu's discovery of history and conceptualization of historical consciousness is that he had departed from the theoretical confines established by Lukács's formulations of history; he was ready to concentrate his criticisms on the present. The essays and the poetry that comprise this critique of contemporary culture resonate with the position of the Weimar critic Walter Benjamin, who also adopted the iconoclastic belief that in the capitalist system of the late 1920s and early 1930s the author had become a "literary producer."[68]

In his address to the Institute for the Study of Fascism in Paris on April 27, 1934, Benjamin opened by affirming the poet's right to autonomy and rejecting the yardstick of "political tendency" as the determinant of literary quality. Benjamin wanted to ask a new question. Rather than positing a work in relation to its attitude toward the social relations of production of an era, he was concerned with the function of a work within the *literary* relations of production. The European critic stated what Nakano explored in his essay on Akutagawa and in other essays and poems of the late 1920s. He said that society was "in the midst of a mighty recasting of literary forms" epitomized by the unprecedented literary po-

[66] Ibid., pp. 148–55.

[67] See Akutagawa, "Bungeiteki na, amari ni bungeiteki na," pp. 32, 42, 70.

[68] Walter Benjamin, "The Author as Producer," in *Reflections*, ed. Peter Demetz (New York: Harcourt Brace Jovanovitch, 1978), pp. 220–38.

sition of the newspaper.[69] It was not sufficient for a left-wing intellectual to feel solidarity with the proletariat; he must experience comradeship as a producer within a process of production and cooptation, for "we are faced with the fact . . . that the bourgeois apparatus of production and publication can assimilate astonishing quantities of revolutionary themes, indeed, can propogate them without calling its own existence, and the existence of the class that owns it, seriously into question."[70]

Benjamin elaborated on the role of the author as producer in terms similar to the assumptions informing Nakano's discussion of the work produced from within the Japanese revolutionary theater movement in the fragments responding to Akutagawa. According to Benjamin, the author had received an education, which was a means of production, from the bourgeois class, and he and other writers were to become engineers capable of adapting this productive apparatus, which currently worked to convert left-wing writing into entertainment, for use in a proletarian revolution.[71] Walter Benjamin also shared with Nakano a distaste for the academic mode of production, as stated in his miscellany, "One-Way Street." In a scathing segment entitled "Teaching Aid" and subtitled "Principles of the Weighty Tome, or How to Write Fat Books," he attacked the scholarly mode of exposition, opening with seven cardinal points that punctured the painstaking method of the academic who eschews the terseness of the poetic form for a wordiness that overexplains.[72]

The Marxism of Benjamin and Nakano may well have derived from the same source, for in 1924 Benjamin read *History and Class Consciousness* and was stunned at the similarity between its theory of consciousness and his own conclusions.[73] For both intellectuals Lukács's theory of "consciousness as a transformative material force within historical development"[74] provided a theory of change, but both men deviated from Lukács in their examination of contemporary culture. Benjamin produced his theory of cultural reproduction; Nakano's poems captured the process in verse form. These two Marxists had no contact. Rather, the

[69] Ibid., pp. 221–26.
[70] Ibid., p. 229.
[71] Ibid., pp. 237–38.
[72] Benjamin, "One-Way Street," in *Reflections*, p. 79.
[73] Terry Eagleton cites a letter written by Benjamin to his friend Gershom Scholem. Eagleton, *Walter Benjamin: Or Towards a Revolutionary Criticism* (London: Verso Editions, 1981), pp. 152–53. While there is debate as to whether Walter Benjamin should be called a Marxist, my analysis treats Benjamin's materialism as Marxist. For elaboration on this issue by specialists versed in the work of Benjamin, see Richard Wolin, *Walter Benjamin: An Aesthetic of Redemption* (New York: Columbia University Press, 1982), pp. 255–65, and Susan Buck-Morss, *The Origin of Negative Dialectics: Theodor W. Adorno, Walter Benjamin, and the Frankfurt Institute* (New York: Free Press, 1977), pp. 139–50.
[74] Eagleton, *Walter Benjamin*, p. 153.

reality of the urban capitalist culture in which they worked provided the material that enabled both thinkers to go beyond Marx's theory of reproduction of commodities and of social relations as set forth in *Capital* to write, in their own genres and language, of the reproduction of culture. This new capitalist phenomenon demanded new theory and new poetry. Marx and Lukács had provided a theory of history and of change, but both Benjamin and Nakano would have to rely on their vision of the present to transform this theory into a practice of writing which they saw as contributing to a revolution opening into the future.

CHAPTER FOUR

Song II: The Reproduction of Taishō Culture

THE REPRODUCTION OF CULTURE

In February 1927, Nakano published a three-part poem in *Roba* entitled "Train."[1] The ordering of the three segments reversed the logic of history, as the first poem fantasized violent revolution, the second, the appearance of class consciousness, and the third, the production and reproduction of the social relationships comprising an economic order. By working backward to historical genesis Nakano called the reader's attention to the structuring or creation of history. By ending with the beginning, he highlighted the last part of the triptych. This method anticipated Yamada Moritarō's ordering of the three essays contained in *Nihon shihonshugi bunseki* (Analysis of Japanese capitalism).[2] Since the three essays first appeared in 1933, and the monograph, often referred to as the Japanese version of *Capital*, would not appear until 1934, when Nakano wrote "Train" he could not refer to Yamada's problematic of "making concrete the theory of reproduction in the context of Japanese capitalism." But he could easily have referred to *Capital*, which was of course Yamada's theoretical inspiration.[3] For just as *Capital* articulates most clearly Marx's vision of the dynamic of the structuring of society, revealed in his concept of simple reproduction, the third section of "Train" is Nakano Shigeharu's most succinct reworking of Marx's concept of the creation and recreation of social relationships under capitalism. This poetry is, in other words, a changed song.

Marx introduces the concept of simple reproduction by emphasizing the simultaneous, intertwined nature of the process of repetition and reproduction. The premise for change is thus repetition:

> Whatever the form of the process of production in a society, it must be a continuous process, must continue to go periodically through the same phases. A society can no more cease to produce than it can cease to consume. When

---

[1] Nakano, "Kisha I–III," *NSZ* 1:515–17 [*Roba* 2/27]. From the 1931 edition of Nakano's collected poems onward, this poem appeared as three poems entitled "Train I," "Train II," and "Train III."

[2] Yamada Moritarō, *Nihon shihonshugi bunseki* (Iwanami shoten, 1934, 1977).

[3] Regarding Yamada's theoretical premises see his own introduction, ibid., pp. iii–vi. For an analysis of the work as a *Capital* on Japanese capitalism, see Minami Katsumi, "Kaisetsu," in Yamada Moritarō, *Nihon shihonshugi bunseki*, pp. 279–318.

viewed, therefore, as a connected whole, and as flowing on with incessant renewal, every social process of production is, at the same time, a process of reproduction.[4]

Not only are commodities and surplus value reproduced, for Marx is also concerned with the reproduction of the working class in its relation to the capitalist class. This reproduction is concealed from the worker, because of the constant change of employers and in the wage commanded by the employment of his labor power. Both these elements bestow an illusion of freedom, and of change and chance. The unity of the process is thus broken apart into a kaleidoscope of shifting pairs, but the nature of components remains constant. The worker is offered new partners in this dance of bondage and is unable to break out of an existence wherein he is made into a thing, or a commodity, until he can become aware not only that he is living a dehumanized life, but moreover, that he shares this condition with others. Reproduction is not merely repetition. It is also accumulation of both the proletariat and capital. The process leads to the accumulation of misery, ignorance, and degradation while at the same time augmenting wealth for the capitalist class derived from the labor-power of the class that produces.[5]

In Nakano Shigeharu's changed song, the opening rhythms of the third part of "Train," "Bye Bye Bye Bye / Good-bye Good-bye Good-bye Good-bye," introduce the idea of the repetitive nature of capitalist reproduction through the dulling rhythm of the words of the factory girls arriving home from their labors in the textile mills, on New Year's break. By the end of the first stanza Nakano has hinted at the meaning he will elaborate in the remaining stanzas as he follows the girls off the train to the scene of their reunion with family. He captures, through the articulation of one scene, the notion of the production and reproduction of the working class: Capitalist society is in constant, repetitive movement, just like the train that stops only to start again along the northern coast of Japan. The train is to deposit its load of young girls, who will return from the villages on the same train to new employers, and to the life the poet sketches with his blunt question, "What are companies factories chimneys dormitories?" The query is really a series of questions, just as the system of capitalism comprises innumerable units of production:

III

Bye Bye Bye Bye
Good-bye Good-bye Good-bye Good-bye
We saw that
We heard that

[4] Marx, *Capital*, 1:572.
[5] Ibid., pp. 573–74, 578, 613–14, 645.

A hundred factory girls alight
Where a thousand factory girls ride on.

What are factory girls?
What are mill factory girls?
What are companies factories chimneys dormitories?
What does it mean that the girls are wrung out
What does it mean that they are wrung out like wet towels?
And what is New Year's?
What is New Year's break?
Ahh—the girls have been thoroughly wrung out
And pushed out—in the name of New Year's
And we saw that
A hundred factory girls alight where a thousand factory girls ride on
And we saw that
Fathers and mothers and brothers and sisters come out from the snow
Atop their oil-papered raincoats
Atop their capes
Atop their wraps the white snow collecting
And their straw shoes wet all the way along up
And we saw how they and the girls embraced
And we saw that
They and the girls stroking each other
They and the girls stroking each others' heads and faces and shoulders
And how the snow kept falling on

Bye Bye Bye Bye
And the girls knew
That only for a while they were able to embrace
Only just a while for giving pats receiving pats
Ah—the girls knew
Who they themselves are
Where their villages are
And what sorts await in the village

The girls were pushed out   in the name of New Year's
The girls were thoroughly wrung out
And in the villages new buyers for them making all the rounds
Leaving those small stations
Through the snow
The girls are returning to the buyers there in ambush
This they all knew

Bye Bye Bye Bye
Good-bye Good-bye Good-bye Good-bye
That there was Etchū

That there the land of special treats for the rich
Atop the dirt floor exposed to the wind in that small station
Daughters and parents and brothers and sisters each patted the other
The parting words of those who sit and those who keep riding
Of the girls probably to be bought and rebought up again by different
    factories
Of the mill factory girls probably never to meet again
The chorus of their thousand voices
Spun round and round that never stopping sky of snow

Here then is the process of reproduction as played out in the Toyama countryside. The author of "Women in the Rice Fields" could only passively marvel at the labors of the working women, but the composer of "Train" was working from a theory of labor. Nakano implies a historical transition by relating the journey of the factory girl as a transition from factory and chimneys symbolizing the modernity of industrialization to Etchū, the premodern term for Toyama Prefecture.

The poem emphasizes repetition rather than change, through its use of identical phrasings and actions, as Nakano positions another version of the buyer and seller who confront each other in Marx's historicized rendering of Hegel's master-slave relation and of the pairings established in "Notes on Art Written on the Run." In that essay, which emphasized the confrontation between labor and capital, Nakano presented a factory girl hosed with cold water. "Train," written just months before "Notes on Art Written on the Run," establishes the relationship preceding and allowing for such conflict. The factory girl possesses nothing but her labor-power, which she expends at the work-site of the buyer, within the factory. Reproduction occurs because she is "wrung out," a rephrasing of Marx's explanation that "the labourer, on quitting the process, is what he was on entering it, a source of wealth, but devoid of all means of making that wealth his own."[6] The worker who quits the process does not leave it for good but, like Nakano's factory girl, who is prey to the labor procurers lying in ambush, is "bought and bought again." Marx termed this "perpetuation of the labourer" the "sine qua non of capitalist production" and explained how the reproduction was effected: the labor-power was purchased for a fixed period, which was constantly repeated when the term of labor ended. "Train III" captures the moment between the fixed periods of labor, and Nakano appears at first to counter Marx's notion of the pretence of independence, which is maintained by the constant change of employers and by the use of the "fictio juris of a contract," by implying that the factory girls recognize or "know" their true situation. Yet ultimately he conveys the idea that the girls are only conscious

[6] Ibid., pp. 570–71.

of the actual process of reproduction—of their transport between work and family and between successive work-sites. While he implies that capitalist production hurled the factory girls from the organic unity of family ties into a new community of horizontal linkages with women workers, Nakano does not take the poem in the direction of exploring the new class consciousness forged within the urban existence of these daughters of poor peasants.

Four years later, in 1931, the essay "Nōmin bungaku no mondai" (The problem of peasant literature) would refer to the countless daughters of the poor peasants working in textile or spinning factories who provided a source of labor power and numerous bridges between the city's proletariat and the working masses in the countryside.[7] The factory girls in "Train" express no consciousness of this social position. Rather, they "know of their condition" just as the working class described by Marx "knows," because, due to education, tradition, and habit, it "looks upon the conditions of that mode of production as self-evident laws of Nature."[8] The emphasis on repetition in the poem provides no possibility for the factory girl to break out of the cycle of reproduction although, according to Lukács, it is this process that forges the revolutionary consciousness of the worker. By becoming aware of the process of capitalist production, the worker recognizes that capitalism is not "a series of disconnected objects or people." In other words, through his understanding [in this case, of course, it should be *her* understanding] of the process of the production of the commodity, the worker recognizes that he himself is the object of the economic process. Quoting from Marx, Lukács concludes that the worker can make the sort of query reserved only for the narrator in "Train" because he is aware of the true nature of social relationships governing capitalism. The worker with self-consciousness has access to a total view of society *"as a whole"* and can thus place his own immediate self-interests into a historical vision cognizant of the social character of labor, thereby rendering his consciousness and actions revolutionary. This worker himself can ask: "Does a worker in a cotton factory produce merely cotton textiles?" He can provide the answer that indeed not, he produces capital that in turn creates capital, or values that create new values.[9]

Henri Lefebvre's theory of reproduction helps to explain why the factory girls cannot break out of their situation. He explains that reproduction is an inseparable process comprising both linear and cyclical as-

[7] Nakano, "Nōmin bungaku no mondai," NSZ 9:359 [Kaizō 7/31].

[8] Marx, *Capital*, 1:737.

[9] Lukács, *History and Class Consciousness*, pp. 50–71, 149, 168–73, 180–81.

pects.[10] In this sense the third part of "Train" treats of the cyclical and neglects the linear, revolutionary effects of reproduction depicted in the multifaceted scenario of opposing forces in "Notes on Art Written on the Run." The factory girls remain a theoretical abstraction used to illustrate a concept, and the verse succeeds as an examination of the process of reproduction of a preconscious class, but it cannot be taken as an expression of the attitudes of the factory girls, which remain almost unexamined. In later essays, Nakano would recognize the importance of examining the consciousness of the worker, its complexity, and its availability in language. He would discuss how the everyday experience of speaking, literary production, and the political activism of the worker were all colored by cultural vestiges from the past, and by bourgeois values that had seeped into the popular consciousness.[11] Yet the words "Bye" and "Good-bye" are the extent to which worker's language appears in this poem; the way of "knowing" of these girls is not pursued. Herein lies an irony, for the very same *kaeuta* that raised Nakano's awareness when he read *Jokō aishi* provided a good look at the class consciousness voiced by the young women employed in the textile mills in late Taishō Japan.

The ballads in Hosoi Wakizo's *Jokō aishi* express the misery of factory life and homesickness and a deeply felt resentment aimed at factory management. Moreover, the continuing connection between urban and rural is an important historical relationship in Japanese labor history, as Yamada Moritarō argued in his *Analysis of Japanese Capitalism*. In it Yamada created his own language so that he could place the history of the Japanese worker within the process of capitalist reproduction. Employing an idiosyncratic syntax and eschewing a direct translation of Marx's "proletariat" into Japanese, he focused on the textile industry to chart the transformation of "semi-serf small cultivators" into "semi-slave wage laborers" in Meiji and Taishō who commuted between city and country.[12] Nakano was pointing to this historic circumstance when more than once he emphasized the country-city relationship rather than the country to city transition underscored in the *Communist Manifesto*. But what Nakano neglected to develop in "Train III" or in his brief, suggestive commentaries on the "changed songs"[13] was the insight that the numerous

[10] Henri Lefebvre, *The Survival of Capitalism: Reproduction of the Relations of Production*, trans. Frank Bryant (London: Allison & Busby, 1976), p. 9.

[11] For example, regarding the worker's own language, see "Puroretaria geijutsu to wa nanika," *NSZ* 9:349.

[12] Yamada, *Nihon shihonshugi bunseki*, pp. 3–46.

[13] Nakano made reference to the songs in 1976, as cited above. In 1931 he had quoted verses from *Jokō aishi* to illustrate how they conveyed authentic emotion. See Nakano, "Shi no shigoto no kenkyū," *NSZ* 9:373 [Puroretaria shi 7/31].

kaeuta in Hosoi's book do more than give voice to the emotions of the uprooted young girls.

In the classic by Hosoi, the author inserts lyrics into his argument to illustrate fatalism and sentimentality, as well as the resentment and pride expressed by the woman worker. Hosoi is critical of the blindness of the women to the systemic nature of their exploitation in the factory and decries the overwhelming evidence of their inability to focus on the issue of working conditions when they do go on strike. Their militancy is "lacking in cultural significance" because the women are only capable of personalizing their shared experience by demanding the expulsion of specified managers, and factorywide strikes by women are rare because these workers are incapable of experiencing a community of interest with fellow workers. They can only identify with co-workers who hail from the same region or have been placed in close proximity in the workplace or in a dormitory room.[14] At the same time, he treats the songs as new creations actively constructed by a new class producing new words to express relationships within the factory. Hosoi illustrates the closeness of the women to their songs by relating how factory girls at a certain plant responded to a questionnaire that asked them to discuss their thoughts: most respondents chose to compose songs to voice an answer.[15] A reading of the new words and the new songs quoted by Hosoi reveals that the girls both accepted the system, in "unconscious" fashion, and were quite conscious of the created nature of class society.[16] The opening to one ballad, "More than the caged bird, more than jail / Dorm-life is even more hard to bear," shows that the workers knew full well that their freedom, as laborers under contract, was an illusion. Another verse echoes this sentiment: "Working at the company is working at the jail / All we need is

[14] Hosoi Wakizō, *Jokō aishi* (Iwanami shoten, 1982), pp. 324–71. For a critique of Hosoi's position as part of the standard wisdom regarding the consciousness of the factory girl see E. Patricia Tsurumi's revisionist articles, "Female Textile Workers and the Failure of Early Trade Unionism in Japan," *History Workshop* 18 (Autumn 1984): 3–27, and "Problem Consciousness and Modern Japanese History: Female Textile Workers of Meiji and Taishō," *Bulletin of Concerned Asian Scholars* 18, 4 (October–December 1986): 41–48.

[15] The 452 responses from the 4,000 employees broke down into the following categories: 199 miscellaneous, 80 hymns to capitalism, 33 love songs, 27 calls to resistance, 17 accounts of homesickness, 16 laments regarding physical pain, 14 militaristic responses, 13 expressing contempt for men, 11 of self-debasement, 11 expressing filial piety, 9 on pride and triumph, 6 lewd songs, 4 on food, 3 on religion, and 2 extolling success. Hasoi, *Jokō aishi*, pp. 325–26.

[16] The notion of "class unconsciousness" is borrowed from Russell Jacoby, who finds the concept of an "unconscious society" in Theodore Adorno's discussion of history and in the theory of reification propounded by Lukács in *History and Class Consciousness*. Jacoby, *Dialectic of Defeat*, pp. 117–26. The term "class unconsciousness" is used in analogous fashion to signify the partial acceptance by the women workers of the organization of their own society as natural.

metal chains." The singer is fully aware of the power relationships within the factory, which she likens to a hell in which the manager is devil. The relationship of employer to employed is set forth when the narrator of the ballad rants at a fellow worker: "Stop being so proud you and me / Take the money from the same company." Here is a class consciousness, articulating what Lukács terms "the awareness of a common situation and common interests."[17]

There is no sophisticated analysis of capitalism in these songs, but they bear a close reading because they provide a resource for reproducing the consciousness of these Japanese workers arising from this sense of shared experience. The women workers did not talk about "class," but what can be concluded is that the women did have a sense that their position in the factory was qualitatively different from the place of management, and that these sharp distinctions were based on the contrasting tasks assigned them within the factory. The same song also exhibited an awareness that the divisions in the workplace were not fixed or natural; that both classes were created, by scoffing at the working-class origins of the manager with the proud face.[18] The consciousness of these women workers was informed by a doubly brutal domination based on class and gender,[19] and the lyrics of this *kaeuta*, which are most acerbic in their treatment of the relationship between the women and men, make it abundantly clear that the factory girls were bitterly aware of the sexual politics in the factory. They drew attention to the company, calling it a brothel full of prostitutes and wryly commenting on the tendency of male superiors to seduce factory girls: "The boss and me are the thread of the ring / Easy to tie together easy to cut apart." This contempt for the boss spilled over into contempt toward all male factory operatives, which was verbalized in the language of capitalist calculation: "Put a male worker on a skewer—costs 5 *rin* / Stick the factory girl—she's 25 *sen*." The factory girl is warned, in other ways, not to become impassioned over her co-worker who will only throw her out like old tea leaves. The factory girl who gave her eye to the company factory man, another couplet admonished, would end up stark naked, wrapped in bamboo and grass.[20]

---

[17] Lukács, *History and Class Consciousness*, p. 173. The class consciousness in this song also corresponds to E. P. Thompson's determination that "class happens when some men, as a result of common experiences (inherited or shared), feel and articulate the identity of their interests as between themselves, and as against other men whose interests are different from (and largely opposed to) theirs." E. P. Thompson, *The Making of the English Working Class* (New York: Vintage Books, 1966), p. 9.

[18] Hosoi, *Jokō aishi*, pp. 404–406.

[19] The innovative work of Miyake Yoshiko explores the relationship of gender to class in an unpublished paper, "*Jokō aishi* or the Pitiful History of the Mill Girls: A Reality and a Discourse Produced by the Partnership Between Patriarchy and Capital" (1987).

[20] Hosoi uses such verses to illustrate his attempt to counter the impression held by his

On her own, the factory girl analyzed the relationships within the factory, without the aid of outside theorists or lyricists. Nonetheless, the fragment "If the textile factory girl is a human being then flowers bloom on a telegraph pole" adheres to Marx's notion, vigorously seconded by Lukács in his essay on reification, that in a society organized around the production of commodities, relations between people are transposed into relations between things.[21] Yet the bulk of the lyrics expressed an unconscious adherence to values learned during childhood in the countryside. In more lyrics than not, immediate experience—the reality of relations of production in the present—is overwhelmed by the demands of filial piety, a vestige from the past that retains its relevance in the present because the worker is suspended between country and city, between family and factory community. There are numerous variations of the song "Nan no inga de" (By what fate) wherein the factory girl, without questioning the source of her parents' misery, explains away her own misery by concluding that her parents have no resources.[22]

According to Hosoi, the factory girl was also dominated by the machinery in her life. This rule of machine over man is another theme in Marx,[23] and in Walter Benjamin's succinct paraphrase of the problem. According to Benjamin, under capitalism it is "the instruments of labor that employ the workman, and not the other way around. He adds that it is "only in the factory system that this inversion for the first time acquires technical and palatable reality."[24] Hosoi discusses how this inversion manifested itself in the textile factory. After working on the machines for a period of time, the young girls would not view the moving parts as threatening to their safety, and instead the individual factory girl would accept blame for any injuries incurred. The machines also ruled the motions of the young women off the job: even afterhours the factory girls affected a "crab-like" walk necessitated at work by the long aisles of machinery. In the factory, the din of the machinery forced the girl who wished to talk to speak directly into the listener's ear; on the street, the factory girls continued to speak in overenunciated tones.[25]

In his essay on peasant literature, Nakano listed three elements as contributory to the factory girl's psychology: immediate experience, vestiges

---

contemporaries in Taishō Japan that the women workers were promiscuous. He agrees that one-third of prostitutes were most likely ex-factory girls, but he attributes this to the manipulations of factory managers, recruiters, and male co-workers. Hosoi, *Jokō aishi*, p. 332.

[21] Ibid., p. 406; Marx, *Capital* 1:72; Lukács, *History and Class Consciousness*, p. 86.

[22] Hosoi, *Jokō aishi*, pp. 334–35.

[23] See Lukács quoting Marx on this theme in *History and Class Consciousness*, pp. 152–53.

[24] Walter Benjamin, *Charles Baudelaire: A Lyric Poet in the Era of High Capitalism*, trans. Harry Zohn (London: NLB, 1973), p. 132.

[25] Hosoi, *Jokō aishi*, pp. 349–51, 354.

from the past, and bourgeois values.[26] These three elements are all present in Hosoi's account. The young women were controlled by vestiges from the past, by the immediate experience of the machinery, and by the bourgeois value of the division of labor. While the cynical third verse of the ballad of the caged bird, "The role of the thread is to break, my role to tie it / division subchief nearby the glaring role,"[27] indicates that in some sense the factory girls recognized that the spheres of labor were embedded in a class system comprising inequitably apportioned tasks, Hosoi's glossary of her language reveals that the factory girl's adherence to the division of labor was one aspect of her enslavement to machinery. The factory girls did express a critical attitude toward the division of labor in a new language revealing a consciousness of ideological manipulation by a ruling class, when, for example, they talked of "the important man" (*erai hito*) who told a questionable "story" (*ohanashi*) while exhorting the workers through "pronouncement" (*iiwatashi*). But most of the words given by Hosoi in his transcription of the factory girls' language signify that the women thought that work was attached to a certain job, and that the worker's attributes must derive from his or her machine. This conclusion, based on the nicknames used in the factory, indicates that the division of labor instituted to increase production in the factory must have created a hierarchy that worked against the development of horizontal ties among workers, a prerequisite for a class consciousness capable of organizing workers for any effective political action.

Hosoi confirms Nakano's claim that the proletariat had its own language: dyers were "riverboys" (*gawatarō*), because they were always in water; "sparrows" (*suzume*) were noisy because they worked on the ring machine; the "prostitutes" (*oyama*) were thought to act like prostitutes due to the nature of their work, which required them to follow closely on the heels of other workers. New employees were "new rice" (*shinmai*). "Darkies" (*kuronbō*) could be found doing power-related, electrical, or steel work. The glossary also included a term derived from democracy (*demokura*) which hints at some sort of intrusion of Western ideology into the workplace: *Demokura* was used in the mill to denote unfair treatment, and there was also a term for individual slowdown tactics, taken from the word sabotage (*saboru*).[28]

The information provided by Hosoi in *Jokō aishi* supplied Nakano with ample material for documenting the reproduction and the production of factory girl class consciousness, but immediately after his discovery of history, he was more interested in discussing reproduction in the

[26] Nakano, *Nōmin bungaku.*
[27] Hosoi, *Jokō aishi*, p. 404.
[28] Hosoi gives a list of thirty-five common terms. Ibid., pp. 351–54, 404.

context of the manipulation of cultural tradition. In "Train," for example, he disclosed how the reproduction of the New Year ritual concealed the new within an old form. The rural celebration of family and work relationships was being used as an excuse to break social links. The girls were pushed out of their jobs "in the name of New Year's" and sent home for brief reunions before they would again be separated from their families. The term for New Year's (oshōgatsu) had been adopted but its new meaning veiled, confirming Henri Lefebvre's thesis that the cultural reproduction "of the old in the modern conceals the current society which is renewing and reproducing itself."[29] While the factory girls were ostensibly sent home to be reunited with their family, this was merely a momentary break in the process of their reproduction. The third segment of "Train" thus offered an apt example of the "tearing asunder" of family ties among proletarians as their children are "transformed into simple articles of commerce and instruments of labor" mentioned in the *Communist Manifesto*.[30] In "Train," the old concealed the new because the traditional cultural practice of New Year's observances was merely an excuse to reproduce a new, capitalist social relationship. But the theory of cultural reproduction has one more side to it. Just as the old can conceal the new, as in management's manipulation of the traditions of New Year's, so can these terms be reversed, as Lefebvre has noted: "The redundant brilliance and the appearance of newness in everyday cultural repetition conceal total reproduction. Conversely, the reproduction of the old in the modern conceals the current society which is renewing and reproducing itself."[31] Nakano Shigeharu's critique of Taishō culture, developed after his discovery of history, encompassed both sides of this process. Both aspects of his critique—his treatment of the reproduction of the old in new form, "the reproduction of culture," and his response to the mass "culture of reproduction"—informed the second stage in his changing song.

In his essay "Engeki ni tsuite" (On theater),[32] published in January 1928 in *Puroretaria geijutsu*, Nakano discussed how Japanese culture could be freed from the repetition of outmoded forms. In the ringing opening to *The Eighteenth Brumaire of Louis Bonaparte*, Marx had pushed history, literature, and revolution forward with the pronouncement that "social revolution of the nineteenth century cannot draw its poetry from the past, but only from the future." Like Marx, Nakano opposed the recycling of old literary tradition for new political needs. He singled out drama from all the arts because drama was rooted in all of the

---

[29] Lefebvre, *Survival of Capitalism*, p. 34.

[30] Marx, *Communist Manifesto*, pp. 487–88.

[31] Lefebvre, *Survival of Capitalism*, p. 34.

[32] Nakano, "Engeki ni tsuite," *NSZ* 9:117–24 [*Puroretaria geijutsu* 1/38].

senses. Its form of expression thus came closest to the forms taken by human life even in its most fragmentary aspects. This art form had to be taken to the people, but the question was, how? Nakano's answer was organized around the metaphor and history of Kabuki. The drama of Japan, he proclaimed, "will first proceed on the road of development when Kabuki is overcome." The only way to overcome Kabuki was to overcome its form, which stood atop a long accumulation of tradition. Only the aggressive establishment of a new revolutionary theatrical form could achieve such a goal, because the uniquely Japanese form of theater was like a large octopus extending its tentacles. Even the strongest critics of its traditions were often drawn in, with the result that "the ghost hunter becomes a ghost." And the only way to create this new form was to harness the daily experience of the proletariat.[33]

According to Nakano, the bourgeoisie had created its own, modern form of theater, the Tsukiji Little Theater, but while it had established its own nonfeudal, bourgeois expression, it opposed the liberation of the people from feudal ideology. There was thus no way to say that it had fully liberated the drama of Japan from Kabuki. Nonetheless, the bourgeoisie had also created its own opponent, added Nakano, providing a twist to the dialectics of the Japanese proverb of the hunted ghost-hunter: the bourgeois class, a threat to both feudal society and ideology, had in effect empowered the proletariat who threatened it. Nakano's demand for "Overcoming Kabuki" was similar to Walter Benjamin's 1940 call for the reform of appropriated culture. Benjamin warned that the receiver of tradition could become a tool of the ruling classes and gave his prescription for averting this: "In every era the attempt must be made anew to wrest tradition away from a conformism that is about to overpower it."[34] According to Nakano's prescription, when the proletariat could act to liberate itself from the feudal thought wielded as a weapon by the bourgeoisie, its liberation would be complete. The form of its theater had to go both beyond Kabuki and beyond the form of the bourgeois theater which had not fully eluded the grasp of Kabuki's tentacles, and only the worker could create the new art that would extend beyond Kabuki's reach.[35] The "overcoming" implied an absorption of the principles of Kabuki prior to abandonment. In other words, Nakano's dialectic called for a sublation of this indigenous cultural phenomenon. He did not elaborate on the nature of the Kabuki form or *kata*, perhaps because he felt that his

[33] Ibid., pp. 119–21. Marx, *The Eighteenth Brumaire of Louis Bonaparte*, p. 597.

[34] Benjamin, "Theses on the Philosophy of History," in *Illuminations*, p. 255.

[35] Nakano, "Engeki ni tsuite," pp. 121–22. For a discussion of *Shimpa*, the "new-style drama," in relation to Kabuki, and for a history of the Tsukiji Little Theater, see J. Thomas Rimer, *Toward a Modern Japanese Theatre: Kishida Kunio* (Princeton: Princeton University Press, 1974), pp. 14–16, 30–32, 42–45.

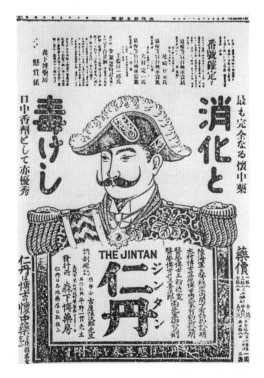

Full-page advertisement for Jintan appearing in the December 9, 1905 issue of *Osaka asahi shimbun*. (From Yamamoto Taketoshi, *Kōkoku no shakai shi* [Tokyo: Hōsei University Press, 1984]; courtesy of Yamamoto Taketoshi.)

Nakano Shigeharu and Hara Masano in May 1930, soon after their marriage and one week before Nakano's first long imprisonment. (Courtesy of Hara Izumi.)

Nakano and Hara out on the town during the early 1930s. (Courtesy of Hara Izumi.)

Cover page from *Musansha shimbun*, September 1, 1927. Nakano's poem, "The Young Girls of Korea," appears in the center of the page, accompanied by an illustration of students with clenched fists. It is surrounded by advertisements for a biography of Marx and Engels; a book about the Sacco-Vanzetti incident; and the journals *Marxism*, *Proletarian Arts*, and *Literary Front*.

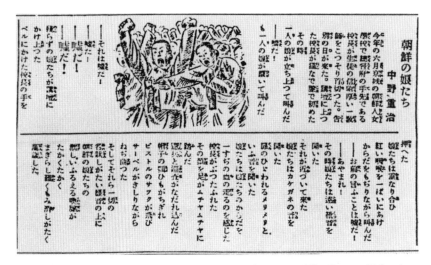

Enlarged detail from the preceding illustration, featuring "The Young Girls of Korea."

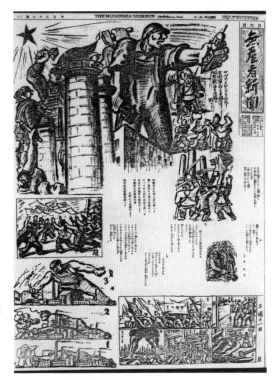

Cover page of the New Year's Day 1928 edition of *Musansha shimbun*. Nakano's poem, "Just Wait You Evil Landlords" is in the center of the page, marked by small corner brackets. The six-part cartoon narrative at the bottom of the page is entitled, "One Day in the Factory." The polemic accompanying the cartoon at the top of the page calls for support of Soviet Russia and the Chinese Revolution.

Miyamoto Yuriko's colleagues gathered at her home after her arrest in May 1935. *Front row, from left*: Tsuboi Shigeji, Ebisui Niheiji, Yanase Masamu. *Middle row, from left*: Kubokawa Tsurujirō, Yamada Kiyo, Hara Izumi. *Back row, from left*: Nakano Shigeharu, Matsuyama Fumio, Tsuboi Sakai, Sata Ineko, Nakano Suzuko (Nakano's sister). (Courtesy of Hara Izumi.)

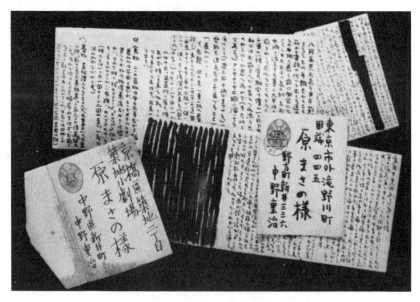

Nakano's prison letters, addressed to his wife and written on prison-issued stationery, with censored portions inked out. (Courtesy of Hara Izumi.)

audience was more than familiar with how in the Kabuki tradition the actor's technique is constructed from highly stylized gestures, body movements, and facial expressions created to symbolize both specific emotions and social types. He did not elaborate on how, through such forms as a stylized gait or saunter, the actor conveys his identity in terms of gender, caste, and age.[36] Yet while Nakano did not offer his readers an analysis of the Kabuki *kata*, he retained it as an ideal, implying the necessity for the reproduction of theater capable of adapting the Kabuki method of accentuating form while rejecting its feudal content. There was, of course, no extant *kata* to represent a new proletarian language and body-language, but both had to be centrally featured in a new cultural form based on the old.

Nakano's method for overcoming the attractive threat of Kabuki implied the need for a new set of *kimari*, or set poses: "To overcome Kabuki the proletariat has laid its life bare open. His very life—his way of walking, way of talking, way of running, his gatherings, his demonstrations. It is as though all of his actions in use of his body are our source for overcoming the production and dramatization of Kabuki."[37] The message was simple and clear, but in the poetry he wrote during the second phase of his changing song, Nakano used verse to work out the problem of the reproduction of culture rather than to document the new gestures of the working class. Marx's discourse in *The Eighteenth Brumaire* offered him an eloquent account of the ideological meaning adhering to the reappearance of familiar cultural objects and expressions in the passage that is reworded with such force in Nakano's changed songs:

> Men make their own history, but they do not make it just as they please; they do not make it under circumstances chosen by themselves, but under circumstances directly found, given and transmitted from the past. The tradition of all the dead generations weighs like a nightmare on the brain of the living.[38]

History is "consumed" so that the false cannot be distinguished from the authentic, and the reproduction of antiquated forms, ripped out of his-

[36] As Mark Oshima notes in his study of the history of Kabuki, *kata* can refer to all aspects of a role, including gestures and costumes. In addition, a *kata* associates a certain style with a specific actor. Oshima's insightful discussion of the tension between the demand for the preservation of *kata* from the Meiji era onward and the push for innovation provides a context for Nakano's appropriation of the term. See Oshima, "Kabuki: Structure and Change in a Traditional Artistic Institution," senior thesis, Harvard College, 1983, pp. 61–64, and *Engeki hyakka daijiten*, 1960, s.v. *kata*.

[37] Nakano, "Engeki ni tsuite," p. 123. The *kimari* can be differentiated from another frozen pose in Kabuki, the *mie*: the former is like a comma in the action, whereas the latter constitutes a period or full stop. *Engeki hyakka daijiten*, 1960, s.v. "*kimari.*"

[38] Marx, *Eighteenth Brumaire*, p. 595.

torical context, legitimizes both the absence and the myth of creativity.[39] This is Nakano Shigeharu's position in his attack on the abuse of history in Taishō Japan. The blunt language of his poem "Pooru Kurooderu" (Paul Claudel)[40] discloses how the reproduction of culture in contemporary Japan produced an exoticism distancing the Japanese from their own ever-changing tradition. The poem, which appeared in the January 1927 issue of *Roba*, attested to the fact that the young Shinjinkai member and labor organizer was taking a political stand in a literary journal by placing his Marxist theory and his anger into verse about the French poet and dramatist.

PAUL CLAUDEL

Paul Claudel was a poet
Paul Claudel was an ambassador
And France occupied the Ruhr

Romain Rolland fled to Jesus
Vladimir Ilyich returned to Russia
And Paul Claudel wrote poetry

Japan sent troops to Siberia
Fatty Semenov came running
And Paul Claudel wrote poetry

The farmers of France saved their money
The rich took that away
And the rich prayed to Mary
And Paul Claudel prayed to Mary
And Paul Claudel became the French ambassador to Japan
And Paul Claudel wrote poetry

Paul Claudel wrote poetry
Paul Claudel circled the moat
Paul Claudel played the shamisen
Paul Claudel danced Kabuki
Paul Claudel did foreign relations

Ahh   and then
Finally one day
Paul Claudel

---

[39] This is the gist of Lefebvre's exegesis of the relationship of repetition to modernity. He talks in terms of the "voracious consumption of past *oeuvres*" and of the making authentic of "*both* the *absence* of creativity and the *myth* of creativity." Lefebvre, *Survival of Capitalism*, p. 33.

[40] Nakano, "Pooru Kurooderu," *NSZ* 1:513–14 [*Roba* 1/27].

Memorialized Charles-Louis Philippe
The Ambassador on Philippe!

Ahh the great Paul Claudel!
Paul Claudel Ambassador they say is a poet
"Our little Philippe" will
From within his humble grave most likely say
"Paul Claudel became ambassador!"

The technique of repetition reveals the false logic of bourgeois ideology, as history is replaced by nonsensical sequence. The poem does narrate one aspect of Taishō history following the First World War, the implication of Japan in counterrevolution in Soviet Russia. Other data are implied: Romain Rolland was a popular hero of the earliest Japanese left-wing writers before the earthquake in September 1923, and France had occupied the Ruhr in January of that same year. Yet, in the first verse, there is no logical link between the three occurrences, because sequence replaces causation. There is no apparent connection between Paul Claudel's vocation as poet, his work as ambassador, and France's occupation of the Ruhr. The second verse contrasts personal and political choices available to intellectuals. The reference to the cossack commander, Gregory Semenov, who received aid from the Japanese is based on a logic of historic causation, but Claudel is not given a history until the fourth stanza. Here, Nakano connects ideology to power through the image of the appointment of the poet as ambassador after he, too, has "run to Jesus" by adopting the religious ritual of the rich.[41] Claudel's poetry is thereby discounted, as are the traditional Japanese cultural forms alluded to, but Paul Claudel's place in Taishō culture is preserved, for Nakano Shigeharu did not underestimate the power of the ambassador who wrote poetry.

The poetry of the devout Catholic poet-playwright who served as France's ambassador to Taishō Japan between 1921 and 1927 has been termed modernist by scholars of literature because of his iconoclastic approach to language and imagery resulting not only from his allegiance to symbolism but also from his study of Chinese and Japanese culture during his eighteen years of residence in the Orient, in the service of the French diplomatic corps. Claudel wrote and translated poetry while in Japan, and the allusions to the moat, the shamisen, and Kabuki are more than evocative symbols of Japanese culture. They can be read as a shorthand of Claudel's writings on Japan, although here, as elsewhere, Nakano left

---

[41] Claudel's "prayer to Mary" in the poem may only refer to his renowned religious zeal, or it may be a chronological reference to "Tidings Brought to Mary," the drama that established Claudel's reputation as a playwright in 1912.

the historian no definite confirmation of the background reading informing his composition.[42]

It may be that Nakano did read *Cent phrases pour eventails* (A hundred sentences for fans), the collection of short verses inspired by traditional forms of Japanese poetry. It was published in 1927, and Nakano's poem appeared in January of that year. It is questionable whether Nakano was aware of Claudel's 1923 poems inspired by the outer wall of the Imperial Palace; an identification of the hero's "encirclement of the moat" with these poems would demand a stretch of the metaphor. It is more likely that Nakano had in mind Claudel's poetic tribute produced on the occasion of the death of the Taishō Emperor:

> Taking advantage of this gaping tomb,
> The Japan of the living on one side
> And the Japan of the dead on the other
> Communicate.[43]

The reference to the shamisen may or may not refer to Claudel's creation of a dialogue between a poet and a shamisen, published in 1926, but the Kabuki reference is more readily indexed. The French ambassador's frequent visits to Kabuki performances were public knowledge in Japan, and in 1923 the Imperial Theater in Tokyo put on what has been termed the only Kabuki play to have been written by a foreigner. It should also be noted that Paul Claudel did indeed "memorialize" Charles-Louis Philippe in a eulogy written in 1922. Nakano may have read Claudel's tribute to the popular French writer of the late nineteenth century, whose semiautobiographical works on the life of the poor found a wide readership in Japan during the early 1920s. In any case, in the poem Nakano mocks the French functionary's patronizing appropriation of the author, implying that Claudel's expressed appreciation for Japanese culture and his sympathies with the poverty in the literature of Philippe mask the callous self-interest of the ambassador, who represents both the bourgeoisie and the French state.[44]

[42] Regarding Claudel's modernism see Wallace Fowlie, *Paul Claudel* (London: Bowes & Bowes, 1957), p. 91, and Edward Lucie-Smith, "The *Cinq grandes odes* of Paul Claudel," in *Claudel: A Reappraisal*, ed. Richard Griffiths (London: Rapp & Whiting, 1968), pp. 79–90. For the most detailed biographical account of Claudel's years in Japan, refer to Louis Chaigne, *Paul Claudel: The Man and the Mystic*, trans. Pierre de Fontnouvelle (New York: Appleton-Century-Crofts, 1961), pp. 186–209. Claudel's writings on the Far East are identified in Sylvia E. Bowman, gen. ed., *Twayne's World Author Series*, vol. 92: *Paul Claudel*, by Harold A. Waters (New York: Twayne Publishers, 1970), pp. 125–27, 130–33.

[43] Chaigne, *Paul Claudel*, p. 207.

[44] See "Le Poete et le Shamisen" (Paris: Gallimard, 1926). Claudel's Kabuki composition, "The Woman and Her Shadow," came out of a collaboration with the famous Taishō composer Kineya Sakichi. Regarding Claudel's infatuation with and appropriation of Kabuki

By choosing Claudel as a subject, Nakano chose to attack his own mirror-image. Here was another poet who had absorbed the classics of his literary tradition as a youth. In fact Nakano shared the European canon available to the Frenchman, comprising works of Hugo, Goethe, Renan, Voltaire, Balzac, Keats, and Baudelaire. Both had determined to combine politics and culture in their careers, and Nakano recognized that Claudel, too, saw that the two spheres were not at all separate. The Japanese Marxist poet realized that the French Modernist diplomat, hailed as the "Poet-Ambassador" in the Japanese press, was not an emissary who happened to be a member of the French cultural elite. Rather, he was an ambassador who recognized that culture could be wielded as a political tool. Yet what is most important about the poem "Paul Claudel" in the context of Nakano Shigeharu's changing song is that it is an attack on Claudel's Orientalism.

Claudel belongs to the group of ideologues whom Edward Said has grouped under the rubric of "imaginative" orientalists. Claudel's works provide rich documentation of his orientalism. For example, his meditations on China and Japan, *Connaissance de l'Est* (The East I know), published in 1900 after Claudel's first tour of duty in China, present sensual landscapes of Japan and China, devoid of demarcations denoting boundaries of space or time.[45] In Japan the poet feels himself so oriented that one glance allows him "the whole plan of the country." It is as though modern Japan can be contained within one landscape: In the background are the "deep forests and the folds of cumbrous mountains"; in the foreground lie the "detached foot-paths which bar the way one behind the other, like spaced and parallel barriers." Claudel feels so at home that he reaches for an allusion from within Catholicism to be used as a modifier for his Japanese experience: Mt. Fuji is "like a virgin throned in the clarity of the Infinite."[46]

---

and Noh, see Leonard Cabell Pronko, *Theatre East and West: Perspectives Toward a Total Theatre* (Berkeley and Los Angeles: University of California Press, 1967), pp. 131–33, and Jacques Petit and Jean-Pierre Kempf, eds., Christine Trollope, trans., *Claudel on the Theatre* (Coral Gables: University of Miami Press, 1972). Claudel's memorial, "Charles-Louise Philippe," dated December 1922, was first published in *Siwakai* in January 1923. See also another memorial to the same writer with the same title: Paul Claudel, "Charles-Louis Philippe," *Oeuvres completes*, vol. 1: *Poesie* (Paris: Gallimard, 1950), pp. 314–15.

[45] Edward Said, *Orientalism* (New York: Pantheon Books, 1978), pp. 2–3. Claudel says the structure of the pagoda "gathers all nature into the offering that it constitutes," and he is "entangled in a maze of Chinese streets, murky and moist with domestic odors" amid "a people mixed in with their dwellings as bees are with their wax and honey" (*The East I Know* [New Haven: Yale University Press, 1914], pp. 6, 108, 117–18). These brief essays bear a strong resemblance to the self-consciously orientalist work of Roland Barthes; see *Empire of Signs*, trans. Richard Howard (New York: Hill and Wang, 1982).

[46] Claudel, *The East I Know*, p. 121.

Claudel also belongs within the history of Orientalism in its institutional manifestation. As a diplomat posted to China, and even more clearly as French ambassador to Japan, he belonged within a corporate structure for "dominating, restructuring, and having authority over the Orient." As Said has made clear, for the orientalist, the East is a career, and Claudel did use the East for his own professional ends, both as a cultural figure and as a government official. His most visible achievement as foreign envoy was the establishment of the "Maison de France" (later renamed the "Maison Franco-Japonaise"), an organization dedicated to facilitating Franco-Japanese cultural relations. As a result of this effort, the diplomat received the title of commander in the Legion of Honor in 1924.[47] Yet the poem does lean toward a characterization of Claudel as an orientalist in the first sense; he is an imaginative producer of an idealized Japanese culture.

In "Paul Claudel," shamisen music and Kabuki are deprived of value not only because they are adopted by one who is working for the rich, but also because they have become free-floating commodities. These cultural forms, the product of centuries of indigenous history and years of training in the discipline by the performer, are here picked up as a means of "doing" foreign relations. The first four lines of the fifth verse are in that sense equated with the last line. Japanese tradition has become a product to be consumed by the Frenchman because culture is now naturalized as timeless and without spatial boundaries. Paul Claudel and his cohorts, in other words, cannot view Kabuki as something feudal, to be overcome. In a subtle wording, Nakano also implies that hypostatization of culture serves the Japanese state when he has the poet-ambassador circumambulate the moat, the site of the Emperor of Japan, who is thus implicated in this manipulation of culture. Claudel's vision of Japan would be further developed after the appearance of "Paul Claudel," in the 1929 publication of the prose-poems written during his tenure as ambassador, collected under the title *L'oiseau noir dans le soleil levant* (The blackbird in the rising sun), in his essays on the Japanese theater, and in his last play, "Le Soulier de satin" (The satin slipper), which made use of lessons he had learned from Kabuki, bugaku, and bunraku theater. Nakano would move on to other issues, for his unmasking of the ambassador was but part of his critique of the appropriation of culture under capitalism. In Nakano's eyes, Claudel was an orientalist who took from the East what he wanted to see and to use for his own purposes, but he

---

[47] A study investigating Claudel's performance as ambassador to Japan discussed how his plan to establish political and economic relations advantageous to French interests rested on the training of a corps of French orientalists well-versed in the Japanese language. Chujo Shinobu, "Paul Claudel Ambassadeur de France au Japan," *Claudel Studies* 11, 1–2 (1984): 32–55. Said, *Orientalism*, p. 3.

was also one aspect of the economic and cultural expansion of capitalism from Europe into the East set forth in the *Communist Manifesto*:

> In place of the old wants, satisfied by the production of the country, we find new wants, requiring for their satisfaction the products of distant lands and climes. In place of the old local and national seclusion and self-sufficiency, we have intercourse in every direction, universal interdependence of nations. And as in material, so also in intellectual production.[48]

It was this process that Nakano addressed, in one of his most angry, if not most overtly violent, poems, entitled simply "Teikoku hoteru" (Imperial Hotel).[49] Here he related how the reproduction of culture in Taishō Japan was more than the repetition of the old within a new socioeconomic context (his concern in "Train"), or the appropriation by the European of the Japanese (his subject in "Paul Claudel"). He wanted to demonstrate how culture moved both ways, as contemporary European culture was reproduced in commodity form to be sold in Japan, just as Japanese culture was broken into profit-producing units to be sold in the market.

IMPERIAL HOTEL

I

This is the West
The dogs use English

This is the proper West
The dogs invite me to the Russian Opera

This is the West A Western Exposition
The Japanese marketplace for kimono and shop-worn curios

And this is a prison
The guard jangles his keys

This is a dreary, damp, dank prison
Neither the prisoners nor the wardens trade words with a soul

And the prisoners are called by number
And the guards stand in the exits/the entranceways

And then this is a cheap dive
The old fat guy is roaring drunk

And also this is a cheap whorehouse
The women walk naked

---

[48] Marx, *Communist Manifesto*, p. 476.
[49] Nakano, "Teikoku hoteru," *NSZ* 1:510–11 [*Roba* 11/26].

And this is a hole
Black and fetid

II

A large hole
A large whorehouse
A large saloon
A large dampish prison
A big and seedy sample Japanese marketplace
Undestroyed even by the earthquake
In the center of Tokyo
Over our heads
Squats, letting loose a stench

The opening lines of "Imperial Hotel" suggest a rejection of the West and of the Japanese urban citizenry's desire to adopt its cultural fashions, but by the third stanza, Nakano's real target is evident. His intent here is not to overcome but to do battle with the bourgeois values of capitalism, which is responsible for the deformation of human beings into things or numbers and the transformation of the site of daily intercourse into a marketplace. Japan, like the Japan of Paul Claudel, has become a source of antiquarian objects, its culture a warehouse. Moreover, the European bourgeoisie has created the site for the sale of their own cultural commodities. This is Marx's argument. The bourgeoisie covers the globe in search of locales in which to expand its market and thus gives a cosmopolitan character to production and consumption throughout the world. This class forcefully introduces what is termed civilization into other nations, creating "a world after its own image." Marshall Berman's paraphrase is a most appropriate wording of Nakano's reading of Marx: "Culture becomes an enormous warehouse in which everything is kept in stock on the chance that someday, somewhere, it might sell."[50]

Nakano's method of interpreting Marx is to strip the veneer of civilization from the hotel, revealing the freedom of movement in the corridors to be confinement and the items for sale to be objects that will only satisfy vulgar cravings. The second part of the poem is thus devoid of human actors and retains only the metaphors for the hotel. The conclusion, which takes the hotel itself as subject, stresses Nakano's intent. He is revealing an eroticism gone sour in an urban world that offers no real ties between human beings, while it continually promises new excitement through the reproduction of new commodities. This culture provides con-

---

[50] Marx, *Communist Manifesto*, p. 477; Marshall Berman, *All that Is Solid Melts into Air: The Experience of Modernity* (New York: Simon & Schuster, 1982), p. 162.

stant new images and texts, and conceals a reality wherein "no words are traded."

The Imperial Hotel appears in Nakano's postwar autobiographical prose as part of a vignette illustrating the discomfort of the hero of *Churning* with the politics of the labor movement, with his cultural heritage, and with contemporary culture. In the work, Yasukichi takes on the role of interpreter for a German labor organizer, and thinly veiled references to political theorist Yoshino Sakuzō and to reformist labor leader Suzuki Bunji are used to emphasize the split between the communist and non-communist factions on the Japanese left in the 1920s and the hero's bewilderment with this political reality. He is equally confused by the splendor of the Imperial Hotel, where he first meets Lienhardt, his charge. The hero's visits to the hotel provide a logical context for the prewar poem on the Imperial Hotel. First of all, a hotel official, a form of guard, blocks Yasukichi's entrance into the hotel, demanding to know his destination. After Yasukichi has established a routine of avoiding the elevator and the crowds at the desk by dashing up the side stairs to the German's second story room, he is stopped by a "dog" (a slang term for spy) who offers him tickets to the Russian opera after a mild series of questions. The segment alludes to the transformations informing Taishō culture when the hero senses a "modern something-or-other" atmosphere permeating the room where the daughter of the Yoshino Sakuzō figure and other young people are visiting, and when he is loathe to interpret working-class culture for Lienhardt, who expresses interest in the movies playing in the worker's neighborhoods. But the looming presence of the Imperial Hotel itself is the clearest indication of the novel's concern with Taishō culture, for in postearthquake Tokyo it was the meeting place for Japanese eager to participate in the ways of the West.[51] What is missing is Nakano's Marxism. Just as Nakano's hero in *Muragimo* is depicted as lost in a society of young Marxist intellectuals in the Shinjinkai dormitory, in Nakano's postwar rewording of the "Imperial Hotel," his hero cannot place his experience in any critical perspective. The Marxist concept of cultural reproduction, central to the poem, is missing from the postwar prose. Yet by the second half of the 1920s, the poet who was grounding his writing in a Marxist conception of historical change and of the figuration of human relationships governed by commodities under capitalism was directing his anger at a modern capitalist phenomenon that first confronted Marxists in the twentieth century—the political power of the mass media. Between 1926 and 1929, Nakano's concern

[51] Nakano, *Muragimo*, NSZ 5:251–64. The reconstruction of Tokyo after the earthquake is one of the themes of *Muragimo*. For another view of the place of the Imperial Hotel in Taishō culture see Seidensticker, *Low City, High City: Tokyo from Edo to the Earthquake* (New York: Knopf, 1983), pp. 275–76.

with the reproduction of Japanese cultural artifacts for capitalist consumption was accompanied by his indictment of a cultural process capable of obliterating all historical and cultural distinctions whatsoever, the process of cultural reproduction, which could and did homogenize human experience in the name of an objective truth that served capitalist interests.

THE CULTURE OF REPRODUCTION

Nakano's Marxist analysis of the reproduction of culture was a Japanese response to the modern packaging of indigenous tradition by Western capitalism which accompanied the sale of Western commodities in Japan. He criticized the dual nature of the reproduction of culture whereby cultural innovation conceals social continuity and the appropriation of cultural tradition obscures the emergence of new relationships in society. In contrast, Nakano's writings on mass culture, herein referred to as the culture of reproduction, highlighted universalistic aspects of Taishō history. His analysis transcended national boundaries to encompass discussion of such modern phenomena as the urban crowd and the ideological implications of the unprecedented ability of modern technology to reproduce culture in the mass media. Now, in his second phase of changing song, like his contemporary Walter Benjamin, but separate and apart from Benjamin, he wrote about the production of the cultural commodity.

In many ways the young Nakano Shigeharu matches Walter Benjamin's characterization of Baudelaire, his urban hero of nineteenth-century Paris. Like Benjamin's "social poet," Nakano oriented himself to the city very quickly and thereafter "viewed the literary market without any illusions."[52] Both poets were forced to go underground and to produce poetry on the run; both assumed guises. Benjamin claimed that Baudelaire, as a modern hero, chose to play roles because in the end he was not motivated by any convictions. He could thus appear as a flaneur, an apache, a dandy, or a ragpicker. Nakano's pose as an amateur and a "simple man" was closer to disguise and more consistent, possibly because it was premised upon a single-minded political purpose that contrasts with Benjamin's depiction of Baudelaire's rapid abandonment of his "revolutionary manifesto."[53]

While Benjamin may have been critical of Baudelaire's "profound duplicity," which allowed him to support the oppressed in his poetry while repeating their illusions, he credited Baudelaire for recognizing the importance of the appearance of a new phenomenon, the urban crowd, dur-

[52] Benjamin, *Charles Baudelaire*, pp. 25, 33.
[53] Ibid., pp. 26, 47, 97–98.

ing a moment of historic transition. This crowd was about to be transformed into the reading public within a commodity culture that processed all information into standardized newsprint. According to Benjamin, Baudelaire recognized the significance of this change.[54] The city emerged as the eroticized site of the production of commodities and of the crowd in Walter Benjamin's studies of Baudelaire. There, Benjamin introduced into Marxist theory the notion of the historical emergence of the crowd, expanding on Marx's analysis of class in the context of the transformation of the agricultural populace into an urban proletariat. Benjamin wanted to examine how relationships were altered by urban life, as the activity of the eye began to take precedence over the ear when the city-dweller aboard the new modes of transportation—the buses, the railroad, and the trams—was forced to look at his temporary companions for extended periods. But coexistence on the streets was the theorist's main concern, and in Baudelaire, Benjamin found a poet who wielded the crowd as a new subject for lyric poetry because he presented the crowd in the context of the "life of the erotic person."[55] For Benjamin, the crowd is but an assemblage of private individuals who share space on a street, at a fire, or possibly at the site of a traffic accident. It is analogous to the customers at a market who gather by accident to fulfill their unshared needs because "the accident of the market economy brings them together." It is the role of the flaneur who strolls the avenues of the Paris of the Second Empire to endow the atomized grouping of the passers-by with a soul.

Benjamin's flaneur is separate from the crowd, observing it, whereas, ostensibly, Baudelaire's flaneur abandons himself to the crowd and to the intoxicating draw of the commodity. But in fact, while he recognizes that the excitement of the city is but surface glitter during a passing moment, he, too, is entranced by it.[56] The city also held an awesome attraction for Nakano Shigeharu before and after his discovery of history, but he was too critical to be Baudelaire's hero and too hurried to be Benjamin's leisurely critic. In an early love poem, entitled "Kyō mo" (Again today),[57] written a year after his move to Tokyo and before his turn to a Marxist

[54] Ibid., pp. 26, 120, 154. Essays written by Benjamin at different times appear together in this work. I have treated them as part of the same argument. Regarding this issue see Buck-Morss, *The Origin of Negative Dialectics*, pp. 155–62.

[55] *Charles Baudelaire*, p. 45.

[56] Benjamin's ambivalence has been captured by Marshall Berman: "His heart and his sensibility draw him irresistibly toward the city's bright lights, beautiful women, fashion, luxury, its play of dazzling surfaces and radiant scenes; meanwhile his Marxist conscience wrenches him insistently away from these temptations, instructs him that this whole glittering world is decadent, hollow, vicious, spiritually empty, oppressive to the proletariat, condemned by history. . . . He cannot resist one last look down the boulevard or under the arcade; he wants to be saved, but not yet." Berman, *All that Is Solid Melts into Air*, p. 146.

[57] Nakano, "Kyō mo," *NSZ* 1:497 [*Razō* 2/25].

politics, Nakano had begun to examine urban relationships from a critical distance as he covered the sensual draw of city congestion noted by Benjamin:

AGAIN TODAY

There are crowds of women in the street again today
Chattering in showy tongues
Can they all have a place to go
With bright pink earlobes swinging arms
Rapidly I find myself passed by
You are not here in this big city Tokyo
You are not here in this big city Tokyo—what does that really mean?
Passed by even by such women
From morning onward
Tensing my heart and tensed
Pale of face I have no place to go

There is an erotic quality to this scene of young women in motion, but the narrator is no flaneur, for even as he feels lost, without a place in the city, he recognizes that the intensity of the women is forced. There is neither the awe nor the admiration aimed at the working women in the rice paddies present in "Women in the Rice Fields," which appeared in the same issue of *Razō* in February 1925. A second city poem, "Hataki wo okuru" (I offer you a dust mop),[58] is even stronger in its rejection of Tokyo culture. "You know, don't you/ This place called Tokyo's a brutal city," he demands of the friend to whom the verse is addressed. The lines that follow are an indictment of his friend's everyday activities and manner of speech. In other words, Nakano is noting and rejecting an urban *kata* exhibited by a new personality in Japanese history, the young bureaucrat:

You know don't you
This place called Tokyo's a brutal city
It's brutality reflected in the soot and grit concealed like shadows
And everyday you wear down your life among those junior officials
And that is why your language is becoming rough

In 1925, Nakano had not begun his serious study of Marxism, and had thus not yet formulated language to universalize his feelings of loss and estrangement. The lonely young man in "Again Today" was unwittingly witness to a new phenomenon in Japanese society—women were being allowed a place in the public sphere as purveyors and consumers of a new commodity culture; they too were new personalities. The process of using

[58] Nakano, "Hataki wo okuru," *NSZ* 1:499 [*Razō* 3/25].

women "without reservation in the production process outside the home," cited as a nineteenth-century phenomenon by Benjamin, had also begun in Japan by the end of that century, and by the second decade of the twentieth century it had extended beyond the factory to encompass new places of work.[59] Yet while Nakano's plaintive address to the young girls passing by sounds similar to Benjamin's concern with the crowd as the refuge "of love which eludes the poet" and his focus on "the stream in which the woman moves past, borne along by the crowd"[60] he could not place into a context the female procession composed possibly of factory girls on their day off, department store employees, or possibly cafe waitresses. His description of the busy young women and his remonstrance to his colleague working for the state hint at the emergence of new modes of social interaction, but they lack the exactitude of Benjamin's notations on the activities of the urban bourgeoisie committed to the collection of things in order to compensate for the vacuity of private life in the city.[61] By 1929, when Nakano published his commentary on a debate about contemporary folk music surrounding the popular song "Tokyo March," he had formulated his account of the reign of things in city life within a Marxist framework. By then he was an established critic of an urban locale that no longer overwhelmed him.

Although Nakano did not seize the chance to elaborate on the issue of the reproduction of popular culture, the history of "Tokyo March" provides an evocative illustration of the rationalization and repression of late Taishō popular art. The song was conceived of as a publicity gambit for Nikkatsu Pictures, because the company was producing a cinematographic version of Kikuchi Kan's popular pulp novel, *Tokyo March*, first serialized in *Kingu*, the forerunner of the popular family-oriented magazine, from June 1928 through October 1929. Nikkatsu convinced Victor Records of the mutual advantages of the endeavor, and the recording company turned to the poet Saijō Yasu, who decided "to depict the mod-

---

[59] In a passage betraying his prejudices relating to gender roles, Benjamin notes: "The nineteenth century began to use women without reservation in the production process outside the home. It did so primarily in a primitive fashion by putting them into factories. Consequently, in the course of time masculine traits were bound to manifest themselves in these women." Benjamin, *Charles Baudelaire*, p. 93. For a comprehensive social history of woman's work in new white collar, consumer-oriented occupations during the Taishō era, see Murakami Nobuhiko, *Taishōki no shokugyō fujin* (Domesu shuppan, 1983).

[60] Benjamin refers to Baudelaire's wistful poem, "To a Passer-by," which opens as follows: "Amid the deafening traffic of the town / Tall, slender, in deep mourning, with majesty / A woman passed, raising, with dignity / In her poised hand, the flounces of her gown." Referring to the same motif of a woman passing by in a poem by Stefan George, Benjamin notes, "The poet has missed the important thing: the stream in which the woman moves past, borne along by the crowd. Benjamin, *Charles Baudelaire*, pp. 45–46.

[61] Ibid., p. 46.

ern mores of Tokyo for them." Upon reviewing the lyrics about urban play in a café-crazed Tokyo, the company decided to preempt government censorship by deleting references to a "Marx Boy" and to Alexandra Kollontai's novel *Red Love*. Their precautions did not prevent sensation.[62] In "Mō hitotsu no Tokyo kōshinkyoku e" (Toward another Tokyo March),[63] Nakano joined in the debate about the censored hit tune of 1929. While the other guest columnists, including the lyricist of the song, Saijō Yasu, focused their comments on the merits of intrinsically Japanese melodies as opposed to such Western popular music as jazz, struggling to determine definitively what made a Japanese popular song or *ryūkōka*, Nakano chose to talk about the power of changing song in its urban context. Labeling "Tokyo March" both absurd and dull, he agreed with Saijō that it was an apt accompaniment to the contemporary corruption of Tokyo. Rather than echoing the lyricist's defense that the tune could not encourage degeneracy, he elaborated on why "Tokyo March" was an apt and insidious accompaniment to Tokyo life in the year 1929. According to Nakano the song would have been a hit even had it not been associated with the movies or the radio, for it floated atop the veneered, gaudy, unresisting life of the modern city and thus inevitably drew anyone who sang it into that kind of life.

The statements made in "Toward Another Tokyo March," including its ending, which called for an alternative music capable of rising from the depths of society,[64] remained undeveloped in Nakano's contribution to the controversy, but other essays and poetry contribute to the conclusion that by the end of the 1920s, Nakano, like Benjamin, had integrated a theory of commodity culture into his vision of urban life. Benjamin concerned himself with the attraction of the actual products of mass production, the commodities "bathed in a profane glow," and with the ideological masking of the process of consumption which in urban society had

[62] See Ishikawa Hiroyuki, ed., *Goraku no senzen shi* (Shoseki kabushikigaisha, 1981), p. 157. Only because record sales were climbing toward a total of 250,000 were the Victor executives able to persuade disgruntled Odawara Railway officials that the line "let's run away on the Odakyu" (shorthand for *Odawara Kyūkō*) was an advertisement and not a defamation of their company. See Tsurumi Shunsuke, *Ajia kaihō no yume*, Nihon no hyakunen (Chikuma shobō, 1962), 4:48–49, and Isoda Kōichi, *Shisō to shite no Tokyo: Kindai bungaku shiron nōto* (Kokubunsha, 1978), pp. 85–96. For a chatty account of the production and reception of the song focusing on the "Queen of the new folk song," Satō Chiyoko, refer to Yūki Ryōichi, *Ahh Tokyo kōshinkyoku* (Kawade bunko, 1985), pp. 85–92. The debate regarding the censorship of the song and the nature of contemporary Japanese popular music and its relationship to jazz was waged in the pages of the *Yomiuri shimbun* on August 4, 10, and 13–16.

[63] Nakano, "Mō hitotsu no Tokyo kōshinkyoku e," NSZ 9:261–63 [*Yomiuri shimbun* 8/20/29].

[64] Ibid., p. 263.

as strong a hold as the denial of the true relations of production by bourgeois ideology. In this context the international world exhibitions were "places of pilgrimage to the fetish Commodity" symbolizing its "enthronement." While Nakano's Imperial Hotel, which was both a Western exposition and an oriental bazaar, was just such a mecca, he did not pursue this topic, nor did he choose to showcase the department store. Instead, he focused on the object for sale in one corner of the marketplace of the "phantasmagoria of capitalist culture," the literary commodity. And indeed, the expansion of print culture in late Taishō was a phenomenon that Nakano could not ignore. Between 1914 and 1923, four hundred new magazines had appeared on the stands, and by 1927 the leading publishers were selling forty million copies of entertainment magazines each year to men, women, and children.[65] Like Benjamin, Nakano determined that the intellectual was in no way a flaneur gazing over the urban landscape for the pure pleasure of the view; he was a producer in search of customers for his commodity.[66]

In 1926 Nakano had illustrated the idea of the commodification of Japanese tradition in "Paul Claudel." In 1927 "Imperial Hotel" introduced the transnational nature of commodity culture, and in 1928, in the closing sections of his essay on Akutagawa, Nakano identified the man of letters as an actor in the capitalist marketplace. In the following year, in the nonproletarian, mainstream magazine *Shinchō*, he published an explicit exposé of the production of the literary commodity. "Bunshō wo uru koto sono hoka" (The selling of writing and other matters)[67] opens with an ironic caveat premised on Nakano's materialist vision of historical progression:

> There are all sorts of issues where he who does not have something can tell the truth all the much better than he who does have it. The slaveowner never once gave a thought to freedom; the taker of tribute was never burdened with a headache over the real nature of taxation. Therein lies the reason why a poet has qualifications to talk of money.[68]

The issue Nakano wished to raise was the nature of the commodity demanded by those who exacted commodities from writers like himself.

[65] Benjamin, *Charles Baudelaire*, pp. 104–5, 165–66. Regarding the explosion of mass-produced magazines and the emergence of centrally located department stores, see Ishikawa, *Goraku no senzen shi*, pp. 88–92, 116–17.

[66] Benjamin notes how Baudelaire often referred to himself as a whore and concludes that "Baudelaire knew what the true situation of the man of letters was: he goes to the marketplace as a flaneur, supposedly to take a look at it, but in reality to find a buyer." Benjamin, *Charles Baudelaire*, p. 34.

[67] Nakano, "Bunshō wo uru koto sono hoka," *NSZ* 9:264–72 [*Shinchō* 9/29].

[68] Ibid., p. 264.

To this end he offered a parable: One day, he had gone off to sell some writing to a newspaper. He knew the type of writing newspapers wanted and had painstakingly conformed to those standards, but the article had not sold. Thus, even more painstakingly, he had written a second article. This second one also had not sold. To explain the moral of the story, Nakano gave his metaphor for the contemporary mass culture within which history obliged him to work: it was a Jintan (sen-sen) culture. Nakano placed this metaphor within an analogy from prison life, in one of his earliest allusions to an experience increasingly shared by Japanese intellectuals associated with communism after the sweeping nationwide arrests on March 15, 1928, and April 16, 1929. Without mentioning his own recent arrests, he introduced into his work the topic of everyday life in prison, with an understated irony that could only have been gained through experience.[69] Nakano was quite aware that a separate prison culture was being institutionalized by the late 1920s (at the same time as capitalist culture appeared to offer the public an ever-increasing choice of literary items to consume), and the poet managed to strike at both in deadpan fashion:

> In jail even if you get sick they won't buy you medicine. Sometimes they will buy you just Jintan. That's because Jintan can't be "either poison or medicine." The reason that Jintan is sold so widely is this characteristic of convenient usefulness. Probably writing which is like Jintan sells quite well. That sort of writing probably has as good an effect as Jintan. And I have the utmost faith in the efficacy of Jintan.[70]

The subject here was not overt repression, but the hegemonic aspect of cultural control.[71] Clearly, Nakano did not really accept the value of the sort of writing he had likened to the glittering, uniformly round pellets of silver-coated mint so easily reproduced in quantity for the market; the metaphor allowed him to attack the commodified nature of literature produced for profit. One decade later Benjamin would define the goal of the materialist method to be the sundering of truth from falsehood. In

[69] Nakano joined the Communist-backed campaign of the Labor-Farmer candidate, Ōyama Ikuo, and was arrested at a rally on February 27, 1928. He was released on March 5, after spending time in five different prisons, and placed under arrest for the second time during the March 15 dragnet. For a fictional account of the effects of the March 15, 1928, incident on activists and their families, see Nakano's famous short story, "Harusaki no kaze," NSZ 1:203–14 [Senki 8/28].

[70] Nakano, "Bunshō wo uru," p. 264.

[71] This is not to underestimate the institutionalization of repression, which led to what I have termed "prison culture." According to Shiota Shōhei, 8,368 people were arrested under the Peace Preservation Law in 1928 and 1929, and more than 800 were prosecuted. For a discussion of the arrests and the trials beginning in 1928, see Shiota Shōhei, Nihon shakai undō shi (Iwanami zensho, 1982), pp. 101–6.

very similar language, Nakano here explained why it was so painful for him to produce "Jintan writing." Through the act of writing, he noted, authors have the opportunity to approach the truth; the closer to the truth, the farther the writing from Jintan prose. In a passage that can only be read as a reworking of the opening section of the first volume of *Capital*, Nakano claimed that "to sell writing is to produce it as a commodity. Commodities, as everybody knows, are produced for the market and not so they may be used by people. The truth is the opposite of this."[72] Exchange value, in other words, has been substituted for any use value, as implied in Nakano's advertisements in his essay about Akutagawa "and other matters." There is no elaboration on Marx's conception of the fetishism of commodities, a process that serves to hide the human labor behind the product, other than Nakano's lament that he has no other method of making money and has thus been forced into a "spiritual prostitution" that "skirts around the truth, neither approaching nor straying far from it." This mercenary situation is in fact a notch below prostitution, as the author (like Benjamin's Baudelaire) likens his situation to the position of a dance-hall dancer. According to Nakano's logic, the dancer is forced to sell herself because she lacks the talent to be a prostitute. The writer of Jintan prose who works so that he may be bought, rather than working to be read, is in a similar position.[73]

Nakano's Jintan culture, in its bland uniformity pandering to the needs of the capitalist press, appeared under another name in Walter Benjamin's work. In his language, such culture belonged within the category of "the work of art in the age of mechanical reproduction." In an essay by that name, written in 1936, Benjamin expounded on the fact that while in the past a work of art could always be reproduced, its mechanical reproduction was a historically unprecedented development, isolating the art object—now a product—from its history, and thereby depriving it of authenticity, by effacing what he termed its "aura." Art was emancipated from tradition, or from ritual, when the photographic negative was reproduced, and when the modern cinema ripped art from its cultural heritage. Art now served politics and not ritual, but the conclusion to the essay made clear the political ambiguity inherent in the new phenomenon of mass culture. In other words, the modern technology allowing for mass reproduction could be used for politically antithetical purposes: just as fascism was aestheticizing politics, so communism responded by politicizing art.[74]

---

[72] Benjamin, *Charles Baudelaire*, p. 103; Nakano, "Bunshō wo uru," p. 265; Marx, *Capital* 1:35–83.

[73] Nakano, "Bunshō wo uru," pp. 265–66.

[74] Walter Benjamin, "The Work of Art in the Age of Mechanical Reproduction," in *Illuminations*, pp. 217–51. Richard Wolin states that this essay contains Benjamin's "most con-

Benjamin's essay focuses on the power of film, a medium barely mentioned in Nakano's Taishō writings, but his argument confirms Nakano's message about the historical transformation of Japanese culture. Nakano's concerns in the beginning of the second half of the 1920s were in agreement with Benjamin's choice to analyze "the developmental tendencies of art under present conditions of production" rather than under a postrevolutionary classless society. Both writers believed that an understanding of the present, rather than a projection into the future, could aid in bringing about revolution; both men looked at the uses of the past. When Benjamin discussed how an ancient Greek statue, removed from its original context wherein it was worshipped, was treated as "ominous idol" during the Middle Ages, he was both adding his theory of the aura to Marx's treatment of culture in *The Eighteenth Brumaire* and illustrating Nakano's views on the reproduction of culture set forth in "Paul Claudel" and "Imperial Hotel." Both critics supported art's emancipation from outmoded traditions; both were also acutely aware of the revolutionary potential of film and photography and of the pervasiveness of the manipulation of these art forms. Moreover, Nakano met Benjamin's demand for intellectuals to place themselves within the production process. He made it clear that he was selling his writing in order to make a living, but his decision to place his revolutionary energies within the cultural sphere through the production of mass-marketed essays, stories, and poetry printed in both revolutionary and mainstream publications is proof that he recognized the potential of technology to wage revolution. His conclusion in his essay on the selling of writing, which comprises the confession that he had no recourse but to pursue truth within Jintan prose and his claim that he must refrain from expressing his joy in the pursuit of truth in such writing, revealed that he was aware of the double-edged nature of the mass-produced word. During the closing years of the 1920s, he would champion the politicization of art in essays and poems, but in 1926 and 1927, during the second stage of his changing song, he emphasized the first part of Benjamin's equation. His poetry attacked the aestheticization of politics and the homogenization of history and politics in the mass media in the name of culture. Nakano did not develop an actual theory of the influence of the mass media in prose form, beyond his notion of sen-sen culture. Yet by 1929, when the metaphor appeared in the "Selling of Writing and Other Matters," he had already produced a series of poems recording the abuses of technological reproduction by the photograph, termed by Benjamin the "first revolutionary means of reproduc-

---

sistent and forceful argument for the functional transformation of culture along Marxist lines." Wolin, *Walter Benjamin*, p. 184.

tion."[75] His attack on this medium had begun in 1926 with the appearance of the following poem:

PICTURE OF THE ARRIVAL OF THE NEWLY APPOINTED AMBASSADOR TO THE CITY

That man's photo appeared in a hundred newspapers this morning
He'd brought along his wife and daughter
Surrounded by police and officials
What, I wonder, has he planned to do here?
Most likely he plans to tell lies here
Here again and again he probably plans to tell lies
And I wonder for whose sake he's going to tell those lies
And I wonder what path those lies will take
How I wonder how will those lies echo back to us

That liar's photograph
Surrounded by wife and daughter and police and officials
Appeared all at once in a hundred newspapers this morning[76]

Like "Paul Claudel," this poem was about cultural exploitation coated by a gloss of foreign friendship and diplomacy. It may well have referred to Claudel's arrival in Japan, which was heralded in the Japanese press as the arrival of a "poet-ambassador,"[77] but these lyrics introduced a hitherto unexamined aspect of contemporary cultural manipulation into Nakano's theory. When he brought attention to a new use for portraiture by using the word *zu* (ordinarily used for an illustrative sketch or a title of a painting) to denote the photograph, he was alerting the reader to the ideological questions posed by the poem. These problems did not merely relate to the political manipulations of the newly arrived diplomat. Rather, Nakano wanted to investigate and expose the form taken by those lies, which had appeared "at once in a hundred newspapers." His poem corroborated Benjamin's theory that modern man is "increasingly unable to assimilate the data of the world around him by way of experience."[78] While purporting to organize this information for the edification of their readers, newspapers actually isolate the reader from understanding, and the form of the message is as responsible as its content for this

[75] Benjamin, "Work of Art," p. 224.

[76] Nakano, "Shinnin taishi chakukyō no zu," NSZ 1:507 [Roba 7/26].

[77] See the illustrated articles referring to the poet-ambassador's oratory and his welcoming party and to his oration the following day: "Shijin taishi kushi kangeikai no hanagata," *Yomiuri shimbun*, January 15, 1922, p. 5, and "Kangei no yorokobi ni shijin taishi no yūben," *Yomiuri shimbun*, January 16, 1922, p. 3. While neither police nor officials appear in the January 15 photograph, Nakano may have had it in mind.

[78] Benjamin, "The Author as Producer," p. 224.

abuse of the truth. In other words, the "principles of journalistic information (freshness of the news, brevity, comprehensibility, and above all,
lack of connection between the news items)" along with "the makeup of
the pages and the paper's style" obscure contemporary history. Because
the newspaper appears in large editions, the data it contains do not enter
tradition. Shared information is not perceived as privileged and is thus
not passed on. It is available to all, at once, without any transmission
among readers, until the next news item cancels out the previous edition's
revelations.[79]

In the poem about the picture, Nakano wished to freeze this process of
the constant production of items by the press to reveal that the picture is
the product of a history, and that because of this one photograph of the
ambassador (which would not be mentioned in the following morning's
newspaper, or ever again), an ideologically saturated history could be created in a twofold fashion. There would be the actual lies told by the new
ambassador. (Nakano here was not concerned with the additional layer
of deformation of truth caused by any misquotation or misrepresentation
by the press of the ambassador's language.) Second—and this is the real
subject of the poem—there would be the impression left by the photograph, naturalizing the official as a given entity, without questioning his
personal history or his future intentions. In the poem, Nakano's seemingly naive questions are his way of voicing his sophisticated insight that
a photograph, like any other cultural text, must be read with a critical eye
for the highly coded messages, which are not overtly articulated. He knew
that in twentieth-century culture there are presumptions about the place
of the photograph and how a photograph should be read. Benjamin also
warned his readers to turn their attention away from the question of
whether photography was an art, toward an examination of the transformation of a work in the photograph.[80]

Like Nakano, Benjamin was interested in a certain sort of photographic image, the picture that was captioned and commodified in the
illustrated press. Both men worked from the premise that photojournal-

[79] Benjamin, *Charles Baudelaire*, pp. 112–13.

[80] Walter Benjamin, "A Short History of Photography," *Screen* 13, 1 (Spring 1972): 5–
26. Alan Sekula discusses what he terms the "photographic discourse" wherein the meaning
of a photograph is "subject to cultural definition." He calls the photograph an "utterance"
carrying or embodying a message: "the photograph is an 'incomplete' utterance, a message
that depends on some external matrix of conditions and presupposition for its readability.
That is, the meaning of any photographic message is necessarily context-determined. We
might formulate this position as follows: a photograph communicates by means of its association with some hidden, or implicit text." Alan Sekula, "On the Invention of Photographic Meaning," in *Thinking Photography*, ed. Victor Burgin (London: Macmillan,
1982), pp. 84–85.

ism attains meaning through the use of captions; accordingly, Benjamin put the photograph in the service of politics with the following stipulation: "What we require of the photographer is the ability to give his picture the caption that wrenches it from modish commerce and gives it a revolutionary useful value."[81] In Nakano's poem the title words, "Newly Appointed Ambassador to the City," denote the caption that can instantaneously create a personality out of a man who is in fact a liar. It also illustrates Benjamin's theory of the emergence of the celebrity as part of the expansion of commodities following the invention of photography. The poem was a statement that the press had created a commodity, the "poet-ambassador," as a form of advertisement to extend its market. And just as the press could create newsworthy entities, it could also appropriate ideas that were originally produced to question the capitalist culture that encouraged the commodification of words and images, a point made most explicitly by Benjamin: "the bourgeois apparatus of production and publication can assimilate astonishing quantities of revolutionary themes, indeed, can propagate them without calling its own existence, and the existence of the class that owns it, seriously into question."[82] Both the form of the newspaper and the newspaper writer, the journalist, were responsible for this subversion, for the journalist sought and created truncated, isolated occurrences, which appeared as arbitrary, historically unmediated events.[83] This work of the journalist was Nakano's subject in "Shimbunkisha" (Journalist),[84] a second poem about the world created by the newspaper:

JOURNALIST

Did you know
We were "talking"
You came on in
You saw me and were shocked
You took heed of me in front of the whiteman
You asked the whiteman
Does he speak English
No that he does not
You were relieved
I see I see hm hm
Ahh your chatter was ultra-leftist   [stanza break]

[81] Benjamin, "The Author as Producer," p. 230.

[82] For Benjamin's notion of the personality as commodity, discussed in the context of the phenomenon of the film star, see "Mechanical Reproduction," p. 231. He ruminated on the appropriation of contestatory ideas in "The Author as Producer," p. 229.

[83] Benjamin, *Charles Baudelaire*, pp. 112–13.

[84] Nakano, "Shimbunkisha," *NSZ* 1:511–12 [*Roba* 11/26].

You knew
That I speak no English
But did you know
That I understand a small amount of English

Did you know
What you asked of that whiteman
What you forced that foreigner to say
In front of me
From that whiteman of my circle
What you robbed from him and how

And do you know?
When you flew out like a crow
What that whiteman said to me
That whiteman said it
Dringend neugierig!
And the base of my ears turned red

But worry not
We'll probably talk tomorrow
About you
About newspaper journalists
About Japanese newspapers in general
And we'll probably laugh jovially
Ahh—Fatty
You be loyal to your work
That itself can be the topic of our talk

The poem paints a suggestive setting. The narrator and a German friend, who appears to be a fellow revolutionary, seem to be visiting in a cafe when their conversation is interrupted by an aggressive newspaperman whose "chatter" is leftist. He is a poseur who has neither an understanding nor a genuine interest in revolution. Instead of recognizing the bond between Nakano and the foreign man (the crude term *ketō* has been translated as "whiteman" to denote its vulgarity), which transcends the Japanese poet's inability to communicate in English, the journalist immediately affects a conspiratorial, cosmopolitan air in order to presume an intimacy with the German. The dialogue is sketchy; the reader knows no details of the exchange between the German and the reporter, and even a translation of the German phrase reveals only that "Dringend neugierig" means "insistently curious." Moreover, when this scene and this term reappeared in Nakano's postwar fictional memoirs in the account of Yasukichi's relationship with the German labor leader staying at the Imperial Hotel, the additional detail served to dilute rather than explain the meaning of the prewar poem. In 1954 the encounter was presented in the following version in *Churning*:

> Once while Yasukichi was in Lienhard's room there was a knock at the door and a Japanese journalist entered. He could speak English, and Lienhard answered in what appeared to be poorer English. The journalist kept putting in "I see, I see . . ." but even to Yasukichi who could not understand the conversation the journalist seemed rude and overly persistent. Lienhard seemed to be faltering. As soon as the journalist had left and the door had shut, Lienhard spit out "Neugierig!" and the sound of "gierig" seemed so bitter that Yasukichi felt embarrassed.[85]

In the poem, as in the postwar prose account of the Imperial Hotel, the author draws attention to the hero's isolation, but this is not the subject of the poem, for "Journalist," like "Imperial Hotel," is an angry, assured statement of the author's rejection of Taishō culture. The Taishō version places the Japanese journalist's "insistent curiosity" in perspective in the concluding stanza. The "topic of our talk"—the work of a new urban personality, the "loyal" Japanese newspaperman—is the topic of the poem. As in "Imperial Hotel," Nakano's approach is neither theoretical nor direct, and yet there is no doubt but that the poem alludes to the nature of that work. Journalism is sensationalist, relying on the instant creation of news or a "happening" before the writer can rush on to create his own subjective shaping of a situation in another instant article, or before the photographer can caption an illusion without having to elaborate through either photographs or more elaborate written explanations. The poem illustrates Benjamin's view that the press has served to replace politics with a curiosity that is never sustained; there is no other organizing principle to the newspaper than "that imposed on it by the readers' impatience." Newspaper fact is inseparable from fiction, as the newspaper incorporates advertisements, serialized novels, and any other pieces of writing that can be indiscriminately utilized to present the experience of novelty to the reader. Yet, the very task forced on the reader by the nature of the newspaper, to make disparate items coherent, could be used to insert politics into the news, if the reader could become a writer, capable of prescription and not merely description.[86] This is the process set forth in Nakano's third poem about the politics of the press in Taishō Japan:

---

[85] Nakano, *Muragimo*, pp. 258–59.

[86] For Benjamin's view of the commodification of the news as novelty, see *Charles Baudelaire*, pp. 27, 29, 172. On the role of the reader as producer, refer to "Author as Producer," pp. 224–25. Benjamin presents this vision in almost identical terms yet again: "[Thus] the distinction between author and public is about to lose its basic character. . . . At any moment the reader is ready to turn into a writer." Benjamin, "The Work of Art," p. 232.

THE PHOTOGRAPH IN THE NEWSPAPER

Look
Look at this man two down from here
This is my big brother
It's your other son
Your other son   My big brother   Here   Looking like this
Made to wear gaiters
Made to lug his lunchbox
Wrapped round and round with heavy ammunition
Made to aim
Made to load
Made to fix his bayonet
Here
In front of the wall of the **** Association
Legs astride he is made to stand with the face of a murderer
Look   Oh Mother
At what your son is trying to do
Your son is trying to stab people to death
The people who appear in front of that wall
There at the hands of your gentle other son
Will abruptly have their trembling chests gouged through
So that they can be all the more suddenly all the more sharply gouged
    through
Oh Mother
Look at how your son's arm contracts like a viper
And look
On the other side of the wall
At the other side of the wall
Inside that building
Inside its many rooms and halls and basements
Sons of mothers elsewhere who look very much like you
Are twisting broken locks
Wrenching open safes
That they're turning floor and ceiling upside down doing a house search
That they're stealing things
And all the chests refusing this
Round chests and chests with breast and chests like yours all wrinkled
With the very same bayonet as your son's
Look how they're stabbed in and out from in front and behind
Ahh
Do not turn your face away   Oh Mother

Do not take your eyes from the fact that your son's now made into a
    murderer
That your son's been made a murderer
That that murderer's look and stance are here in the newspaper in the
    photograph
Do not cover it with those trembling palms
In front of the fact that your beloved son's been made a murderer
In front of the thousand mothers who like you had their beloved sons made
    into murderers
Wrest your beloved son from your arms
And in front of the existence of the thousand mothers with spikes pushed
    through their chests
And in front of the fact that you are only but one of them
Oh Mother
Oh my one only Mother of me and of my big brother
Do not shut those ever blinking faded eyes[87]

Benjamin made a statement similar to his plea that the reader become
a writer when he demanded that the writer become a photographer.[88]
This is what Nakano has done in "The Photograph in the Newspaper."
He has constructed a photograph in the course of leading the mother
through the process of writing her own caption to the untitled photograph. The real goal, however, is not to make the man of letters into a
photographer, but to teach the reader who identifies with the mother that
the photograph in the newspaper must be given a meaning. Alan Sekula
has illustrated how "photographic 'literacy' is learned" by relating the
experience of an anthropologist showing a Bush woman a photograph of
her son. The social scientist must "read" the photograph to the mother,
isolating out each detail, in order for the mother to recognize the picture
as an image of her son. This is the narrator's task in the above poem, as
the writer gives the mother an opportunity to organize the pictoral news
made available to her in the newspaper. He gives her a language to help
her see that the photograph is in fact a close-up bringing into view what
has been hidden.[89]

Making use of the same insight remarked on by Lichtwark in 1907
and repeated by Benjamin in 1931, that "there is no work of art which is
regarded with as much attention as a photograph of oneself, one's closest
relatives and friends, one's sweetheart," Nakano entreats the mother to
view her son's face close up. Four years before Benjamin's short history
of photography would trace how the photographic reproduction of the

[87] Nakano, "Shimbun ni notta shashin," *NSZ* 1:519–20. [*Puroretaria geijutsu* 7/27].
[88] Benjamin, "The Author as Producer," p. 230.
[89] Sekula, "On the Invention of Photographic Meaning," pp. 85–86.

human face had been transformed, so that the picture of a face was no longer a detailed, life-like portrait of an ultimately anonymous elite minority but an instrument for understanding the detail of the photograph's social and political context, Nakano zooms in on the look of the murderer who is the mother's son and demands that the mother do the same.[90] He makes use of the mother's need to feel proximity to her son, in order to illustrate how this one being is no different from thousands of others, just as she is no different from countless other mothers viewing the photograph. Here also Benjamin's theory is relevant. According to his idea of mechanical reproduction, the contemporary masses wish to bring objects into proximity and are therefore capable of seeking the specific or the unique from within a photograph, but the reproductions in the illustrated newspaper and magazine also universalize the particular. In his words, "Today, people have as passionate an inclination to *bring things close* to themselves or even more to the masses, as to overcome uniqueness in every situation by reproducing it."[91] Nakano demands both inclinations from the mother.

As in "The Journalist," there is an ambiguity to the poem. As with the content of the journalist's conversation and the identity of the two colleagues in the café, in "The Photograph in the Newspaper" it is never clear whether the narrator is being literal when he calls the man "my big brother." The phrase *watashi no aniki* is jarring, calling attention to the problem of relationality and the complicity of the mother, because of the unlikely juxtaposition of the softer, feminine-sounding term *watashi* for "my" and the much more brusque term for older brother. The anonymous narrator demands that the mother confront her involvement by responding to the photograph as unique, but at the same time she must overcome the uniqueness. She must recognize the murderer as her son and then reproduce her horror in order to feel just as intensely about any of the soldier-murderers in China who appear in this picture or in any other presentation of the Japanese soldier. The poem may or may not be about one individual mother and two brothers, but it is most clearly about the violence of Japanese imperialism, which is perpetrated by the Japanese state "for no reason." In this sense, Nakano's third poem referring to the press is not merely about the reproduction of print culture. Reproduction here refers to the content of the narrative as well as the technical duplication of the artifact, because Nakano was talking about the production and the reproduction of the soldier and the soldier's work.

Like the photograph of the new ambassador, this photo does not tell all, but Nakano fills in the gaps for the mother who is his audience and

[90] Benjamin, "A Short History of Photography," pp. 8, 21–22.
[91] Ibid., pp. 20–21.

potential collaborator in this act of constructing the social and political implications of the photograph. He depicts what lies on the other side of the wall, but this is of less importance to the poem than the process that brought the Japanese man, clothed in gaiters and equipped with bayonet, to the wall to perform his acts of murder. The soldier has been produced through training—he has been made to wear the uniform and carry the weapon visible in the photograph. His training, his clothing, and his actions have been duplicated without variation, and thus thousands of men share the same facial expression and stance. Likewise, their old mothers must have identical responses. The unique identity of both son and mother is denied "in front of the fact" of the killings. By attaching his own form of caption to the anonymous photograph, Nakano has given a specificity to the imagery. He has made use of the political potential inherent in the cultural product for his own political end. When he states that the murder by the soldier was for "no reason," he does not mean that the act was random, with no explicable cause. He means that neither mother nor son is aware of the reason, for they have no perspective on the relationship between Japanese capitalism at home and Japanese expansion abroad.

This poem, which first appeared in the July 1927 issue of *Puroretaria geijutsu*, was transitional, for the level of violence abroad and at home, expressed in terms of labor and tenant union unrest and in the state's response to organized protests in the mass arrests of 1928 and 1929, was to call for a different approach to poetry. In active response, Nakano's poetry and essays would move away from the topic of the reproduction of commodity culture. By the summer of 1927, Nakano experienced the dynamic of revolutionary struggle, followed by repressive response in his own work, when censorship forced the displacement of the site of the murder in "The Photograph in the Newspaper" by asterisks.[92] From 1927 until 1929, he was to accommodate himself to the escalation of cultural and physical violence perpetrated by the authorities in two ways. Nakano's first mode of changing song had expressed his discovery of history. He had used the second stage to explicate the commodified urban culture within which he worked as an artist advocating revolution. During the two years constituting the third stage of his changing song, his essays and short stories would contribute to the canonization of Japanese Marxism. At the same time, in a series of violent scenarios in verse form, specifying the dialogue of social conflict in the cities and the countryside of late

---

[92] In the 1931 version of the poem the word "murderer" was excised from the phrase "face of a murderer," as was the verb "stabbed." Nakano, *Nakano Shigeharu shishū*, (Nappu shuppan, 1931), pp. 43, 45.

Taishō Japan, Nakano Shigeharu would prophesize an apocalyptic end to Taishō commodity culture. The next poem Nakano published after "The Photograph in the Newspaper," which was also about the press, would be about the replacement of reproduction by the eruption of violent revolution.

CHAPTER FIVE

Song III: The Dialogue of Revolution

Taishō Dialogues

The August 1927 issue of *Bungei kōron* carried the poem "To Those Who Make the Newspapers."[1] This violent vision of the end of the Taishō culture of reproduction signaled the poet's new preoccupation with revolutionary transformation through class action:

To Those Who Make the Newspapers

You newspapermen
You who make newspapers
You who write articles with your own hands
The ones who assemble them
The ones who print them
The ones who deliver them
You all
The ones who push new incidents and also bloody incidents inside people's
    eyes
Who with shame and anger and inability to withstand it
The ones who roast to crackles other people's hearts
You who make newspapers
We are waiting   We are

We're all waiting
For accurate reports and reports that have no lies
With no deference to anyone
And forgetting not one any thing
Reports of facts just as they are
For the first of those reports
For the raw report whose warmth we feel in the palms of our hands
We are the ones who will hear it right away
For the report on which we're the ones who right away must take steps
The ones to hand it over to us will be you all
For the report for which our being grateful will be to you all
Ahh you who make newspapers
You all

[1] Nakano, "Shimbun wo tsukuru hitobito ni," *NSZ* 1:520–22 [*Bungei kōron* 8/27].

We are all waiting.
For the report that the mounds of supplies have all rotted to gunk
For the report that next to that teacups and beanpaste strainers and sieves
　　and rice half-cooked have left their sticky stamp
And that babies were torn from shriveled breasts
That mouse-grey, starved thin to the bone they died
And for the report that they did not even raise a crying voice
That their mothers were slapped　pulled out by force　chased after
For the report that ashes were smashed in their eyes and they nailed down
For the report that their fathers hung upside down from the ceiling of the
　　gym their ribs smashed broken by a bamboo sword
Clamped in a wooden vise
Their pleas for a formal trial grasped and smashed
For the report that they were made to drink TB germs while stuck in a
　　moldy hole
And the reports that policemen pushed off the very end of cliffs
Principals beaten black and blue by schoolgirls
And then that the soldiers have escaped
And also that the *yobo* and the *chon* throughout the village ** in one big
　　clump[2]
For the report that the *aigo*[3] of the mother and daughter were heard all the
　　way to the far city
And also that the paddies and fields of all the village did change hands
For the report that exposed dirt dumpling dug out turned over and an eight-
　　lane road dashed forth
For the report that armored cars raced forward on the eight-lane road
And that on it the ruddy-faced mercenary murderer turned right back
For the report that the teacher beat his students with a saber
And that a memorial rose on that very spot
And for the report that all and everyone could not take it any more
And for the report that they all rose up
For the report that they rose up and proclaimed "No more!"
For the reports that here and there Hunger Federations were now begun
In the factories the whistle sounding
Straw banners beginning to move
Bamboo staves now being carved
For the report that their tips had already been bloodied
For the report that nothing can be done
Write it clearly in big clear print

　[2] *Yobo* is the Korean term for addressing a spouse. In this context it has been appropriated as a slur. The term *chon* refers to a Korean youth. The censored words translate as
"burnt up and killed."
　[3] Nakano used the Korean exclamation of surprised pain.

Write it recklessly
You the ones who run fastest in the world
The ones who write the fastest
Entering any alley
Cutting through the night
The ones with countless wires plugged into your ears
The ones with the "material"
Open those hands and come on out with all of it
Write and write and keep on keeping writing
Do it on the large and small roads in the narrow streets
In the trains and in the cinema
Spread it round officials offices and in the public baths
On cars and benches and toilets and fences and even on people's backs
Stick it stick it stick it all around

Language is consciously contoured in Nakano's poem, in both the pounding rhythm of the long stanzas and the tortured syntax, but this journalistic montage is a tribute to the resilience of language—even after the commodities of the culture of reproduction have rotted, the revolutionaries will still rely on journalists to relay news through the printed word. The twisting of the language points to the inversion of the use of violence: at the moment of revolution, the urban workers, farmers, and Korean laborers who are currently subjected to torture by the state will turn against the ruling segments of society. This bloody vision of an entire society disrupted evokes Marx's narrative of the total upheaval accompanying the transition from capitalist reproduction to proletarian revolution set forth in the *Communist Manifesto*:

All fixed, fast-frozen relations, with their train of ancient and venerable prejudices and opinions, are swept away, all new-formed ones become antiquated before they can ossify. All that is solid melts into air, all that is holy is profaned, and man is at last compelled to face with sober sense, his real conditions of life, and his relations with his kind.[4]

Nakano's revenge on the newspaperman was prefigured by the first stanza of "Train," which had appeared half a year earlier. There, in the introductory segment to the three-part poem that concluded with the tale of the reproduction of the factory girls, he had first mapped out a scene of mass domestic violence:

I

Who wants to trample people's feet?
But we ground them all the way down

[4] Marx, *Communist Manifesto*, p. 476.

With shoes and with narrow-toothed clogs
Then—realizing—we trampled other feet
And were trampled 'til it smarted
Felt like we would lose our bodies buffeted by waves of folks
We had to wrench our bodies from among the waves of folks
We clung to our baggage
We clutched and crushed our tickets
The crying children's voices screamed out under our thighs
The faces of the women dried up before our noses

Who wants to trample people's feet
But we trampled them to pieces
Even as we trampled we could not see below
We could not turn our faces
We wanted to raise up our bodies
We did not rise up
There were no spaces on the ground
Countless feet were stuck together
We ground them til way down
Always til way down[5]

This segment of the poem had expressed an ambivalence toward an inevitable violence to be experienced by unidentified combatants. The narrator was within a crowd, struggling with other individuals for his own survival. He used the term "We," but there was a sense of unplanned reflexive action shared with others whose common interests would be maintained only for the duration of one train ride. The "We" seemed motivated more by the motions of the arms and legs propelled forward by the motions of a train than by any consciousness of social conflict, but, as stated in the opening discussion of chapter 4, this first of three segments can be read as a fantasy of violent revolution resulting from the emergence of a class consciousness. By the time Nakano wrote "To Those Who Make the Newspapers," the notion of class had appeared in his poetry: the relationship of those who trampled and those who were trampled was transformed from a vague "We" pitted against an undifferentiated mass, to clear-cut social groupings in urban factories, in the countryside where tenant farmers enacted land reform, and in the school, where pupils confronted authority. The transition from the blind violence of the first segment of "Train" to the structured scenario of "To Those Who Make the Newspapers" occurred in the second section. Here again the narrator is on a crowded train, struggling with others to reach a destination, but the expression of violence is more subtle. It is the violence

[5] Nakano, "Kisha," NSZ 1:515 [Roba 2/27].

perpetrated through the opportunity and comfort granted a limited number of passengers while the majority is forced to suffer:

II

The corridors and the toilets were crammed with folks
The ma was yelling at her baby who'd begun to wail
The cigarettes and the stuffiness and the tangerines consumed and the lunch
    leavings were thickly smelly
Steamrolling forward and pushing folks apart the conductor came on
    through
All pulled out crumpled tickets and showed them to the man

There was a man and there was a woman there
Instead of showing tickets, they showed slips of paper
And then the conductor bowed
Over this way please over this way he said to them
They did not move with magnanimity
The conductor kept repeating his over this way over this way
They moved
Trunk and basket and overcoat and parasol were all pulled out
The conductor divvied up the load
They all set forth
They and the conductor and the baggage
Steamrolling forward pushing folks apart to disappear beyond the door
From start to finish we all looked on
We burned our eyes into their backs
Our hearts alike and desperate had all begun to move.[6]

In the poem the crowd of passengers is transformed into two clearly distinguishable entities when one class of riders begins to recognize another as a railway official singles out a couple and their possessions for special treatment. In clipped, blunt terms Nakano has thus introduced the idea of class relations, which would emerge as the unproblematic premise of the third segment about the reproduction of factory girls via the reproduction of culture. Yet while the three parts work backward from revolutionary violence to the unconsciousness of the factory girls, the poem can also be read forward, in order, as an expression of the move from blind, unfocused rage in the first stanza to the clear-cut class consciousness expressed by the author (if not by his heroines) in the concluding segment. When this poem is put within the larger narrative of the change in Nakano's poetry, the latter interpretation must prevail, for by the summer of 1927 when "To Those Who Make the Newspapers" made its

[6] Ibid., pp. 515–16.

claims, the division of Japanese society into sharply conflicting sectors had been established in Nakano's poetry. It remained for him to elaborate on the nature of the contrasting, contending voices speaking for these groups. During the ensuing year Nakano would write poetry that met his requirements of specificity and simplicity as an expression of class antagonism. In verse form, he organized his intense emotions and his vision of power struggles in Japanese society. While Nakano's writing on the packaging and purchasing of city life calls forth comparisons with Benjamin's Baudelaire, who was also attuned to a culture of reproduction, in his poems enacting revolution the Japanese writer came closer to a figure championed by another contemporary, with whom he had no contact but shared a history. Nakano's poetry written from 1927 until 1929, during the third stage of his changing song, had the attributes lauded in Dostoevsky, the hero celebrated by Mikhail Bakhtin, the Russian theorist of language in culture and society.[7]

In 1928 Nakano did in fact laud Dostoevsky for putting his entire being into his writing by making "stories out of his own flesh."[8] But this was not Bakhtin's argument. According to his theory, Dostoevsky's greatness lay in the dialogic nature of the story-telling in Bakhtin's novels. His praise for Dostoevsky, written in 1929, serves as an interpretation of the third stage of Nakano's poetic production. In the words of Bakhtin:

> Dostoevsky possessed an extraordinary gift for hearing the dialogue of his epoch, or, more precisely, for hearing his epoch as a great dialogue, for detecting in it not only individual voices, but precisely and predominantly the dialogic relationship among voices, their dialogic interaction.[9]

[7] There is heated debate over whether Bakhtin can be called a Marxist. Tony Bennett has said that Bakhtin, along with Pavel Medvedev, attempted to "chart a terrain for Marxist criticism" as part of his "attempt to develop a comprehensive theory of ideology within Marxism." Bennett, *Formalism and Marxism* (New York: Methuen, 1979), pp. 75, 78. Along even more vehement lines, Terry Eagleton points to Bakhtin's materialist poetics and calls his *Discourse and the Novel* "one of the most superb documents of Marxist literary criticism of the century." Eagleton, "Wittgenstein's Friends," *New Left Review* 135 (1982): 76, 80. Robert Young gives a comprehensive summary of how Bakhtin, who provided a materialist approach to language missing in Marxism, has been claimed as Marxist by Marxists. He concludes that such problems as the distinction between dialogue and dialectic, recourse to the word as a "guarantor of freedom," and an absence of teleology make Bakhtin a "somewhat treacherous way out for Marxist criticism." Young, "Back to Bakhtin," *Cultural Critique* 2 (Winter 1985–1986): 71–74, 84. The presumption herein is that Bakhtin's interrogation of the place of language in society, history, and ideology and his critique of capitalism were informed by Marxism. As such it comes closest to David Carroll's middle ground. Carroll recognizes how Bakhtin can be used to support "diverse and conflicting" methodology and ideology yet accepts the strong Marxist coloring to Bakhtin's ideas. Carroll, "The Alterity of Discourse: Form, History, and the Question of the Political in M. M. Bakhtin," *Diacritics* (Summer 1983): 67, 73.

[8] Nakano, "Soboku to iu koto," p. 174.

[9] Bakhtin, *Dostoevsky's Poetics*, p. 90.

According to Bakhtin's reading of Dostoevsky, these voices represented "a world of consciousnesses mutually illuminating one another." No one voice reigned supreme; what was important was the relationship or orientation of the plurality of the vocalized world views "meant to triumph," voices which illuminated each other through their interaction.[10] In "Discourse in the Novel," written in 1934 and 1935, after Nakano had ended his work as a poet, Bakhtin would note that language is ideologically saturated because conflicting linguistic interests (of social groups or professional groupings or generations) come into contact with the pull toward verbal unification as every utterance appears and disappears within a fleeting social and historical context. Discourse exhibits its dialogic tendency in three ways: within a single language, as a social language within a national language, and as a national language inhabiting a different national culture.[11] Although Bakhtin excluded verse from the dialogic realm of literature, the language of Nakano Shigeharu's poetry at all stages, especially during the third stage of his changing song in the closing years of the 1920s, was dialogic in all three aspects. When the poems of this era are put together to be read as a political statement of a social moment, languages belonging to different classes and eras collide as farmers and intellectuals, students and soldiers, and colonizers and colonized confront and engage. In Nakano's poetry no one voice reigns; a group of voices are meant to triumph. These are the voices belonging to the beleaguered individuals in the scenario from "Notes on Art Written on the Run."

In September 1927, one month after "To Those Who Make the Newspapers" introduced the theme of revolutionary upheaval, "Chōsen no musumetachi" (The young girls of Korea)[12] worked from one happening reported in the media to combine the voice of the Korean "speaking his own language" and the topic of "the student who has begun to think of things honestly." This poem opened with a journalistic narrative setting the scene:

THE YOUNG GIRLS OF KOREA

In June of this year, at a Korean girls school in Seoul, a principal working for the Governor General secretly fired a teacher who was deeply respected by students. The day for his leave-taking arrived. At the moment when the principal climbed to the lectern and began in a purring voice

One young girl stood up and yelled
—That's a lie!
Another young girl after her yelled out

[10] Ibid., pp. 90, 93, 97, 204, 207, 279, 296.
[11] Bakhtin, "Discourse in the Novel," in *The Dialogic Imagination*, pp. 259–75.
[12] Nakano, "Chōsen no musumetachi," NSZ 1:524–25 [*Musansha shimbun* 9/1/27].

————It's a lie!
————That's a lie!
————That's a lie!
————That's a lie!
The girls with no exception rushed up to the podium
They held down the hand of the principal that reached out for the bell
The girls stacked together
Opening their red lungs wide
While twisting their bodies they yelled right out
————What you say is a lie!
————Damn you apologize!
At that moment the girls heard far away footsteps
These were coming closer
The girls heard the sound of the latchkey
They heard the sound of the door split open with a crack
The girls felt one thread of blood race through the bodies of the girls
The principal fell over
Feet stamped on that face to pulp
The MP's and police rushed in
The chin-straps of their hats came off
Their holsters flew up in the air
Sabers squeaked as they twisted round
And above all that
Clamor defying description
The great trembling cries
Of the young girls of Korea
High so high
Defied deception defied suppression when they went Banzai

If the reader of "The Young Girls of Korea" had any doubts as to the intensity of the emotions organized within the poem, the ink illustration in the *Musansha shimbun*—three grimacing young women, their arms stretched forth boldly, their fists clenched, heading row upon row of similarly positioned arms—conveyed an outraged militancy. But Nakano's goal was not merely a photographic or even stylized rendering of the resistance of a colonized people. Elsewhere, Nakano would note how the bourgeoisie denied the colonized peoples their own language, when he demanded the unification of the exploited colonial peoples with the proletariat of Japan.[13] Here he was interested in the process whereby class consciousness could lead to the voicing of class action. The poem does not make clear whether the girls used their native language to counter the colonial voice, but conflicting social languages are engaged in battle. The

[13] Nakano, "Puroretaria geijutsu to wa nanika," *NSZ* 9:352–53.

yell, "That's a lie," challenging the principal's authoritative purr, is the first step toward the group's denial of its place as passive subjects and students.

The battleground shifted to the countryside in a poem published the following month, a brief torrent of words that would only later be given the title "Sweep Up All the Bastards Kith and Kin." By 1927, when the verse appeared, 7 percent of Japanese farm families (more than 365,000 men) belonged to tenant unions, and the two thousand or so tenant disputes that took place between 1921 and 1925 provided the context for the verse, which referred to landlords who could obtain court orders to prevent tenant farmers from entering the fields during a dispute. In Nakano's brief litany of prescribed actions, it is the oppressor who is treated with contempt:

Sweep up all of the bastards kith and kin
Tie on your back this great living shame of our living under the whip of the
    bastards and beat it out of sight
Shave off the bastards who cling
Trample and smash the bastards who cry in apology
Rub them off, tear them off
Sweep them away then clean them out[14]

This cry for blood was the first of a trilogy of poems documenting rural class conflict. Three months later, "Mattero gokudō jinushimera" (Just wait you evil landlords)[15] appeared on the cover page of the New Year's day issue of the *Musansha shimbun*, in the center of a series of greetings by other lyricists who hailed Soviet colleagues, called workers to war, demanded food and work from the capitalists, and alerted workers not to be fooled by the illusion of order offered by the smoke rising from industrial chimneys. Nakano's poem, addressed to the powers in the countryside, was an extension of his threat to "sweep up the bastards." Its language was equally blunt:

JUST WAIT YOU EVIL LANDLORDS

Gang with whoever all ya like
Puttin' up weird don't enter signs the way ya want
We're sharpenin' our sickles
Rubbin' 'em real good
Wait ya wait just there

[14] Nakano, "Yatsura no ikkakenzoku wo hakidashiteshimae," *NSZ* 1:527 [*Puroretaria geijutsu* 10/27]. For figures on union membership and on the number of disputes see Shiota, *Nihon shakai undō shi*, p. 66.

[15] Nakano, "Mattero gokudō jinushimera," *NSZ* 1:528 [*Musansha shimbun* 1/1/28]. The poem first appeared with no author named.

We'll cut ya down there too
Rub ya out real good
And cut off your two legs, ya too

The two raw visions of violence were given a social context in Nakano's final poem in the set. In October 1928, "Yokari no omoide" (Memories of night harvesting)[16] offered a woman's narration of a rural version of the landscape envisioned in "To Those Who Make the Newspapers." But there was an important difference between this and the first two poems, for in this story, the female narrator and her revolutionary accomplices have been defeated. Nonetheless, Nakano refuses to abandon his threatening tone, and in a rural dialect he talks about the terrorist actions of tenant farmers who remain undaunted by arrests and other maneuverings of the law. While the first two poems about rural class conflict should be read as threats, this third, changed song, which expressed Nakano's sensitivity to the interplay of class, region, and gender in language, demanded a response—an affirmation that the speaker's voice had registered.

MEMORIES OF NIGHT HARVESTING

Didn't we all go and do the night harvest
Were our backbones weak and tremblin'

So indeed you've brought the court
The numbered acres you'd carefully made up had signboards stuck on them
And when we looked around
All the men called men had all been pulled away
Then and then didn't we stand rooted to the ground
To the night harvest then
It is the mob'lization
Couldn't our voices reach your ears then
The teeth of our sickles weren't they sharpened
Our bicycles outfitted in gloves and gaiters
From village then to village they flew like locusts didn't they
Our torches flamed up high along the paddy footpaths
The fire burned the heavens
The soot stuck on the frightened necks of all your wives
And then didn't we
Not leave one clump of fox-colored nonglutined rice or maize-colored
    glutinous rice
Leaving no cause for accusation by straw-sandaled policeboys

[16] Nakano, "Yokari no omoide," *NSZ* 1:528–29 [*Musansha shimbun* 9/5/28].

And then again you pulled away all the men   [stanza break]
It's been 'bout half a year since the pained bound figures left the village on
    the third
And then don't we got rags and old tires at our place
Don't we got a dribble there of oil
The number of the torches made from them
Are they less than the number of rafters on your roofs
Daughters take the side of sons
Wives take the side of husbands
Don't matter how many times you try to change the laws
Trying not to let us hear the voices of the men * * [17] in town
Don't matter how many times you paint the prison walls so thick
Do ya think you can stop the coming of autumn that way
The coming of autumn
The coming of autumn
Ahh ya masters of the villages
Lit all red by the torches
Won't we all go and do the night harvest
Are our backbones then
So narrow

In all three poems Nakano talks through the peasant to give voice to the belief that power, of historical necessity, is transferred from one class to another; and that art should articulate the organization of contesting emotions of classes in conflict. There is thus a consistency between Nakano's poetry and his early theory. His focus on the ascendant side of the relationship of oppressor to oppressed required, however, that another voice join the chorus composed of Korean students and farmers. The worker had to be heard, and in this regard Nakano offered more prose than poetry. In an essay entitled "E ni tsuite" (On pictures),[18] which appeared in the February 1928 issue of *Puroretaria geijutsu*, he demanded art that would provide a specific picture of the proletarian—his factory, his machine shop, his gatherings. The stereotype he drew for his reader to characterize how the worker was represented in the revolutionary press was as formalized as a Kabuki stance:

Our workers as depicted are merely crying out. They are always marching forward, their hammers raised above their heads. In between the belly of the capitalist bloated by his moneybags and the sabers of the dogs on the payroll, our

[17] The censored word was "tortured."
[18] Nakano, "E ni tsuite," *NSZ* 9:125–32 [*Puroretaria geijutsu* 2/28].

workers as depicted are always yelling "in true form." Red stars hang in the
sky. And that's it. (p. 125)

The problem was that the socialist artists had acted as though they had
only one tool or a single carpenter's square. The scope of art had expanded to include the proletariat in various guises—the proletariat strik-
ing, the proletariat at a meeting of factory representatives, the proletariat
in the Chinese Revolution, the proletariat participating in the elections.
All had been duly depicted, but the issue was the way they had been
drawn:

> Beyond the horizon "political freedom" glitters. In the foreground a member
> of the lower middle class in a wool hat, and a farmer heaving a scythe, and a
> Korean in white garb, and in the foreground a young worker is standing, grasp-
> ing a hammer. On each back is written "petit-bourgeois," "farmer," "colonized
> person," "laborer." And the body of the worker is especially bigger than the
> others." (p. 127)

When Nakano noted that the workers appearing in pictures were being
pushed into *kata* or molds, he might well have been referring to the New
Year's day cover of the *Musansha shimbun* which had featured his poem,
"Just Wait You Evil Landlords," one month earlier. Cartoon workers,
captured in bold black socialist realist strikes, had covered the front of
that roughly ten-by-twelve-inch tabloid. Among them stood a four-inch-
high worker marching forward, his hammer raised high. Beneath him a
saber stabbed at a worker at his labor, and directly atop the text of Nakano's poem, capitalists in top hats and soldiers waged battle. A red star
shone over all.

It was not enough, the poet claimed, for the Japanese artists to intellec-
tualize that it was time to graduate from the method of Georg Grosz (p.
129). Through a series of questions, Nakano broke out of the mold he
had rejected, to give his version of how the Japanese working class should
be depicted:

> A sturdy, beardless 24 or 25 year old wearing a cap with a visor, overalls, wield-
> ing a hammer, in shoes. He may be a most militant worker. But to what indus-
> trial sector does he belong? Where is his factory? And what work does he ac-
> tually do there? How does the belt revolve there, and how are his arms drawn
> into it? Assuming he reads *Musansha shimbun* there, does he read it at a desk,
> or is that crumpled newspaper in which his lunchbox was wrapped the recent
> *Musansha shimbun*? What is in that lunch he eats? (p. 128)

In seeking new visual constructs, Nakano was aware of the tension between the need to represent the reality of the individual worker's everyday
life which encompassed both production and political activity, and his

desire to maintain the concept of class uniting those in the factory. He used the metaphor of a magnet to express this relationship of individual to class experience, likening the formation of class consciousness and therefore of class power to the process whereby steel filings are drawn to an enormous magnet and are thereby themselves magnetized: "All peoples who pant under the weight of capital, when they are drawn toward the enormous magnet, they take a specific direction, and unite and of themselves present the point of a needle" (p. 130). Nonetheless, this tension was not manifested in Nakano's poetry during the third stage of his changing song, for no individualized factory workers appeared in his poems of the late 1920s. Yet while his lyrics did not answer his own questions about the beardless worker, in two essays he did create a close approximation to the sturdy member of the proletariat imagined in "On Pictures." This was the fictional character, Makita Eizō.

In the essay introducing Makita, "Kondō Eizō shi ni tou" (Asking of Mr. Kondō Eizō),[19] Nakano defined the act of reading as a revolutionary act in a passage that made use of one of the central images from "Train," the picture of the worker who is wrung out in the capitalist workplace:

> I'm just a worker. Work every day. Squeezed dry every day. But I'm not just squeezed dry. It's so that soon I can squeeze them dry. I've never been to Korea or China. Of course never been over to Russia. Think I'd like to go once, though. But even if I don't go anywhere I work in Japan. I've read a few books. Even now read a little each day. I'm not showing off just because I read books. (If you read on you'll understand.) I just read the necessary books. If there's any strength to me, to us, to us workers of Japan squeezed dry everyday it's that while we're being squeezed dry, we've been in our struggle in Japan where we've been living. Reading the written materials which we just must read, and even though tied down by Japan's special conditions, inside the reality of Japan, we are truly, concretely, fighting. That's why we don't have much knowledge or scholarship. That's why we keep trying to get new knowledge. (p. 78)

Nakano, the leading socialist activist-writer, engages in factional politics within the literary left: he wants to make sure that his readers know that this character, who has only read two books in his life, thinks that *Bungei sensen*, the magazine competing with *Puroretaria geijutsu* (the forum for Nakano's faction), is a strange journal. In the midst of such rhetoric Nakano answered his questions about the reading and eating habits of the worker in overalls in "On Pictures." As he puts his recollection in

[19] Nakano, "Kondō Eizō shi ni tou," *NSZ* 9:78–82 [*Puroretaria geijutsu* 10/28]. Kondō Eizō (1883–1965) was a colleague of Yamakawa Hitoshi and Sakai Toshihiko and a founding member of the Japanese Communist Party. In 1924, he was also a Japanese delegate to the fifth congress of the Comintern in 1924. In 1926 he returned to Japan and broke with the Japanese Communist Party.

a context, Makita Eizō remembers reading "some bourgeois newspaper" in a chink-noodle joint on Kurumazaka. The allusion is fleeting, but Nakano has given the worker a neighborhood, a menu, and an everyday habit of skimming the newspaper in a local restaurant (p. 79).[20]

When the fictional worker Makita reappeared one month later in the November issue of *Puroretaria geijutsu*, as the author of "One Laborer Welcomes the Tenth Anniversary of the Russian Revolution,"[21] he was still couching his opinions in terms of his reading. He had read of the Russian Revolution in the newspapers and recalled how the journal *Marxism* had explained the significance of Japan's recognition of Russia as an actual recognition of the Russian Revolution. Speaking in the worker's voice, Nakano related Makita's life story. He had drifted to Tokyo ten years earlier, after involvement in a local strike. He had then become a simple laborer, had become involved in the worker's movement to support the Soviet Union, and had been jailed. In the context of relating the emotional attraction of revolution to the day laborer, Nakano had Makita talk about work:

> Through the four seasons I had no settled work; didn't have a workplace. Did all sorts of work. Cut ice. I was a helper at a herring fishery. Bicycle factory. Then when I was in the bicycle factory I heard there was a revolution in Russia. I mean this was Kerensky's revolution. Of course I didn't even try to find out what kind of characteristics Kerensky's revolution had. But I thought it a great deal of fun. (p. 92)

Makita Eizō's story was one man's history, but it relates a transformation in consciousness Nakano wished to associate with an entire class. When Makita criticizes Japanese government policies toward the Ainu and Koreans and expresses satisfaction at the growth of the labor movement, exhorting the working class to engage in struggle from a "Marxist vantage point" and to give itself new customs, his voice stands for many. Nonetheless, even in this essay Nakano did not show old or new working-class habits in the detail called for in his criticism of the caricatures of the worker, or in his demand to show the worker's way of walking and talking in his essay on overcoming Kabuki.

It would be too simplistic to conclude that Nakano, because he was an intellectual who never worked alongside laborers, except during his brief stint in the Kyōdō strike, was ignorant of working class culture. His description of the furnishings of the worker's room in "Farewell Before Dawn," his evocation of the community of factory girls in "Train," and even the passages featuring Makita's voice reveal a familiarity with the

[20] The slur for the Chinese restaurant is *chansobaya*.
[21] Nakano, "Ichi rōdōsha to shite Roshia kakumei jusshūnen wo mukaeru," *NSZ* 9:92–94 [*Puroretaria geijutsu* 11/27].

texture of everyday life among Japanese workers in the late Taishō era. Yet when Nakano's reproduction of the voices of Taishō culture is reviewed from the standpoint of the first, second, and third stages of his changing song, the figures who emerge most vividly are the workers within the culture of reproduction—the intellectuals, like the loud journalist hounding Nakano's German friend, and the students attending the most elite of Japan's educational institutions. Nakano's rejection of the culture of the apolitical Tokyo Imperial University student was expressed in his own words at that time, in "Tokyo teikoku daigakusei" (Tokyo Imperial University student).[22] The poem represented the language, the uniform, and the everyday activities of the young Taishō intellectuals garbed in *haori*, or kimono jacket, and *rubashika*, a peasant-style shirt modeled after the Russian garment:

TOKYO IMPERIAL UNIVERSITY STUDENT

There are some with yellow faces
There are glasses
Haori
Rubashika
There are overcoats with buttons a whole inch wide
There are also some like beggars
And they promenade along Ginza
When they're drunk using nasty country talk on purpose
The innovation of knowledge
Cultivation of the personality
And they say
"The Symbol of Anguish really gets one reading"[23]
It's vomit
And they hang around the school front gate
There are some who just keep kicking footballs

Nakano distances himself from this world. He achieves this not only through his value judgment that the literary taste of his colleagues is nauseating, but also through his use of language when he employs the term *iru* to denote the presence of spectacles and overcoats, instead of the term *aru*, which would ordinarily refer to inanimate objects. Through his personification of the accouterments of the young men, Nakano says that the world of the scholar is fetishized. This does not detract from the vivid quality of the imagery; life at Tokyo Imperial University emerges in all its self-conscious splendor.

[22] Nakano, "Tokyo teikoku daigakusei," *NSZ* 1:506 [*Roba* 6/26].
[23] Nakano is referring to *Kumon no shōchō* (Symbol of anguish) by Kuriyagawa Hakuson.

Nakano also recorded the talk of politically engaged young intellectuals who were not his colleagues in the Marxist movement, in "Museifushugisha" (Anarchists),[24] a poem that appeared three months after "Tokyo Imperial University Student":

ANARCHISTS

We were all listening to a great grand speech
We were all listening ardently
Sometimes we gave forth fierce applause
Then nearby us
Was a group of men with long hair
Who threw forth incorrect words with lowly heckles
Their words
Like one sort of politician
Like a bully-boy
And like a merchant at a temple fair somewhere

The biting detail drawing attention to "wrong words" is reminiscent of Nakano's condemnation of the "varying sorts of language" to be burnt and swept away in "Cleaning," which appeared in the same issue of *Roba* in September 1926. Here, in an illustration of Nakano's sensitivity to the multiplicity of Taishō languages, the poet sets forth and passes judgment on a variety of interacting speeches. These young men, along with a certain type of politico and a fair vendor, share a way of talking expressive of their incorrect political views. Their language contends with the correct words of the narrator which are in dialogue with an unspecified speaker whom the anarchists continually interrupt. Three dialogic pairings appear in this short verse. The narrator and his colleagues respond to the language from the lectern with applause as part of their active participation in the event described as "intent listening," which differs from the passive acceptance of information disseminated by journalists in the mass media. The anarchists break into this exchange with their jeering, and the poet then recounts the cacophony for the reader. Presumably the reader shares the language of Marxist precepts with the narrator, which makes it unnecessary for Nakano to give the specific content of either the "great speech" or the "incorrect words." He and the readers share one political position. While the words of the anarchist youths are never quoted directly, the youths have chosen to set themselves off from others through a visual code: They wear their hair long, an affectation that serves as the sole identification for the reader who has been given a detailed itemization of the clothing of the Imperial University student. The language of the anarchists is not unique because it is the same as the words used by

[24] Nakano, "Museifushugisha," *NSZ* 1:510 [*Roba* 9/26].

politicians, bully-boys, and merchants. In other words, it is the shared language of those who choose to obscure the truth, and to silence the words of those like the poet's comrades, the "We" or *bokura* who work to establish the truth through the cultural work of lectures, the production of newspapers, and poetry.

An additional voice emerges from the two-year period ending in 1929, the era when Nakano's verse turned from its exploration of mass culture to imagine revolution in the city and countryside during the third stage of changing song. The voice belongs to a soldier whose unrelenting listing of acts of violence is quite similar to the phrasings of "To Those Who Make the Newspapers." His presence throughout urban culture in the trams, on the trains, in the Sunday streets, and in movie theaters is not unlike the ubiquity of the journalist. But this soldier has no specified geographic place from which to speak, and unlike the journalist who moved in and out of the cafés creating news and history, he cannot move at will. The mercenary, mobile nature of his work counters association with a home, conversation, or social revolution; without a place to speak from he cannot demand a change. "Heitai ni tsuite" (On soldiers),[25] which appeared in August 1927, at the same time that readers were studying "To Those Who Make the Newspapers" in the pages of *Bungei kōron*, is a poem about the damming up of the dialogic; it is about voices not allowed to come together:

ON SOLDIERS

Did you see
The shrewd-looking mournful face
The sweat shaped like a knapsack
The young soldier whose whole body smelled of leather goods
Did you sense
That he flashed a glance at you
That he tried to say a word to you
That he tried to talk but he just could not get through to you

The guy did try to say
—Look at me will you
  I'm a soldier
  I'm a common soldier
  And for me being common soldier's everything
  The big old armory
  Raises loud its roaring clank
  And for us its *[26] of people practice year in then year out

[25] Nakano, "Heitai ni tsuite," *NSZ* 1:522–23 [*Puroretaria geijutsu* 8/27].
[26] The censored word was "murdering."

And they say "Go *27 'em"
Won't let you say just yes or no
So it's shoes and slaps and ration cuts and lugging your own bed
Rubber and the wooden club
By shoving fist and knuckles under someone's ma's arms and * in and
   crushing some baby's head with the *28 butt that you've got
Putting a blindfold on someone's wife and stringing her right side down
Hurting folks in those ways and by *29 them
Makes our hands grow bigger
Makes them sturdier
And sweating is our work
Rock torture in the form of bricks
Picked on taunted constantly haunted stabbed by *30 pols
At any place for any whys when seeing anyone
We cannot say the one thing "Knock it off"
We've committed suicide just countless times
Run away just countless times
We're common soldiers
And being common soldier's everything
Do ya got it now?

The guy did try to talk like this
With his shrewd and mournful face
And he was looking for an answer
He wanted you to lend a hand
For you to raise yourself right up
The guys were all always
Even in the trams
Even in the trains
Even on the Sunday streets
In the movie sheds on flag days
And at public lectures somewheres
Here now there now signaling with their eyes
With their smart and mournful looks lots of them came and stood close by

The poem is framed in terms analogous to the schema of "Journalist," written the previous year, during Nakano's examination of cultural reproduction. In the opening and ending of "Journalist" the narrator had addressed the journalist and the newspaperman had spoken; when the narrator of "On Soldiers" asks the reader to recognize the tearful face of

---

27 The word was "kill."
28 The words were "pound" and "gun."
29 The censored word was "killing."
30 Part of the term for military police, the *pei* of "*kenpei*" was excised.

a young soldier and to listen to his conversation, Nakano seems to be repeating an earlier form, but there is no dialogue whatsoever in this poem. The reader of the poem is an observing, nonspeaking third party, and the would-be speaker, the soldier, is silent. Nakano, the narrator, has only said what the soldier would have said if he could. In addition to being a monologue without a specified respondent, like the mother in the poem about the carnage in Shanghai, it is also an imagined monologue. Yet while there is no dialogue between social groups, the relationship of individual to class of individuals (if not class) is implied in this poem. In "Journalist" the manipulation of language by one newspaperman was expanded to imply the machinations of an entire order of journalists when in the last stanza the narrator told "Fatty" that he and the German would talk about him and about "Japanese journalists in general." The same shift occurs in "On Soldiers" (the title "*heitai*" can mean either soldier or soldiers), which moves slowly from a discussion of one individual's identity as a soldier to his training in the group. By the end of the narrative the reader is following the story of not one "guy" but a number of guys, with knowing, mournful expression, who stand in wait.

"On Soldiers," like "Journalist," takes place within the realm of cultural production. Although the military man cannot move freely through Taishō society like the newspaperman, he shares a work site with him and with the cultural revolutionary in the moving picture shed and the lecture hall. But his work, like the job of the mother's son in Shanghai in "The Photograph in the Newspaper," is very different, for integral to his role as surveillant of culture is his ability and responsibility to kill. "On Soldiers" reports on the details of this labor, and on the training, but the poem is most clearly about the ideology of his work. In other words, it is about the young man's experience of his role. His position has been naturalized so that being a soldier "is everything." Nothing can or need be questioned. Nonetheless, the soldier is ambivalent; his declaration on being a common soldier repeats too many times. Like the factory girls who criticized the division of labor in their ballads while at the same time incorporating the language produced by the segmentation of labor in the factory, the soldier expresses both acceptance of his job and anguish. The censored words in "On Soldiers" were all accounts of the violent acts sanctioned and encouraged by the military as the poem portrayed an ongoing process, rather than a series of separate actions that could be erased in isolation. The poem thereby pointed to the reproduction of the soldier, just as "Train" alluded to the reproduction of the factory girl. The account of the disciplining of the young recruits told how the reproduction of the soldier, through an education in soldiering, took place continually. Moreover, it was a linear process causing the presence of the military in Japanese society to grow. Earlier in the decade when uniformed soldiers had made a public appearance in urban society, their fellow passengers on city trains had responded with cold looks, and the media had coined the pejorative term "military clique."[31] In this poem Nakano was commenting that this was no longer true by 1928.

Nakano's poems set in the countryside were utopian, but they also forecast how in the city and the countryside both tenant farmer and labor disputes would more than double within a decade, reaching their peak in 1937 during an era that would be called "the season of strikes."[32] But Nakano could not ignore the history surrounding him. Yet, by 1928 no theorist dedicated to the sundering of truth from falsehood (Benjamin's definition of the materialist method)[33] could see a revolution in the streets. Nakano Shigeharu's poetry ceased abruptly with "Memories of Night Harvesting" in September 1928, and when "Ame no furu Shinagawa eki" (Shinagawa Station in the rain)[34] appeared the following February, it added the last voice to the dialogue of contending figures but turned away from fantasy, and the often graceless rhythms of his revolutionary poetry, back to the representative, closely structured mode of the third segment of "Train." In its setting and wording it resembled the verse about the reproduction of the factory girls, while introducing a new theme in the poet's history, a theme that must account for Nakano's recent silence. In form and content the poem revealed that intellectuals were being silenced by the state. In this poem a revolutionary bids farewell to Korean friends who are neither workers nor students. One is Lee Buk-Man, a fellow poet:

SHINAGAWA STATION IN THE RAIN

Commemorating * * *
To Lee Buk-Man and Kim Ho-Yong

Good-bye Shin
Good-bye Kin
You board from Shinagawa Station in the rain

Lee Good-bye
The other Lee Good-bye
You return to the land of your father mother

The rivers in your land freeze in cold winter
Your heart which rebels freezes at the instant of parting

---

[31] Takemura Tamio, Taishō bunka (Kōdansha, 1980), p. 185.
[32] Shiota, Nihon shakai undō shi, pp. 62–66. This "season of strikes" saw the number of labor disputes go up from 397 in 1928 to 576 in 1929 and leap to 907 incidents by 1930.
[33] Benjamin, Charles Baudelaire, p. 105.
[34] Nakano, "Ame no furu Shinagawa eki," NSZ 1:529–30 [Kaizō 2/29].

The ocean wet with rain in the evening raises the voice of the sound of
  waves
The pigeon wet with rain dances from the depot roof down in all the smoke

You all wet with rain remember [the Japanese Emperor who pursues] you
You all wet with rain remember [him with moustache spectacles stooped
  shoulders]

In the spraying rain the green alert goes up
In the spraying rain your dark eyes burn bright

Rain pours in the walkway stones and falls onto the dark sea's ledge
Rain disappears upon your fevered young cheeks

Your black shadows pass through the ticket gate
Your white *mosuso* waves about the darkness of the connecting corridor

The green alert light changes color
You all climb aboard

You all will depart
You all will leave

Ohh
You men and women of Korea
You colleagues who are shameless to the depth of depths
Front and rear shield of the Japan Proletariat

Go and break apart that hard thick ice
Cause the dammed up waters to gush forth
And then once again
Leap across the channel and dance right back
Passing through Kobe Nagoya entering into Tokyo
Nearing the ****
Appearing at the ****
Thrust hold up ** jaw
* * * * * * * * * * * *
* * * * * * *

Cry laughing in the great of ** being warmed[35]

[35] The uncensored original version of this poem is not available, and the bracketed words,
indicating censored words in the original version, are taken from the *NSZ* version. Nakano
rewrote this poem more than once, and in its most recent reconstruction, half a century after
his first attempt, the author himself rearranged the politics of the language of the poem so
that the bodies of colonized Koreans could not be used as shock troops to shield the bodies
of Japanese revolutionaries from the worst of battle. Referring to the original wording,
"Rear and front shield of the Japan Proletariat," he admitted to an ethnocentric egoism. See
Nakano, " 'Ame no furu Shinagawa eki' no koto," *NSZ* 22:78 [*Likan sansenli*, Summer
1975].

In "Shinagawa Station in the Rain," the poet was bidding farewell to non-Japanese colleagues, but the censored words in the 1929 version of the poem bracketed the real topic. Nakano was identifying the enemy; it was not simply a matter of proletariat against bourgeoisie or even landlord and capitalist against proletariat and farmer. The poet left the censors no room for doubt as to the identity of the photographic close-up he had sketched. The face covered by moustache and glasses atop stooped shoulders was clearly the face of the Emperor of Japan. Revolution meant that the imperial state ceremonies and structures surrounding this man must be destroyed by a force comprising the proletariat of Japan and those rising up from across the ocean, in Korea.[36]

The new resignation in the clear language and brief lines of the poem contrasted with the dense imagery and fast pace of the revolutionary poems of the preceding years, but this poem was undoubtedly a product of Nakano's third stage of changing song. The black shadows in "The Beach at Kitami" had been clearly defined, and while Nakano still anticipated the revolution, he knew that it would not come soon, nor could he paint its picture. "Shinagawa Station in the Rain" was the last of Nakano's revolutionary poems. This does not mean that he was silenced, although he was arrested for the third time in April 1929 and again in 1930. As the poetry stopped the song merely changed form. During the last two years of the decade, before his longest incarceration, Nakano employed a different mode of action in order to make revolution as a writer. Between 1928 and 1929 he was engaged in the process of creating a revolutionary body of writings that would place his poems in a consolidated position. If the revolution could not be completed immediately because resistance was being curbed, and therefore poetry could not serve to organize the free rein of emotions, the achievements of the revolution to date were to be collected and collated. Nakano had first used poetry as a weapon in order to discover history. He had then criticized a historical shift in culture in his poems. What had emerged from his revolutionary poetry were images of late Taishō groupings—intellectuals in cafés, activists gathered in barren lodgings, factory girls en route to textile mills, Koreans returning to the colony. The voices in these poems had expressed his attempt to

[36] According to Nakano's reconstruction of the poem in 1975, the word deleted from the subtitle in the original version was "enthronement ceremony." The poem was commemorating the November 10, 1928, ascension of the Emperor and the forced return of Koreans to Korea preceding that event. (He had been imprisoned following the ceremony, on November 29.) He noted that the "Shin," "Kin," and the two "Lees" did not refer to specific individuals, but that the stooped shoulders belonged to Emperor Hirohito. Nakano said he had been inspired to refer to the posture because he had been irritated by the newspaper photographs of the Emperor viewing his troops atop a white horse, which were only taken from a side angle in order to camouflage the unregal posture. Ibid., p. 78.

turn history around. Now, before entering the fourth stage of his changing song, he participated in the construction of a historiography. By the late 1920s his poems were being given a place in the emerging canon of revolutionary culture, but his newest work would shape his vision of his own history and that of his colleagues in a series of prose essays on Marxist literary criticism.

CONSTRUCTING THE CANON

When in 1929 Nakano jeered at the Jintan culture of Taishō he was referring to the sale of culture in such mass-marketed journals as *Kingu*, which had sold 740,000 copies at first printing in 1925. Its inauguration had followed an aggressive promotion campaign that made use of such ploys as full-page advertisements in all the major newspapers, more traditional street entertainments offered by the *chindonya* in outrageous get-up who played raucous music to attract attention to an enterprise, and the *kami-shibai* or paper-theater man who illustrated his narrative with boldly sketched pictures. The promotions worked so well that one out of every one hundred Japanese bought this magazine modeled after such American institutions as *The Saturday Evening Post* and the *Ladies' Home Journal*, and within a year sales had reached the one million mark. While the expansion of the audience for the revolutionary magazines of late Taishō was impressive, the numbers on the left could not compare. For example, when *Senki*—which was to publish Nakano's most famous short stories during the fourth stage of his changing song—first appeared in May 1928, seven thousand copies were printed. By 1930 twenty-two thousand copies were being produced.[37]

The magazine was not the only printed product to be sold for profit. The one-yen book or *enpon* could also be reproduced serially, in uniform size. Knowledge of all kinds was being organized and made available in these easily consumed portions purchased via subscription at one yen per five-hundred-page volume. In 1926, Kaizōsha had put the thirty-seven volumes of *Gendai Nihon bungaku zenshu* (The complete works of Japanese literature) on the market and received orders for 350,000 sets before the first volume went on sale. Shinchōsha's eighty-three volume *Sekai bungaku zenshū* (Complete works of world literature) soon joined the Kaizōsha set in the stores, and between 1928 and 1930 the eager reader could also collect the twenty-four volumes of *Meiji bunka zenshū* (The complete works of Meiji culture). Under the tutelage of such editors as Yoshino Sakuzō, and Nakano's colleague Ishidō Kiyotomo, the series,

---

[37] For one version of the history of the *Kingu* promotion campaign see Ishikawa, *Goraku no senzen shi*, p. 151. Regarding *Senki* statistics, see Shea, *Leftwing Literature*, p. 200.

which opened with a volume on the Imperial Household and included volumes entitled *The Meiji Restoration* and *Newspapers*, divided Meiji history into its "politics," "law," "religion," "thought," "customs," and "science."[38]

The earliest series on social and economic theory had first appeared in 1926 when *Shakai mondai kōza* (Lectures on social issues) offered its readers introductions to Marxism, Syndicalism, and Guild Socialism along with brief histories of women's awakening, the Russian Revolution, the Japanese Leveller's Movement, and the Fabian Society. Three years later, its last volumes included the final segment of Noro Eitarō's Marxist history of the development of Japanese capitalism along with the final installment of Yoshino Sakuzō's political history of Meiji, and a who's who of contemporary activists and social theorists compiled by the editor, Taishō critic of mass culture Ōya Sōichi. That same year the *Shakai keizai taikei* (Series on society and economy) began its two years of publication. Its last volume, number 19 in the series, included an essay by the Marxist philosopher Miki Kiyoshi on "Historical Philosophy" and a treatise on art by Abe Jirō, the humanist beloved by the higher school students of Nakano's generation. Kaizōsha's other one-yen book series, *Keizaigaku zenshū* (The complete works of economics), appeared between 1928 and 1934. In 1929, Heibonsha entered the marketplace with *Shakai shisō zenshū* (The complete works of social thought), the multivolume counterpart to Kaizōsha's *Complete Works of World Literature*, which included *Literature and Revolution* by Trotsky and featured such social revolutionaries as William Morris, Edward Bellamy, St. Simon, Kropotkin, and Ellen Key.[39]

This is where *Marukusu-Engerusu zenshū* (The complete works of Marx and Engels) belongs in the history of Taishō commodity culture, for between June 1928 and February 1934 the thirty-two small red volumes appeared, at the cost of one yen a book. Marx, packaged in *enpon* form, was now truly on the mass market.[40] The preface to the last, supplemental volume to the series, dated July 8, 1933, placed this series in historical perspective. In it the Editorial Committee of the Complete Works of Marx and Engels marked the end of five years of joint effort by

[38] On the introduction of *Gendai Nihon bungaku zenshū* and *Sekai bungaku zenshū*, see Imai Seiichi, *Taishō demokurashii*, Nihon no rekishi (chūō kōronsha, 1966), 23:464. See also *Meiji bunka zenshū*, 24 vols. (Nihon hyōronsha, 1928–1930).

[39] Oya Sōichi, ed., *Shakai mondai kōza*, 13 vols. (Shinchōsha, 1926–1927); *Shakai keizai taikei*, 20 vols. (Nihon hyōronsha, 1926–1928); *Keizaigaku zenshū*, 67 vols. (Kaizōsha, 1928–1934); *Shakai shisō zenshū*, vols. 1–40, with some numbers not available (Heibonsha, 1929–1933).

[40] *Marukusu-Engerusu zenshū*, 30 vols. (Kaizōsha, 1928–1935). The sales of *Gendai Nihon bungaku zenshū* were to reach 230,000. Takemura, *Taishō bunka*, p. 126.

scholars to produce "the complete works of Marx and Engels within the broadest possible limits in Japan at the present time." The editors emphasized that this was the only edition of the complete works available in the world, for their edition contained Marx's writings for the *Neue Rheinische Zeitung*, the *Vorwärts*, the *Volksstaat*, the *Zürich Social Democrat*, and the *New American Encyclopedia*, along with other works from newspapers, journals, dictionaries, and rare books that were not easily brought together, even in Germany. Recognizing that the task of rendering Marx into Japanese required more than skill in translation, they thanked the scores of translators who had lent both their linguistic skills and their advanced understanding of the theory of Marx and Engels to the project. Among the eighty-eight names listed were members of all three generations of Japanese Marxist scholars: Sakai Toshihiko, translator of the *Communist Manifesto*, Yamakawa Hitoshi, and Yamada Moritarō, the leading Lecture School theoretician, whose analysis of the relationships informing the reproduction of Japanese capitalism would set the terms for a Marxist Japanese social science.[41]

In addition to the one-yen set of works by Marx and Engels, there were numerous collections of Marxist scholarship, such as Takabatake Motoyuki's *Marukusu jūni kōza* (Twelve lectures on Marx), a straightforward guide to the life of Karl Marx, his philosophy of history, and such categories in his work as the state, capitalism, the labor theory of value, and the theory of accumulation, which had been one of the very first series systematizing Marxist thought when it appeared in 1926. The series *Shakai kagaku kōza* (Lectures in social science) must be seen as part of the canon on social science, but it was also one of the many Marxist series that made no distinction between culture and politics. Included within its thirteen volumes were articles on the financial world, labor law, the Japanese women's movement, and proletarian mass literature. From 1927 until 1929, *Marukusushugi kōza* (Lectures in Marxism), edited by Kawakami Hajime and Ōyama Ikuo, featured Japanese scholars such as Hattori Shisō, who along with Noro Eitarō would be leading contributors to the comprehensive Lecture School series, *Lectures on the Development of Japanese Capitalism*, which would appear in 1932 and 1933. By 1931 the broad sweep of the four-volume *Puroretaria kōza* (Proletarian lectures) encompassed world labor history, imperialism, colonialism, the development of historical materialism, and the Chinese Revolution.[42]

---

[41] Marukusu-Engerusu Zenshū Henshūbu, "Henshū kōki," *Marukusu-Engerusu zenshū* supplemental volume (Kaizōsha, 1933), pp. 573–77.

[42] *Shakai kagaku kōza*, 13 vols. (Seibundō, 1931–1932); Kawakami Hajime and Ōyama Ikuo, eds., *Marukusushugi kōza*, 13 vols. (Ueno shoten, 1927–1929); Takabatake Motoyuki, *Marukusu jūni kōza* (Shinchōsha, 1926); Puroretaria Kagaku Kenkyūjō, ed., *Puroretaria kōza*, 4 vols. (Kyōseikaku, 1930).

In 1931 and 1932 *Marukusushugi rōdōsha kyōtei* (Marxist workers course of study), featuring translations by such Soviet scholars as Karl Wittfogel, offered a four-volume series on political economy and a three-volume series on the history of the international worker's movement following in the tradition of textbooks written for the Proletarian Free University. Sakai Toshihiko, Yamakawa Hitoshi, Aono Suekichi (the proletarian literature theorist), and others outlined lectures for working-class students in such fields as "Biology and Science," "Japanese History," and the "Proletarian Movement." Many of the books belonging to such series comprised translations from Soviet writers, although the collected works of Japanese Marxists Sano Manabu and Yamamoto Senji were also beginning to be anthologized by 1930.[43] Single works such as *Geijutsu to marukusushugi* (Art and Marxism) and *Chugoku mondai kōwa* (Talks on the China problem), edited by the Proletarian Science Research Center, were published in 1930, and by the late 1920s more than one publishing house was dedicated to the circulation of revolutionary culture. Ishidō Kiyotomo, as librarian of the Shinjinkai, would obtain materials from the Marx Association, which published the monthly issues of *Marukusushugi*, and from publishers with such evocative names as Kibōkaku (Hope House), Dōjinsha (Colleague Society), and Musansha (Proletarian Society).[44]

Japanese reference works to the emerging canon also proliferated. In 1929, *Nihon shakaishugi bunken*, (Documents on Japanese socialism), published by the Ōhara Institute for Social Research, was hailed by a reviewer as "the first complete index to socialist documents in our country."[45] In 1920, the editors of the first edition of the *Nihon rōdō nenkan* (Japan labor yearbook), which also appeared under the aegis of the Ōhara Institute, had divided their almanac into twenty-one categories including a section on "Labor Struggles," unemployment, and the socialist movement. Ten years later, by 1930, the contents of the yearbook had been simplified but expanded, and articles that had been arranged under six headings—"Labor Conditions," "The Labor Movement," "Labor Facilities and Policies," "Social Works," and "International Labor Problems"—were joined by a new topic: "The Movement of Social Thinkers."

[43] See, for example, Puroretaria Kagaku Kenkyūjō, trans., *Marukusushugi rōdōsha kyōtei: Keizaigaku*, 6 vols. (Sōbunkaku, 1931–1932); Kitajima Takehira, trans., *Marukusushugi rōdōsha kyōtei: Kokusai rōdōsha undōshi*, 3 vols. (Chūgai shobō, 1931–1932); S. Semkovsky and Marukusu Shobō Editorial Division, eds., *Marukusugaku kyōkasho*, 7 vols. (Marukusu shobō, 1928–1929).

[44] Puroretaria Kagaku Kenkyūjō, ed., *Geijutsu to marukusushugi* (Puroretaria Kagaku Kenkyūjō, 1930); Puroretaria Kagaku Kenkyūjō, ed., *Chūgoku mondai kōwa* (Puroretaria Kagaku Kenkyūjō, 1930). Ishidō, *Waga itan no Shōwa shi*, p. 53.

[45] *Nihon shakaishugi bunken* (Ohara shakai mondai kenkyūjō, 1929). The review appeared in *Shakai shisō* 8, 11 (November 1929).

Moreover, the appended bibliography of writings related to the social movement had expanded into a two-part guide to magazine articles and monographs on social issues.[46]

Marxist journals carried advertisements for other Marxist series, books, and journals and between 1930 and 1932. *Puroretaria kagaku*, the journal issued by the Proletarian Science Research Center, printed more than seven hundred advertisements for issues of journals and newly translated works, along with the writings of Japanese Marxists. Among the classics advertised during this intensely productive period of less than half a decade were Morgan's *Ancient Society* (Kyōseikaku, 1932), Lenin's *Imperialism, the Highest Stage of Capitalism* (Kibōkaku, 1932), Lunacharsky's *Marxist Art Theory* (Hakuyosha, 1929), and *Marxism and the Woman Problem*, by Lenin and Riazinov (Kyōseikaku, 1930). By the early 1930s Marx's *German Ideology* was also being advertised. During this period of canonization, Nakano Shigeharu was not the only Marxist concerned with the political implications of the explosion of Marxist and non-Marxist print culture. The eleven volumes of *Sōgō jaanarizumu kōza* (General lectures on journalism) presented investigative articles on such topics as bourgeois journalism, the history of the Japanese and proletarian magazines, the place of sensationalism in journalism, and the role of the advertisement. Almost every issue also featured an in-depth analysis of either a publication such as *Kingu* or a publishing institution like Heibonsha, and a brief biographical blurb and photographic portrait on each writer.[47]

Just as Nakano Shigeharu's Marxist essays of the middle of the 1920s belong with the other manifestos introducing the first Japanese Marxist journals of politics and culture, so does he also deserve a central position in this process of organization and dissemination of knowledge that took place at the end of the 1920s. By 1931, when he was given a place in the one-yen book series *Gendai Nihon bungaku zenshū* (Modern Japanese literature) along with the other writers chosen to represent the category of "proletarian literature," more than one anthology had already presented him as one of the "newly rising" revolutionary writers. That year, his story about the response of a tenant farmer's son to the visit of the Crown Prince, *Tetsu no hanashi* (The story of Tetsu), was placed in an

[46] *Nihon rōdō nenkan* (Ōhara shakai mondai kenkyūjō, 1929, 1930). The section on the socialist movement in the 1920 volume included such varied topics as a history of the socialist movement, gratitude owed Kōtoku Shūsui, the imprisonment of a syndicalist in Kyoto, the incarceration by Aomori Prefecture police of a propagandist of Bolshevism, and an account of a tea party of people related to the magazine *Shin shakai*.

[47] *Sōgō jaanarizumu kōza*, 11 vols. (Naigaisha, 1930–1931). See, for example, the article on *Kingu* that asked, "What role does *Kingu* have in the capitalist country called Japan and what role is it trying to play?" (3:163).

anthology of proletarian writers, along with Tokunaga Sunao's account
of the Kyōdō Printers' Strike, *Taiyō no nai machi* (Streets without sun),
and *Kani kōsen* (Cannery boat) by Kobayashi Takiji. Two months later,
the three were included with nine other writers in volume 51 of *Meiji
Taishō Shōwa bungaku zenshū* (The Complete Works of Meiji-Taishō-
Shōwa Literature).[48] Clearly, by the early 1930s Nakano Shigeharu was
recognized both as a "proletarian" or revolutionary author and as a leading modern Japanese writer.

Nakano's revolutionary poetry ended with the publication of "Shinagawa in the Rain" in February 1929, but during the era of canonization,
between 1928 and 1931, he was an active participant in the creation of
both an orthodoxy and a self-conscious history for Japanese Marxist
writers. Categorizing Nakano's life into the three columns of "everyday
life," "literary production," and "political activity," which are at best a
provisional, heuristic device, becomes most problematic for these years,
for "everyday life" is disrupted by the intrusion of a "prison life" four
times between early 1928 and late 1931. Moreover, Nakano's "literary
production" becomes indistinguishable from political activism during
this fourth stage of changing song because the poet was working as editor,
agitator, writer of short stories, and author of a series of theoretical works
inserted into the Japanese Marxist canon integrating writing on society,
political economy, and literature. Although Nakano's critique of culture
and his vision of society in his poetry and his earlier essays, have been
compared with the views of Georg Lukács, Walter Benjamin, and Mikhail
Bakhtin, his essays written for display in the canon did not stray far from
the Communist orthodoxy. His essays repeated conceptions familiar to
readers of such sanctioned writers as Lenin, Lunacharsky, and Plekhanov.[49] These works reveal that the Marxist critic of Taishō culture was a
student of Soviet theory, but even these more derivative essays were not
products of a rigid party line but reflective of an independent, thoughtful
stance toward the making of poetry in Japanese history.

In "Geijutsuron" (Discourse on art), which was anthologized in the

[48] Nakano, "Nakano Shigeharushū," in *Puroretaria bungakushū*, vol. 62 of *Gendai Nihon bungaku zenshū* (Kaizōsha, 1931); Nakano, "Nakano Shigeharushū," *Nihonhen X*,
vol. 10 of *Shinkō bungaku zenshū* (Heibonsha, 1929); Nakano, *Geijutsu ni kansuru hashirigakiteki oboegaki* (Kaizōsha, 1929). The first anthology of his fiction was Nakano, *Tetsu
no hanashi*, vol. 9 of *Nihon Puroretaria sakka sōsho* (Senkisha, 1930). Nakano's novel
appeared with two other recent revolutionary and apolitical classics in "Nakano Shigeharu
hen," *Tanpenshu daiichi*, vol. 51 of *Meiji Taishō Shōwa bungaku zenshū* (Shunyodo, 1931).
[49] Nakano, "Geijutsu ni tsuite," NSZ 9:79–218 [*Marukusushugi kōza*, vol. 10, 10/28
under title "Geijutsuron"]; Nakano, "Seiji to geijutsu," NSZ 9:253–61 [*Puroretaria geijutsu kyōtei*, vol. 1 (Sekaisha, 7/29)]; Nakano, "Puroretaria geijutsu to wa nanika?" pp.
337–55. The Soviet theorists used by Nakano would all be included in the anthology of
translations, *Marukusushugi geijutsu riron* (Sōbunkaku, 1931).

tenth volume of *Lectures in Marxism* in October 1928 along with essays on political parties, labor unions, and world war, Nakano turned to the thinkers then acceptable in the Soviet Union—Bukharin, Plekhanov, Lenin, and Marx—in order to relate Marxism to art.[50] In one of his most rigorously structured works, he cited such non-Marxist thinkers as Goethe, Cocteau, and Ruskin, but his concern was to place Marxist theorists of culture within a comprehensible framework. He mobilized Bukharin's *Theory of Historical Materialism* to argue that Taishō society was in an era of disruption, when the superstructure could no longer absorb the contradiction between productive forces and the economy. The psychology and ideology of class harmony had thus been destroyed, and the proletarian class was now sufficiently conscious of itself as a class to enable it to wield art as a weapon. The essay was informed by a contradiction, for Nakano also adopted Bukharin's analysis of the state to discuss how in Japan, the state still held sway over culture, through such mechanisms as the schools. According to his analysis of contemporary Japan, while proletarian art had escaped the standards of bourgeois culture, "the great troops of proletarians" were "captive within the organs of state control," serving the class interests of the bourgeoisie (pp. 181, 183).

In this essay Bukharin and Lunacharsky are revealed to be the sources of Nakano's concern with emotions in his early manifesto. He paraphrases Bukharin to say that songs and music function to organize the emotions, and that the same holds true for dance, theater, painting, and various forms of literature. Art is a social method for organizing emotions—"social" because the individual cannot be conceptualized outside of society, and because all of man's products are social. For example, music performed in a big hall under grand lights is not made from the stuff of everyday life. It is, in other words, only the form or *kata* accepted by the "fine people" who applaud because they have no feel for music. In contrast, the music produced by a cheap record player in a city bar is for those without any social standing—the wanderers, vagrants, and beggars. Nakano celebrates only the third form of music, which refuses to be commodified. With this music of self-expression there is no commercialized mediation setting up barriers between musician and management or between audience and management; there is no difference between player and audience. Quoting Victor Hugo, he determines that this music is for those who "find stars among the mud" (pp. 185–92).

Nakano associates emotion with class experience. For example, a folk song proclaiming joy at the master's fine harvest is an anachronism, expressive of the consciousness of a serf-like peasant who identifies with his landlord and does not recognize that their interests are at odds. He offers

[50] Nakano, "Geijutsu ni tsuite."

an alternative to such outmoded song: the new lyrics of the changed songs such as the *kaeuta* in Hosoi's *Sad History of the Woman Factory Hand* are emerging from within the factories. These songs sing of "the misery of labor in the factory and resentment aimed at the owners of the factory" instead of expressing joy in factory labor. It appears that Bukharin helped resolve the dilemma, which, according to Nakano's memoirs, he encountered when he turned to poetry in order to make revolution. At a time when no one was asking why or how the factory girls were changing their song, Bukharin's theory that art in all its forms is a social phenomenon, and that the progress of society leads to the birth of new forms of art, which along with manners, customs, philosophy, religion, and language are incorporated into man's "mental" or "spiritual culture," closely associated with the materiality of production, placed poetry into history. Content with Bukharin's statement that culture encompasses "everything that is the work of human hands," Nakano posited art within culture and turned to a discussion of the historical development of art (pp. 195–96).

Nakano then deferred to the Marxist expertise of Georg Plekhanov in an extended analysis of the historical development of art. Quoting from Plekhanov's "Historical Materialism and the Arts," Nakano claimed that the historic development of the feeling for beauty, which organizes art, must be sought within the social context or the conditions surrounding man. In his most complete recitation of his version of historical materialism, he explicated his Marxist way of seeing things, which had transformed his poetry and provided the basis for his actions as an organizer in the revolutionary culture movement: During all past historical stages human existence had been conditioned by nature, by man's relationship within nature, and by man's existence within and negotiations from within nature. In other words, human society was conditioned by labor working on nature, or social production. Labor, labor dances, and labor songs most clearly signifed the production of art from within this social production as human beings transformed nature, thereby transforming themselves. Nakano had already produced his own version of this idea in "The Beach at Kitami" to illustrate Marx's theory of the liberation of man, through his labor on objects, as he continually reconstructs the materials of the external world. The black shadow of a man had been allegorical, but in this essay Nakano brought in such concrete examples from indigenous folk tradition as the Ainu bear festival, a spinning song, and a folk song that accompanied the pounding of rice by farm youth, to make the connection between the technique of an art form and its position within a mode of production. The stage theory of *The Origin of the Family, Private Property, and the State* provided the context for the pronouncement that the content of the peasant's song was thus just changing, after a thousand years of correspondence to feudal conditions. Art was being transformed in a continuous process, as those who had been placed below had risen in resistance. Those who had turned the gears of history were now out front; the proletariat was making history and thus could not but be the agent of new art (pp. 195–204). Introducing yet another figure from the Soviet pantheon, Nakano made use of Lenin to discuss his stage theory of transition from feudalism and to resolve the contradiction, implied by this focus on the working class as culture bearers. Only the proletariat could resolve this contradiction, but they could not create a culture of their own. They were forced to rely on a specific group, attached to another class that would perform the task of spiritual production within the social division of labor (p. 204).[51]

In sum, Nakano had given the intellectual revolutionary work, by putting his ideas about his own labor as expressed in such poems as "Farewell Before Dawn" and "Days" into theoretical form. The manifesto on art offered a glimpse into Japanese cultural history, but on the whole it was a derivative pastiche. Nonetheless, Nakano was not following a party line. The fluidity in Soviet policy had allowed him to look at the production of culture in Taishō Japan, and to reproduce the unique voices of his place and time. In this essay Nakano directed his readers to the open-endedness of Soviet policy by quoting from the "Party's Policy in the Field of Literature" of June 18, 1925, a landmark text, written by Bukharin to legislate party policy in the superstructural domain (p. 213). Although he quoted a passage that stated unequivocally that the laws of class struggle were to apply in the spheres of ideology and literature, the document had laid down no specific guidelines for the control of literature. To the contrary, it claimed that proletarian literature would emerge from within the proletariat, without party guidance as to authorship or determination of form, amidst a pluralistic site of literary production.[52]

[51] Quoting Lenin's assessment of Tolstoy, in "Tolstoy as the Mirror of the Russian Revolution," Nakano concludes that art that cannot conform to the experience of flux will fossilize into a fixed form; it will be forced "to commit suicide" (p. 206).

[52] C. Vaughn James, *Soviet Socialist Realism: Origins and Theory* (New York: St. Martin's Press, 1973), p. 116. This statement did put a decisive end to the debate concerning literature waged by Trotsky and Bukharin. Marx had never used the term "proletarian literature," and Trotsky contended that a separate category of art was not legitimate because there was no need for proletarian literature during the short transition to socialism. Bukharin's statement adopted and legitimized "proletarian literature," but historians of Russian literature disagree as to the implications of the pronouncement. Edward J. Brown claims that the resolution was used by diametrically opposed groups until 1932, when the party actively intervened in literary matters by dissolving the Russian Association of Proletarian Writers, thus ending the era of semi-autonomous literary groupings which had coexisted since the early 1920s. Brown, *The Proletarian Episode in Russian Literature 1928–1932* (New York: Columbia University Press, 1953), pp. 208–20. Marc Slonim has documented the outpouring of novels, short stories, poems, and essays appearing during what he terms

Just as the leading Marxist historians of the era cannot be said to have mimicked Moscow's directives, there was space within which Japanese revolutionary writers like Nakano could maneuver.[53] Yet the flexibility allowed by such a policy during the second half of the 1920s had not resolved the conundrum raised by Marx's writing on consciousness: the ideology of an era belonged to its ruling class, as stated in the *Communist Manifesto*, and a revolution could not take place until tensions in economic relationships had established a battleground. At the same time Marx had claimed that men make their own history. Where and how was the intellectual, almost always, as Nakano acknowledged, from bourgeois background, to act within a schema that seemed to allow for voluntarism on the part of the proletariat in destroying and creating a new culture? How was the revolutionary intellectual to make revolution? When Nakano answered this question in a second essay, written for an anthology, he focused on the problem of the state.

The bulk of "Seiji to geijutsu" (Politics and art),[54] which appeared in *Puroretaria geijutsu kyōtei* (Proletarian art courses of study) in July 1929, was devoted to quotations by Japanese parliamentarians detailing and decrying the torture by state officials of citizens deemed Communists following the massive arrests of March 15, 1928. At issue was the state's refusal, by the end of the 1920s, to allow the writer to write. The Hegelian stand-off of master against servant, which Nakano had transformed into the struggle of groups within his poetry, had escalated to a point where the state and the revolutionary were locked in a struggle for survival. Revolutionary work for the poet could no longer be a matter of raising consciousness through poetry or a theory of history. Yet work had to continue, even as the writer's freedom was being increasingly constrained. Nakano's two other canonized essays, on the relationship of Marxism to poetry, must be read in this light. By the turn of the decade Nakano was too busy with the work of maintaining the revolution to write much poetry, but he wrote about poetry in order to educate his audience in Marxist theory and the need for revolutionary practice. Two additional essays,

---

an era offering freedom to "fellow travelers." Slonim, *Soviet Russian Literature: Writers and Problems 1917–1967* (New York: Oxford University Press, 1967), p. 48. No scholar disagrees with the accuracy of the assessment by Herman Ermolaev that by April 1932, when the Party Central Committee dissolved all proletarian organizations in literature and the arts and placed them under the Union of Soviet Writers, "the party had definitely assumed guidance of literature." Ermolaev, *Soviet Literary Theories: 1917–1934* (Berkeley: University of California Press, 1963), p. 4.

[53] See Germaine Hoston, *Marxism and the Crisis of Development in Prewar Japan*. One example of the autonomy of Japanese thinkers is the fact that the kōza school two-stage theory of revolution propounded by Noro Eitarō preceded the 1932 Comintern Theses.

[54] Nakano, "Seiji to geijutsu," pp. 253–61.

"Studies of the Work of Poetry"[55] and "Studies of Poetry of the Past,"[56] maintained that poetry had a central place in the making of revolution.

In "Kako no shi no kenkyū" (Studies of poetry of the past), written for the anthology *Sōgō puroretaria geijutsu kōza* (General lectures in proletarian art), which appeared in 1931, Nakano positioned poetry within the historic transformation of the Meiji Restoration after placing proletarian poetry within a history of changing forms. According to Nakano, because of content which hitherto could not have been attempted, this new poetry (*shi*) "destroyed the short form of *tanka* and attempted to take on a long form" and therefore had to be considered separately from *haiku*, *tanka*, folk songs, and ballads (p. 452).[57] This analysis emerged from a stage theory of Japanese culture that incorporated respect for tradition, as Nakano made clear in the question opening his essay, "Why study the poems of the past?" His answer, he said, was simple: "We state quite clearly, without the critique of bourgeois poetry, without the study of all sorts of poetry of the past, there can be no construction of proletarian poetry" (p. 440). Proletarian art was the culmination of all art from the past, and to make revolution by making poetry, there had to be an assimilation of the work left by the great poets of the past. Nakano was adopting Trotsky's belief, set forth in *Literature and Revolution*, that "We Marxists live in traditions, and we have not stopped being revolutionists on account of it."[58]

To explicate fully his position on bourgeois poetry, which was to be respected, studied, and superseded, Nakano turned in "Studies of Poetry of the Past" to Walt Whitman. According to Nakano's rendering of history, in 1860, capitalism had been striving to make the world its own, the American bourgeoisie had been locked in a life-and-death struggle with landowners, Whitman was one of its commanders, and the poems in *Leaves of Grass* had been his arsenal. Whitman stood out, capturing the true voice of the American bourgeoisie which was determined to establish a bourgeois democracy, at a time when most poets in the United States had been reproducing outdated content shaped in old forms. While he was guilty of allegiance to bourgeois ideology's myth of freedom and equality for all, it was this very prejudice that made the American poet's work revolutionary, for it was not the content but the ability to articulate a new social psychology that captured Nakano's admiration (pp. 447–

[55] Nakano, "Shi no shigoto no kenkyū," pp. 369–82.

[56] Nakano, "Kako no shi no kenkyū," *NSZ* 9:440–56 [*Sōgō puroretaria geijutsu kōza*, vol. 4, 10/31]. The original title was "Burujua shi no hihan—kako no shi no kenkyū."

[57] From the Meiji era the term *shi* referred to both Western poetry and the Japanese "new form poetry" or *shintaishi* poems written in the new style of the Meiji poets influenced by contemporary Western verse.

[58] Trotsky, *Literature and Revolution*, p. 242.

52). The support of the Marxist poet for the bourgeois cultural hero is illuminated by Marshall Berman's reading of the *Communist Manifesto*. According to Berman, Marx celebrated the activism of the bourgeoisie who created a new world, rather than their actual creations: "What matters to him is the processes, the powers, the expressions of human life and energy: men working, moving, cultivating, communicating, organizing and reorganizing nature and themselves—the new and endlessly renewed modes of activity that the bourgeoisie brings into being."[59] This sort of motivating force excited Nakano, who pointed to "class psychology" as the mediator between art and class struggle in "Studies of Poetry of the Past."

Rather than associating Nakano with the conflict between Yamakawa Hitoshi and Fukumoto Kazuo, Nakano's discussion of bourgeois poetry positions him within the context of the debate as to the nature of bourgeois democracy in Japan between Lecture School and Labor-Farmer factions, which were being canonized at the time. Nakano's argument followed the Lecture School line of reasoning as he placed poetry within a schema of modern Japanese history moved by remnants of the past rather than capitalist transformation.[60] In Nakano's view, the Meiji Restoration had not been fought by a revolutionary bourgeoisie, nor had it produced a bourgeois democracy; the revolution had not been completed. Not only had the Japanese bourgeoisie failed to destroy the landowners; in fact, the new Meiji government had been colored and nurtured by the landowning class. There had been no bourgeois revolutionary, and thus there could

[59] Berman, *All that Is Solid Melts into Air*, p. 93.

[60] For a précis of the positions of the two schools see Hoston, *Marxism and the Crisis of Development*, pp. xi–xii. While one of the aims of this book is to challenge the facile association of the thought of Nakano with Japanese Communist Party policy or Comintern pronouncements, the historiography codified by the Comintern should not be ignored. In this context, it should be noted that "Studies on Poetry of the Past" was written after the abandonment of the 1931 Draft Political Theses of the Japanese Communist Party, which had argued that the Meiji Restoration had been an incomplete bourgeois revolution, and before the 1932 Theses called for a bourgeois revolution to be followed by socialist revolution. The language of this essay is similar to the analysis of the Comintern Theses of 1927, which talked in terms of a bloc of capitalists and landlords and of the transformation of the old Japanese state into a bourgeois state via "the relative strength and the political significance of the industrial, commercial, and financial bourgeoisie," and by "the process of blending the feudal strata with the new bourgeoisie" as the result of economic shifts, fear of the labor and peasant movements, and imperialist policy. From the "Theses on Japan Adopted in the Session of the Presidium of the Executive Committee of the Comintern on July 15, 1927," in George Beckmann and Genji Okubo, *The Japanese Communist Party 1922–1945* (Stanford: Stanford University Press, 1969), p. 297. For the Japanese-language original see Ishidō Kiyotomo and Yamabe Kentarō, eds. *Kominterun Nihon ni kansuru teezeshū* (Aoki bunko, 1961), pp. 30–31. For a summary of shifts in Comintern policy resulting in the three-stage development of the two-stage theory in the Theses of 1927, 1931, and 1932, see Hoston, *Marxism and the Crisis of Development*, pp. 55–75.

be no true bourgeois poet to act as his disciple (pp. 442–43). Thus, when the New Form poets of Meiji attempted to sing of a new life, claiming in their manifesto that "the Meiji poem must be a Meiji poem," their adoption of new form and content was only partial. They opposed earlier poetry for its use of Chinese wording and classical language and its avoidance of colloquialism, but they themselves could not attempt to adopt colloquialism. Their poetry remained a combination of the vulgar and the elegantly classical—corresponding to the incomplete emergence of a semifeudal bourgeoisie after the Meiji Restoration (p. 454).[61]

Nakano's *nenpu* reveals that the poet joined the Japanese Communist Party in the summer of 1931, but "Shi no shigoto no kenkyū" (Studies of the work of poetry), his contribution to *Puroretaria shi no shomondai* (Problems in proletarian poetry), the book he edited for the canon,[62] makes it clear that this political commitment did not signify the loss of his independent voice. Nakano's rhetoric in "Discourse on Art" had given a prominent place to the Communist Party, when he had addressed the issue of the political organization of a proletariat capable of producing revolutionary art. He had stated that the party was to be responsible for agitation and propaganda centered on party cells, especially within the factory. Progress had been made in regard to factory newspapers, flyers, and posters, but the party, like capitalist management, could bring in lecturers with movies. Moreover, such topics as "the eight-hour day," "Fordism," and "rationalization" and the problems of women workers could be strengthened through dramatizations.[63] Here the emphasis was on his militant opposition to the control of poetry by the party. He attacked the mechanistic insertion of slogans into poetry by his Communist colleagues and criticized the rhetoric of Communist critics who claimed that the proletariat could neither see nature nor feel sad at the death of a child. Assertions that such experiences were petit bourgeois were a capitulation to bourgeois ideology. As part of this critique he rephrased Marx's contention in the *Manifesto*, used also by Benjamin, and by the anonymous factory girl who provided the new words for one *kaeuta*, that bourgeois class culture had merely trained the worker to act as a machine: "To treat a living person as a dead thing—merely part of a machine for

[61] In 1882 Inoue Tetsujirō, one of the three translators of *Shintaishishō*, stated in his introduction to "A Psalm of Life" by Henry Wadsworth Longfellow that "Meiji poems should be Meiji poems and not old poems; Japanese poetry should be Japanese poetry and not Chinese poetry." For a summary of the concerns of the New Form poets, see the introduction to A. R. Davis, ed., *Modern Japanese Poetry*, trans. James Kirkup (St. Lucia: University of Queensland Press, 1978), pp. xxxvii–xxxix.

[62] This essay first appeared in the 7/31 issue of *Puroretaria shi*, as cited above, and was included in Nakano's anthology the following year. Nakano, ed., *Puroretaria shi no shomondai* (Sōbunkaku, 1932).

[63] Nakano, "Geijutsu ni tsuite," pp. 214–18.

production of profit—this is cooperation with the bourgeoisie."[64] Na-kano demanded that the Marxist poet see that nature had been stolen from the worker. The worker was denied access to the beauty surrounding him since for two- or three-year stretches of time; the worker locked inside the factory was deprived of the blue sky (p. 380). The beauty of nature and man's rightful place within it were to be reclaimed by revolution. For Nakano, who spoke as a theorist and not as an active poet in 1931, the production of poetry was still one means of working toward that end.

Nakano's image of the worker behind walls proved to be a prophecy. The following year the impassioned revolutionary writer, who had already been imprisoned three times, as he moved from a position within Taishō culture but critical of Taishō commodity culture to a position of leadership in the revolutionary culture movement, would begin two years of everyday life in one small locked room. He was arrested in April 1932, along with other Communist writers, because of his contributions to the Marxist canon. Two months after Nakano's arrest, his colleagues Mori-yama Kei and Itō Shinkichi dedicated *Problems in Proletarian Poetry* to him and to his old friend, Kubokawa Tsurujirō. That inscription expresses the most significant contradiction in Marxist revolutionary culture during the last years of the era. The problem (hinted at in the essay "Politics and Art") was that Nakano and other revolutionary intellectuals pushing to complete the canon before their time ran out were fighting not only a contending ideology of a contending class, but the overwhelming forces of a police state. The contradiction was that Nakano and his Marxist colleagues were writing for an audience that was being denied the right to read. Nonetheless, the construction of a canon was a revolutionary act, because political activists were documenting an approach toward history and politics that was rapidly being silenced. Although in retrospect the tremendous outpouring of Marxist works may seem like a losing proposition, to publish a work of Japanese Marxist theory during the fourth stage of Nakano's changing song was to claim a place in Japanese history. The ironic coincidence of this process of canonization with repression is best illustrated by a glance through the set of red leather-bound volumes of the one-yen "complete works" of Marx and Engels. One work is visibly absent. As the editors explained in their introduction to the set, "given the social situation" in Japan at that time, the *Communist Manifesto*—even in some changed form—could not be included.

[64] Nakano, "Kako no shi no kenkyū," p. 379.

CHAPTER SIX

Song IV: Closing Song

DIALOGUE DENIED

In 1929 Mikhail Bakhtin wrote, "When dialogue ends, everything ends."[1] That same year Nakano also issued a statement on the curtailment of such exchange in an essay prescribing a response to censorship. In a section entitled "Asterisks" in the essay "On Selling Writing and Other Matters," he stated that the issue, as he saw it, was not the avoidance of the asterisks, but the ability to write without asterisks. This subtle distinction was important, for Nakano was asserting that the writer, in total control of his tools, must reject "the language of slaves."[2] He was contending that literature produced in fear, with censorship in mind, could not express the truth, and that it was still possible to produce literature that did not emerge in print as a series of words punctuated by asterisks standing in for deletions. Two years earlier, Nakano had produced an example of such elusive wording in "Hōritsu" (Law),[3] written for a special issue of *Puroretaria geijutsu* that bore the slogan "Fight Against the Unjust Censorship System":

LAW

Eyes and ears had mud packed in
Nose was split and
Tongue pulled out from roots with pliers
Entire face smashed into confusion
The upper arm seems about to come off
All smeared with mud smeared with blood

The poem had not been touched by the authorities, very possibly because its angry imagery in verse was both direct and oblique. Its intentional denial of both a literal approach and a clear language pinning down agency must have confused the censors. The writing undoubtedly evaded them because Nakano's arrangement of the words avoided setting up a relationship between torturer and tortured. The overall impact remained

---

[1] This referred to Bakhtin's belief that being necessitated dialogic communications between at least two voices. Bakhtin, *Problems of Dostoevsky's Poetics*, p. 252.

[2] Nakano, "Bunshō wo uru koto," p. 268.

[3] Nakano, "Hōritsu," *NSZ* 1:525 [*Puroretaria geijutsu* 9/27].

powerful nonetheless. This extended metaphor on the effacing of language in the name of the law was a literal rendering of the torture conducted by state officials. Thus, the six lines of "Law" provided a two-pronged attack on censorship. It protested torture, and, like Nakano's participation in the creation of a Marxist canon, it was an aggressive, offensive move to counter the violence of the censorship of revolutionary language.

During the late 1920s, as Nakano began to produce his Marxist manifestos on art for various anthologies, he turned to fiction for similar reasons. In a series of short stories he recorded the history of his own political movement in order to assert its challenged presence. The bulk of his stories were written after he had stopped writing poetry; along with his prison letters, the essays written for the canon, and journalistic pieces of prose decrying the rapid transformation of Taishō culture, they constitute a fourth stage of his changing song.[4] These works belong to both Taishō and Shōwa culture. They are the products of a transitional moment best captured in "Kinensai zengo" (Before and after the memorial festival),[5] which was written while Nakano was still producing poetry. The story, written in the form of a diary made out of a series of letters to revolutionary colleagues abroad, was Nakano's means of recording and affirming the ironies of the everyday life of a cultural activist who talks of revolution while simultaneously fighting for his own survival. It detailed the work of organizing, editing, and political infighting, and the task of producing new forms of culture in print and in the theater, in the shadow of a strong police presence.

The opening line in the work was the blunt statement, "Matsuyama's been caught." Every other dated segment catalogued either police activity in monitoring or preventing movement or the response of the revolutionaries. Nakano railed against torture, recorded an impromptu parade of children, activists, and spies come to greet a colleague released from prison, and worried about the illness around him caused by tension and prison life. The documentary history in story form ended on December 3, 1927, with the description of the mobilization of police in advance of the enthronement ceremony scheduled for the following November. The nar-

[4] The fiction produced by Nakano from 1926 through 1931 does raise the issues centered in his poetry and critical essays. On the question of language, for example, see "Teishajō," NSZ 1:249–58 [Kindai seikatsu 6/29], and for a picture of urban culture, "Atarashii onna," NSZ 1:259–64 [Bungaku jidai 8/29]. The reproduction of culture is treated in "Nami no aima," NSZ 1:349–67 [Shinchō 5/30]. Most of the fiction produced between 1928 and 1932 records the narrative history of Nakano's political movement. The stories "Teishajō" and "Nami no aima" fall within this category, as does "Doitsu kara kita otoko," NSZ 1:420–33 [Shinchō 7/31], another formulation of the Imperial Hotel story.

[5] Nakano, "Kinensai zengo," NSZ 1:186–202 [Puroretaria geijutsu 1/28].

rator also mentioned the fatal illness of his sister, due to malnutrition, and closed with the dedicated affirmation of the need to produce revolutionary culture: "I've got to rush off thirty-three pages of fiction before eight in the morning so I'll end here" (p. 202).

This short story, like "Harusaki no kaze" (Early spring breezes),[6] which alluded to the physical torture experienced by alleged Communists and told of the death of a baby after the mass arrests on March 15, 1928, was written for the record. When Nakano had his heroine state, "we are living in the midst of contempt" (p. 214), he was looking backward. In contrast his revolutionary poetry facing the future had predicted victory. For example, "Dōro wo kizuku" (Building a Road),[7] an extended double-entendre about revolutionary destruction and reconstruction published in *Musansha shimbun* on New Year's day 1927, had been one of the sharpest fantasies of violent change:

BUILDING A ROAD

Folks boil gravel in order to make a road
Folks stir stones in order to make a road
And what we are building is that road
And for that let's us boil the gravel

For that let us boil the gravel
For that let us turn the mixers
For that let us pull the rollers
Ahh—for that we'll set up a great big cauldron
* * * * * * * * * * * * the bougies and the petit-bougies
All of 'em to * * * * * made * * * * for road-building supplies
Inside that great big stove
Smash in all of both tolerance and pity
Smash in parents and brothers and family
Even babies smash in too
* * * * * 'em all up without regret
To make that road
To let the real whole folk walk down that lively road
Ahh—let's cross over in the midst of *

The poem had grasped the ruling metaphor of the short story "The Letter Inside the Cement Barrel"[8] in order to invert it. In Hayama Yoshiki's nar-

---

[6] Nakano, "Harusaki no kaze," pp. 203–14.

[7] Nakano, "Dōrō wo kizuku," *NSZ* 1:514 [*Musansha shimbun* 1/1/27].

[8] Hayama Yoshiki, "Semento daru no naka no tegami," in *Nihon puroretaria bungaku taikei*, vol. 2: *Undō seiritsu no jidai*, pp. 71–74 [*Bungei sensen* 1/26]. For an English-language version see Hayama Yoshiki, "Letter Found in a Cement Barrel," in *Modern Japanese*

rative, which had rocked the literary world the previous year, a cement worker who is so captive to his machinery that he is unable to break his work motions to unclog his nostrils of the cement that also coats his hair and face finds a letter inside a barrel of cement. It is from a factory girl who recounts how her lover had fallen into the machine to come out "just fine, as cement." The young woman entreats the reader of the letter to tell how her lover will be used in the construction, now that his actual body and not his labor power will be exploited for the benefit of others. In the poem "Building a Road," Nakano reverses the power relationship entrapping Hayama's hero. The workers take conscious control of their labor; it is the bosses who are treated as things to be thrown into the mixing machines. The poem's proclamation of the necessity of violence contrasts with the inarticulate anger of Hayama's hero, who responds to the letter by wanting to get drunk and smash everything in sight. It is the violence of "To Those Who Make the Newspapers" and "Memories of Night Harvesting." It is also a false prophecy of the great insurrection that did not take place in either Taishō or Shōwa Japan. Ten months later Nakano Shigeharu used the image of the road in his presentation of a short story that did foretell the history of early Shōwa. The prophecy of "Kobanmae" (In front of the policebox)[9] was written during the third stage of Nakano's changing song, yet it belongs here because, unlike the revolutionary poetry recording Taishō dialogues or the literary criticism written for the canon, it foretold the transformation of urban culture in the early years of Shōwa from amidst Taishō commodity culture. Moreover, this story, written nine months after "Building a Road," fantasized revolution in a similar urban setting, offering a view of why Nakano's poetry ended.[10] In his effort to disclose the construction of power relations and the opportunity for the transformation of relationships through confrontation and rebellion, Nakano Shigeharu prophesied the power of the early Shōwa state to extend its hold over the actions and movement of the Japanese citizenry during the fourth stage of his changing song.

At the outset of the story, the stage is set at the sight of a highway: "It was a small one, but it was unmistakably an 'incident' " (p. 179). The term "incident" gives special meaning to one of the many rambling, incoherent occurrences of everyday life, the narrator explains. The analysis

---

Stories: An Anthology, ed. and trans. Ivan Morris (Rutland and Tokyo: Charles E. Tuttle, 1962), pp. 204–10.

[9] Nakano, "Kobanmae," pp. 179–85.

[10] Maeda Ai also uses this story, at the beginning of his wide-ranging overview of the relationship of Japanese literature to urban space. His concern, too, is the relationship of power to controlled space, but he associates the poem with the beginning rather than the ending of Nakano's poetry. Maeda Ai, *Toshi kūkan no naka no bungaku* (Chikuma shobō, 1982), pp. 57–60.

continues in a dialectical mode: the one happening contains within it either qualitatively different characteristics or the seed of such differences. Nakano then situates the incident:

> It was a single V-shaped road running from H Ward to S Ward, on an incline. ———This road was reconstructed as a level modern highway, by the government's so-called nationwide road network policy. There were indeed fewer people here. Trains couldn't run there. This sort of road, constructed of cement, concrete, large bricks, bricks, and stone, where no trains ran, and where the comings and goings of people were not intense, ran far and wide through villages and cities. (p. 179)

Henri Lefebvre has theorized that capitalism "absorbed, resolved and integrated" such historical constructs as precapitalist relations of production, agriculture, and apparatuses of knowledge and justice as it "subordinated everything to its own operations by extending itself to space as a whole."[11] In this introduction Nakano describes the process of the fragmentation of space that results from the state's creation of what Lefebvre terms "social space" for the occupation of capitalism, which, in the words of Lefebvre, "took over the historical town through a vast process, turning it into fragments and creating a social space for itself to occupy."[12] In Tokyo, it is not only the urban divisions or wards, marked by letters, that are devoid of historical allusion. In addition, the narrator directs the reader to the exact site of the incident by placing the policebox across from the station, at the intersection of the highway, with the rail line running "from U station to G temple" (p. 179).

This is an urban landscape that offers no delights to any sort of flaneur. All space is organized for the single purpose of transporting citizens from their homes to their places of work, and time as well as space is constrained. Motion is always correlated with time, Nakano explains:

> The major thoroughfare of a large city has a face, and this sensitively expresses the movement in time of a day. Anyone gazing at the gathering in front of this policebox would undoubtedly recognize the expression of "day's end." (p. 180)

The new social order allows no squandering of time, which has been divided and allotted to different tasks just as the members of the crowd have been assigned to different spheres of labor. In his description of the moving chaos of "a certain type of worker," the narrator cuts across class. Laborers, day laborers, elementary school teachers, students going home and setting out for night school, and housewives rushing home to fix din-

[11] Lefebvre, *Survival of Capitalism*, pp. 37–38.
[12] Ibid., p. 19.

ner have all passed in front of the policebox after six o'clock on one April evening.

In Europe in the previous century the state had pacified thousands of workers by employing them on public works projects, some of which, like the broad avenues constructed by Napoleon III, would be used to further control unrest. Berman has recognized these modern boulevards to be the space where people can be "private in public." He uses the term "moving chaos" in his discussion of the boulevard as the symbol of capitalism's contradictions. According to this interpretation,

> The chaos here lies not in the movers themselves—the individual walkers or drivers, each of whom may be pursuing the most efficient route for himself— but in their interaction, in the totality of their movements in a common space. This makes the boulevard a perfect symbol of capitalism's inner contradictions: rationality in each individual capitalist unit, leading to anarchic irrationality in the social system that brings all these units together.[13]

This is the gist of Nakano's picture of urban motion. Each member of the crowd is thus pursuing his or her own private daily course until a portion of the crowd transforms itself into a grouping when an increasing number of people break out of their routine to become witnesses to "the incident."

An officer attempts to arrest a worker because he has been drinking, and the group separates itself from the moving crowd at the sound of his words, "Aren't ya coming!" They discover the very common pairing of an old construction trades worker and a young police officer. Here, in front of the policebox, this man of about sixty years of age who works at constructing roads refuses to bow to the authority of the state; unlike others from his class in his situation, he will not accompany a young policeman to the policebox. Nakano has created another Hegelian pairing in the stand-off of officer and worker; the incident has begun. For a moment, power relations appear reversed, for as the two men confront each other, momentarily the weaker of the two becomes strong and the stronger retreats when the old man attempts to strip the young officer of the dignity accompanying his rank as state official. He pulls loose from the policeman's grasp, and the circle of spectators opens to allow him to head toward his train, but the younger man regains his position after reaffirming his power to himself: "The police officer could no longer stand it. Wasn't he a uniform? Wasn't his body the gate, door, handle to the law?!" (p. 183). He wrenches the old man into the policebox, and for the second time the laborer escapes, this time by slipping out of the sleeves of his worn jacket, which is imprinted with the insignia of his work group.

[13] Berman, *All that Is Solid*, pp. 150–52, 159.

After a second police official comes to the aid of the young man, the cluster of people recognizes that the incident is ending as the construction worker comes "swimming toward them" in the grasp of the two officers who are clearly taking him to "Y police station." They are headed away from the policebox, toward the S Ward:

> "To the police!"
> A faint movement had begun among the people gathered. The police! Those who do not know hell know the police! The degree of atrocity of which the Judicial Division of the Police Station was capable—atrocity proceeds no further beyond this. When this is transcended, to move forward there is only death. (p. 184)

The people break the shared circle they have formed, in order to disperse. Passive before the power of the state, they return to their disconnected yet fully controlled positions within the urban crowd. The contending voices in the marketplace of private, personal exchanges have been silenced.

SHŌWA SONG

The prophecy of "In Front of the Policebox" anticipated such brute violence of early Shōwa as the mass arrests of 1928 and the forced dissolution of the Labor-Farmer Party, the Labor Union Council of Japan, and the All-Japan Proletarian Youth Federation, incidents all listed in an essay by Nakano about the "hook of repression" driven into the Proletarian Movement by May 1928.[14] But there were also quieter responses to the voices of the Taishō era that proclaimed cultural revolution, for the state was creating its own counter-canon. It appeared in the form of censorship laws aimed at newspapers, radio broadcasts, movies, magazines, and recordings.[15] And like the Marxist manifestos of Taishō, this counter-canon also appeared in periodicals—albeit those not available over the counter—that tracked the reproduction of subversive thought. The synchronicity of canon to this counter-canon is illustrated via one dual reference: Nakano Shigeharu's treatise "Discourse on Art" shared a publication date of October 1928 with the inaugural issue of the monthly *Shuppan keisatsu hō* (Police report on publications). At the same time as Nakano was placing a Marxist critique of culture within the canon, this

---

[14] Nakano, "Bungei sensen wa doko ni mon wo hirakuka," *NSZ* 9:137–44 [*Senki* 5/28].

[15] For the most comprehensive listing of censorship laws restricting the mass media during the Taishō and Shōwa era, see *Gendai shi shiryo*, vol. 41: *Masumedia tōsei*, ed. Uchikawa Yoshimi (Tokyo: Misuzu shobo, 1975). See also Gregory J. Kasza, *The State and the Mass Media in Japan, 1918–1945* (Berkeley: University of California Press, 1988), and Richard H. Mitchell, *Censorship in Imperial Japan* (Princeton: Princeton University Press, 1983).

guide to periodicals and other publications was explicating "The Antiwar Discourse in the Arts." It also offered a "Survey of Treatises Anti-Marxist in Tenor in Recent Magazines" and an overview of forbidden incendiary Socialist songs. The Shōwa counter-canon kept close watch over all print published and unpublished, for indexes to books not allowed into print were also available to the readers in the Home Ministry, and this archive continued to grow because Marxist writers like Nakano continued to write into the first decade of the Shōwa era.[16]

The work facing Nakano and his colleagues was overwhelming, for not only did the state manifest its control in censorship, via the production of alternative in-house publications to monitor the canon, and in the physical detention of writers; it also attempted to replace authors through the production of a state culture. Government authorities were moving to exclude all threatening forms of writing or entertainment through a monopoly of the mass media, which broadcast an ideology extolling Japan's unique position in the world along with the necessity for Japanese expansion into Asia. Nakano watched and responded to the construction of this new culture, which had so little in common with the popular culture he had decried in his critique of "Tokyo March." By April 1930, in an essay entitled "Handōki no sakusha seikatsu" (The life of the writer during a time of reaction), Nakano had begun to theorize about the mobilization of cultural forces by a bourgeoisie working to solidify the philosophy, science, and art that directly and indirectly protected the relations of production, the state, and the law. The following month, in an article written for *Senki*, he reported that on his return trip from inspecting youth groups affiliated with the tenancy movement in the villages of Saitama Prefecture, on the outskirts of Tokyo, he had identified a revolving searchlight illuminating the urban sky. He recognized this advertisement for the state-sponsored "Exposition of Sky and Sea" not as a leisure activity for private citizens with money and time to spend, but as a "demonstration for an imperialist war."[17]

By November 1931 Nakano was documenting the "waves of reaction" rising high in the cultural sphere.[18] In an analysis of the educational pro-

[16] In 1930 the *Shuppan keisatsu hō* would be joined by the annual *Shuppan keisatsu gaikan* (General survey of publications), which kept close watch over the publication and censorship of domestic and foreign books, magazines, and newspapers. The seven-volume *Shuppan keisatsu shiryō* (Police materials on publications) offered the state's analogue to the *enpon* by organizing knowledge for the Home Ministry's surveyors of literary production in such volumes as *The Theory of Fascism*, which appeared in 1932, and the last volume in the series, *The May 15 Incident as Seen in Publications*, which was published in 1936. See Yui Masao et al., eds. *Shuppan keisatsu kankei shiryō: Kaisetsu. Sōmokuji* (Tokyo: Fuji shuppan, 1983).

[17] Nakano, "Tokyo. Saitama nōson shōnen no katsudō," NSZ 9:317 [*Senki* 5/30].

[18] See "Handōki no sakka seikatsu," NSZ 9:309 [*Teikoku daigaku shimbun* 4/21/30].

gram submitted to the Ministry of Education by the Commission on Social Education he recorded how women and youth were being mobilized by this aggressive movement of the state and industrialists who utilized such media as sports events, youth groups, military reservist groups, and religious organizations. The mass media were also to blame, claimed Nakano. Such varied print sources as the journals *Nozomi* (Hope), *Ai to ase* (Love and sweat), and *Fujin kurabu* (Woman's club) fanned the flames of fascist and social fascist ideologies. By year's end Nakano was making the connection between the transformation of culture and the Japanese invasion of Manchuria. He followed literary energies being channeled into the production of eroticism and jingoism and proclaimed that the dispatching of troops to Manchuria only served to release the folkish patriotism of most writers, including those who were bourgeois and social democratic.[19]

In a two-part article written in early 1932 Nakano attacked the state control of radio as one facet of the creation of a monolithic military culture that denied the existence of alternative voices.[20] Affecting a matter-of-fact tone, he quizzed his readers on the experience of the Tokyo citizen walking the streets of the city:

> Among you folks there are undoubtedly those who listen to the radio. Even if you don't listen yourselves, there should be many among you who listen to the voices on the public speakers as you walk down the street. What do you folks hear on the radio these days? Every evening the radio broadcasts all sorts of news, and it broadcasts the speeches and talks of officials and scholars. However, what is it among those programs that especially stands out as having increased these days?

The author answered his own question: "Broadcasts of items related to war."[21] The spokesmen for the protection of the national honor were always military officials from the army or navy (it was never rank-and-file soldiers), or priests, school principals, or members of parliament. Nakano offered yet another variation on the dichotomy of oppressor and op-

---

[19] As part of his argument Nakano reproduced the Japanese government's ten-point program for the creation and implementation of "social education" through the use of lectures, movies, radio, the political education of women, students, and members of other organizations, and the establishment of museums and libraries at all levels of government throughout the nation. See Nakano, "Bunka remmei no koto," *NSZ* 9:460–62 [*Kaizo* 11/31]. On the nationalist ideology see "Sanjūichinendo bungeikai no kaiko," *NSZ* 9:482 [*Shinchō* 12/31]. Nakano noted that Saijō Yasu, the lyricist for "Tokyo March," was one of the writers whose volkisch fervor was enlisted to aid the bourgeoisie in "Saikin bungakujō no arekore," *NSZ* 9:524 [*Sarariiman* 2/15/32].

[20] Nakano, "Toki no mondai I," *NSZ* 9:527–34 [*Taishū no tomo* 2/32]; "Toki no Mondai II," *NSZ* 9:534–38 [*Taishū no tomo* 4/32].

[21] Nakano, "Toki no mondai I," p. 529.

pressed set forth during the high tide of revolutionary possibility in 1927 in "Notes on Art Written on the Run" during the high tide of revolutionary possibility:

> [But] these sorts of people are not people like us who all work in the factories, or till the fields, or suffer unemployment, or have children who go hungry. They live in fine houses, fill their bellies with nourishing food, are warm in cold winter, and take large salaries; using workers they make a lot of money, and take in taxes that do not even exist; they are the gang that wrings out and takes annual tribute of 50 percent and 20 percent from the tenant farmers and the poor farmers. (pp. 529–30)

Nakano asks why "we comrades" have not once conferred over the radio to share stories or to gain support for strikes. Why have the soldiers suffering in Manchuria not been heard from, and why have the unemployed not called out over the airwaves, "let's all together make them give us jobs," and finally, why has there not been a group refusal to pay taxes? He offers one "simple" answer to his queries: The radio, a most convenient item, is used only to further the class interests of the capitalists and landlords; this is why the "May Day March" has never once been broadcast on May Day. In sum, state policy put into practice by the Ministry of Communications and the radio stations posits a harmonious unity "of the country as a whole" that does not in fact exist in contemporary society (p. 530).

In his own way Nakano was grappling with what Antonio Gramsci called "hegemony" in his theory of the creation of consent, by nonviolent means, in the interests of a ruling class. Gramsci, who was interested in the realm of culture in the broadest sense, gave credit to Lenin for the insight that the state did not work only through the coercive apparatus of political dictatorship. The Italian Marxist analyzed how political passivity was created through ostensibly private institutions within civil society such as the church, trade unions, and schools. These mediating structures created a "spontaneous consent" for the state and for the values of the ruling class.[22] The Japanese state had never made a pretense at hiding behind private institutions, but as Nakano noted in his essays, by the early 1930s its move into the cultural sphere was becoming more aggressive, as it incorporated more and more facets of Taishō culture into its orbit and systematically destroyed any opposition. The destruction of the Proletarian Culture Movement, through the suppression of the activities

---

[22] Gramsci, *Selections from the Prison Notebooks*, pp. 12, 56, 210. James Joll offers an excellent, simple paraphrase of Gramsci's notion of the function of hegemony, which imposes values and leadership on the majority by the minority. In his words, hegemony "explains how a class can establish its cultural and moral superiority independently of its direct political power." Joll, *Antonio Gramsci* (New York: Penguin Books, 1977), pp. 19, 89.

and publications of the Japan Proletarian Culture Federation (KOPF), including the arrests of the members of its Writers' League beginning on March 24, 1932, was part of that process. The site of Nakano Shigeharu's political activity as writer, editor, and organizer through the second half of the 1920s and into the 1930s was being destroyed,[23] but Nakano continued to sing out, in a poetry reading at the Tsukiji Little Theater as part of an evening of literary readings organized by the Writers' League. One week later, on April 4, 1932, he was imprisoned for the last time, on suspicion of having broken the Peace Preservation Law. He was to remain in prison for two years and one month.

The rhythm of Nakano's literary production and political activism had already been broken by three brief incarcerations in 1928 and 1929. From May until December 1930 he had spent his first sustained period in jail. Upon his release he had written "Iyoiyo kyō kara" (Finally from today),[24] which proclaimed that for him the revolution was far from over. His work would continue in one *tsubo*, a space of little over three square meters:

FINALLY FROM TODAY

Finally from today it's life in this one tsubo
The guard shuts the door from behind
Shut it   Shut it   Lower the bolt
I'm not the one to be discouraged with that
In the corner of the room I look round in there is a chamber pot
On the walls and high windows steel latticework

Oh? They've come knocking from next door already
I will knock back, comrade next door
I will knock I will knock
To knock on the wall is my freedom
To pass this on next door is the freedom of the wall
Though my freedom can be robbed from me
The freedom of the wall to pass it on next door cannot be taken away
Putting metal bars on the windows
Will not stop the moon from shining through

Now then, today finally, it's life in this one tsubo
In this one tsubo it's continuation of my own work
If you want to steal footsteps to peer in then peer in
While you're secretly staring in
My own heart keeps growing

[23] The Writer's League would last another year, but there was no infrastructure after the crackdown of March 24.
[24] Nakano, "Iyoiyo kyō kara," *NSZ* 1:530–31 [*Nappu* 7/31].

My own heart etches rings for all the years
It grows broad
It grows strong
The lines for the years are layered upon layers
One day I shall have the colleagues examine the cross-sections

Finally from today it's the continuation of the important most important work

Like the earlier poems, "Farewell Before Dawn," "Days," and "Cleaning," Nakano's first account of life behind bars was premised on his commitment to his work, but it was also different. Here, his sense of time contrasted with the urgency dominating these poems and his acknowledgment of place reworked his earlier Marxist commentaries on the distinction between authentic and apparent freedom. In "Train," he had described how under capitalism the apparent liberty of the worker to sell her labor value on the market without coercion merely veils a new form of bondage succeeding the feudal form of serfdom. In "Imperial Hotel," he had removed the glitter of the marketplace of Western wares to reveal it for what it was—a prison in disguise. Now, in a real jail cell, he was contending that he had maintained his own freedom. His awareness of the true relations of power and his commitment to changing consciousness rendered him free. The overriding continuity expressed by this poem was Nakano's unabated determination that poetry could yet make revolution. Nonetheless, the rhythm of his production of poetry had been broken. He had written no poetry between the winter of 1929 when "The Rain at Shinagawa Station" had appeared and July 1931 when "Finally from Today" was published. Only one additional poem had appeared before his arrest in 1932. This highly personal poem, in the September 1931 edition of Chūō kōron, was about work, but it was also Nakano's first love poem since before his discovery of history, and as such it expressed the unavoidable truth that revolutionary dialogue was being closed off. Increasingly isolated from joint action with fellow revolutionaries, he could no longer depict the clash of society with state in the imagery of class struggle stretching from the urban landscape into the countryside. In "Konya ore wa omae no neiki wo kiiteyaru" (Tonight I will listen to you sleep),[25] he focused in but not inward, away from the panorama of class struggle in city and countryside, to an affirmation of the political dimension to the most intimate aspect of his now severely constrained daily existence:

[25] Nakano,"Konya ore wa omae no neiki wo kiiteyaru," NSZ 1:531–32 [Chūō kōron 9/31]. Cf. the eroticism of the earlier love poems, "Tsume wa mada aruka," NSZ 1:494 [Razō 1/25], and "Me no naka ni," NSZ 1:495 Razo 1/25].

TONIGHT I WILL LISTEN TO YOU SLEEP

Tonight I will listen to you sleep
I will praise you for your loyalty to your work
When I was sent from police to police
You passed from one to the next carrying your small packet
That was like an ant changing nests carrying its white eggs
But because of that if you had left your work even for a while
I could not have accepted your consideration most likely
Finally when I was sent to prison
You came again waving your hand
But if you
Had not used our being ripped apart as a moment for raising the level of
    your work
I could not have taken that woven hat at the reception room
You were always loyal to work and now too you are loyal
Tomorrow, following work, you go to Kawagoe
All by yourself you bustle preparing
Now you are breathing softly
I count your sleeping breaths
And laud the exactness of your breaths
Exact breathing belongs to those faithful to their work
You always being faithful to your work
That alone is enough
We who were ripped apart before maybe will be ripped apart again
But as long as we are loyal to our separate work
There is nothing that can truly tear us apart
Even those from whom all methods have been taken away cannot lose
    methods based on devotedness
I count your sleeping breath and praise it for tranquility
Crossing into the future go be tranquil
Standing secure on your loyalty to work

Nakano's homage to his wife's dedication also voiced the theme of allegiance to work which had infused "Farewell before Dawn" and "Days" and had provided the bite to the closing line addressed to the ambitious fat man in "Journalist." There the poet's admonition to the newspaperman to be "loyal to your work" had been offered in irony; here the words were repeated almost verbatim, but the sentiment of the poet speaking as a revolutionary and as the husband of an actress in the Proletarian Theater Movement was offered in sincerity. Nakano's wife had not interrupted her work after her marriage to him on April 16, 1930, nor after Nakano's arrest three weeks later. The poem commemorated their reunion after his six-month imprisonment in Toyotama Prison, but it was also a farewell predicting a much longer separation. When "Tonight I Will Listen to You Sleep" was published in September 1931, the censors had merely obliterated the first reference to being "taken away," but their response to Nakano's work was escalating. The following month authorities confiscated all but one copy of the first edition of the collected poetry of Nakano Shigeharu, barring its publication. The manuscript was saved only because another political poet, Itō Shinkichi, happened to be at the publishing house when the authorities arrived. He hid one copy and returned it to Nakano, who would write no more poetry for almost five years. Yet while Nakano produced no poems during his two years in Toyotama Prison beginning in the spring of 1932, nor for almost two years after his release in 1934, his belief that the written word could make a difference in changing consciousness and his critique of culture were reworked into a critique of Shōwa society during the fourth stage of his changing song, in prison letters and essays written following his liberation from prison.

Between April 1932 and May 1934, Nakano Shigeharu was denied direct access to literary production, but during these two years he worked from his own everyday life, a life organized around the study of writing. During this time, as he channeled his commitment to political action into over a hundred letters to family and colleagues, Nakano's Marxist manifestos took on a new medium, but there was a continuity to his concerns as he reworked his belief in historic transformation and his focus on the commodified nature of Taishō culture to respond to the contingencies faced by the imprisoned cultural revolutionary. Nakano's earliest contact with the state had been in the form of postcards received from his father, an employee of the Meiji bureaucracy. Now, in the early years of Shōwa, his means of communication with family and friends came full cycle, as he was only allowed to share his experiences on the limited number of cards distributed by prison officials. The writer would take advantage of this form to give meaning to his daily existence, and to then move outward, from within his jail cell, to adjust his Taishō critique of the commodification of culture.

The opening line of his first prison letter, dated August 5, 1930, later rephrased in the resigned bravado of "Finally from Today," expressed no surprise. It began with the words: "At last I am to write this letter." In this letter he began the project that would continue until his release in December. Nakano used his first long-term imprisonment to assert his respect for the detail of everyday life by refusing to see his imprisonment as exclusion from a textured order or things, or from a life structured by work. After expressing deep affection for his bride of one month (adding that he thought of her as the old lady who'd been through a decade with him), he reserved matters of the heart for a future letter and went on to "business requests." He first divided his immediate needs into the three columns of clothing, food, and books, noting that he could purchase to-matoes and cakes. He sought to enrich his new routine by requesting that his wife occasionally send chocolate bars, fruit drops, and fruit to supple-ment the prison fare. But his main concern was that she send books: he needed a German-Japanese dictionary in order to read Heine, who was included on a list of European novels, works on Japanese history, and poetry. He wanted books by Murō Saisei, Shimazaki Tōson, Tolstoy, Stendahl, and others, along with Whitman's *Leaves of Grass* and a copy of the *Old Testament*. He was settling in for the duration, planning for a period of intensive work, anticipating that he would still be reading when a section of Tokutomi Sohō's *History of Japan* (covering the end of the Tokugawa era and the Meiji Restoration), then being serialized in the newspaper, appeared.[26] Nakano's request for clothing was modest. He wanted only two sets of shirts and kimono to supplement the black un-lined kimono he had worn into prison. If his wife would send him cloth-ing once a month, this would suffice because there was a laundry service in the prison; there was no rush on bedding. In the margin of this first letter, Nakano asked for one additional item. He wanted a mirror, but this was not vanity speaking. If he could not maintain a dialogue with other human beings, he would at least maintain contact with himself, as he explained in his third letter to his wife: "A mirror's a good thing, isn't it? Giving it the eye raises the spirits" (pp. 7, 16).

Six letters later, by September 1, Nakano had begun monitoring the inventory of censored periodicals available for purchase by prison in-mates. The mass media staples of *Ekonomisuto*, *Gendai*, *Fuji*, and *Asahi*, and a house organ produced by prison officials, entitled *Hito* (People), could also be read "inside."[27] Moreover, he had constructed a theory of confinement in order to challenge his isolation:

> Speaking of what goes on in society, it does not even require thought for one to see as a totally mistaken notion, the idea that jail's not the real world and that outside the jail's real and is society. It is in fact jail that is, so to speak, a con-densed version of society itself. (p. 22)

Within this new existence, domestic detail was as important as the study of political events, which must remain part conjecture. Such study, and control over his own affairs, were the only political acts allowed. Political action and the detail of everyday life had been merged, just as they blended in the same letter, which gave the exact measurements for his

---

[26] Nakano Shigeharu, *Itoshiki mono e*, 2 vols. (Tokyo: Chūō kōronsha, 1984), 1:7–8.

[27] In one attempt to circumvent censors, Nakano conjectures as to whether the two gaps in the September 1930 issue of *Gendai* were articles on Stalin and unemployment (p. 22).

zabuton or cushions and asked for the German election results while teaching his wife the names of the five different German parties. Nakano chose and catalogued the items allowed into his life and his responses to them with the same intensity that reproduced the squalid interior of the borrowed lodgings in "Farewell Before Daybreak." He wanted pickled scallions and plums, expressed joy at the receipt of new furnishings—"I am at a distance from anything like a colorful design, so the bedding pattern is really breathtaking"—and transformed quotidian activity into new sensations. The contents of one care package caused him to wonder how he had never before even heard of "chocolate raisins" (pp. 43, 24), and the desire for ham became the occasion for a half-mocking report of triumph over authority:

> The other day I had them open a can of ham with a can opener, but I opened the remaining one with my bare hands. I even surprised myself. There can't be too many who have opened a can with their hands (since there is nothing else to do it with) other than me. (p. 21)

During this first long period in jail, Nakano was compelled to discover the logic of the unwritten laws of prison culture; he teased a theoretical context from his deprivations as when, in another reference to canned food, his thought took the following course:

> Thanks for the drops. The can the drops were in was confiscated (the canned goods cans were not—if you take away the cans they can't be canned goods. Does this mean that drops can be drops even without the can?) (pp. 19–20)

The poet wields language, playing with it, creating order from the absurdities of a life dictated by the decisions of officials who set the limits of his routine, but who cannot prevent him from mocking their controls. With glee, he reports that the guards have been stunned by the number of loincloths (more than ten) sent in to him. If those with lots of money are called "money holders" (the literal translation of the term *kanemochi*, for wealthy), he puns, and those with kimonos clothing holders, then, he wonders, is he allowed to claim the title of "loincloth holder"? The language of his poetry has been retained, as has his commitment to the organization of human emotion informing his theory and practice of poetry. He lives in isolation, but he identifies with his unknown, unidentified colleagues, and their feelings: "here, from yawns, sneezes, coughs, one realizes how people can express complex emotions under certain conditions" (pp. 15–16, 20). Dialogue can be constructed from the most inarticulate of voicings.

Yet while Nakano could pretend that the "inside" was but one manifestation of a totality of social relationships, he could not deny one profound break between "inside" and "outside." He was given only minimal access to nature, and this absence haunted him. In a letter to his sister he admitted that "when one comes to a place like this, one remembers that bugger nature." Visions of flowers and scenery he had not thought of for years preoccupy him, he said. He enumerated how each stop on his way to prison—the local police stations, the courthouse, the road to the courthouse—was associated with a different flower. In the following letter, written to his wife on August 14, 1930, the prisoner shared a strong emotion evoked by a view from his cell, invoking sustenance from his own imagery:

> I think I once wrote you that I can see a small forest from this prison. The sight of that forest hit by storms was splendid beyond words. Leaves tear off and fly, branches bend in disorder, entire trees moan in agony, and while I could see their creaking it seemed as though I could hear it also. But in any case, those roots holding them up are admirable bastards. Since they hang tough under the ground when above ground, trees five hundred *kamme* in weight sway back and forth. I thought those root bastards must really be sweating.[28] (pp. 18–19)

By September 8 Nakano had become wistful: "I would like to see flowers, or trees, or a river, just for a moment." Two days later he wrote, "I can no longer see the moon. In other words it does not come out until after we have gone to bed." It was in this letter that he rewrote one of his earlier poems. Without openly alluding to "Urashimatarō," he repeated the same setting, rephrasing the experience of the intellectual unable to talk. On Sundays, he said, they could somehow hear a phonograph. It seemed to be a fine one, and the sound of both vocal and orchestral music, including Japanese folk songs, reverberated from all directions. The allusion to the music was for Nakano a counterpoint to his enforced silence and isolation: "If it's going to be that loud, I'm not the only one who must be thinking they might as well let me sing out at the top of my lungs" (pp. 32–33).

During this confinement Nakano retained his belief in the power of work and in the possibility of revolution, as revealed in words more suggestive than openly Aesopian, found in his fourteenth letter from prison. The last several lines of this letter to his wife have been censored, but the intent is clear:

> While I am here there are times when I am able to embrace feelings combining extreme courage and joy. The courage flows through my arms/legs/torso, ringing out. Then I clench my fists, wave them about, stamp my feet and up and dance in my narrow cell and facing the mirror I make faces in order to radiate the feeling. All of a sudden laughter wells up. I will leave it to your imagination to figure what sorts of special situations give rise to this highspiritedness and to

[28] One *kamme* is the equivalent of 8⅓ lbs.

the splendid feelings of happiness, but in any case I plan to write this up in a poem. Wherever we are, there is no change in that one source from which we draw courage. I hope that all can go on living with that grand strength. (p. 36)

Nakano expanded on this notion in another letter, the following month, when he expressed gratification at the news of the work of his colleagues in the revolutionary movement: "The work of those on the outside sears into my chest like the flame from a fire." He wished to elaborate, but neither content nor space on the card permitted such an act (p. 62).

Extensive writing was not allowed, but it was possible to read, and Nakano kept track of the literary world through the advertisements he found in journals and books, while demanding that friends and family also tell him about the most recent books, theater, and movies (pp. 26–100). During the six months of his incarceration his letters were filled with lists of works ordered, works not allowed past the prison authorities, and texts he was studying. Dante's *Inferno*; Charles Louis-Philippe, the literary hero alluded to in his poem "Paul Claudel"; *The Origin of Species*; Bashō's classic, *The Narrow Road to the North*; Sharaku; the Psalms; Mori Ōgai; Watsuji Tetsurō, *David Copperfield*; Tsuda Sōkichi's *Studies of the History of the Age of the Gods*; *The Red and the Black*; and dozens of other texts made their way into his letters, along with histories of premodern culture, industry, and the complete works of Heine he had used in his tongue-in-cheek advertisement in the essay on Akutagawa. The earthenware Korean doll mentioned in that same so-called advertisement also reappeared, in a letter to his wife dated November 4, 1930. He told his wife to sell the doll if she found herself strapped for funds. Referring to the essay wherein he had placed the small treasure for sale, he explained that the price, then placed in jest, was based on the cost of a work by Maillol he had seen at Mitsukoshi. He was now serious; he had given the matter much thought but had finally arrived at the determination that there was nothing else to sell (p. 66).

Nakano did, of course, have one other possession for sale—his own writing—and in his letters he voiced concern about their commodification. During this imprisonment, in June, the first collection of his novellas had been produced as volume nine of *Works of Proletarian Writers*. Now that an anthology of his writings, including novellas, poetry, essays, and literary criticism, was being edited, he feared that the reproduction of this new one-yen book could "lose its reason for existence." Aside from one story, he did not want the contents of the first work to be duplicated, even though this might mean lower revenues (p. 84).[29]

---

[29] The collection of novellas was *Tetsu no hanashi*. The anthology was *Shinei bungaku sōshō*, vol. 25: *Yoakemae no sayonara* (Kaizōsha, 1930).

Like Benjamin, Nakano recognized the double-edged nature of the mass reproduction of culture. As a critic of Taishō culture he had been able to choose the images he would have his readers understand, and he had chosen the photograph of the family of the newly arrived ambassador and the image of the mother's son sent to kill other sons for the sake of his nation. Now, during his first long stint behind bars, such images were to be chosen for him, but he wanted this form of reproduced culture to give his life meaning. His attack on photo-journalism had been premised on his respect for its power; now he merely asked for one photograph, as he acknowledged that prison authorities would not allow pictures of May Day or of any gathering of his colleagues in the movement. He conjectured that only photographs falling within the category of "family" would be allowed, and he asked his wife for such a photo (pp. 65–66).

During these first six months in Toyotama, Nakano maintained a strong sense of his purpose. In November 1930 when he received a postcard from the poet Lee Buk-man, to whom he had dedicated "Shinagawa Station in the Rain," he cannot but have seen the reversal—now he was the one addressed in exile. If the irony caused him pain, Nakano did not let on. One of his last lists of requested reading materials during this stay was organized around poetry: he wanted "all sorts of poetry collections written by Japanese," and he enumerated the poets contained in the canonization in *The Complete Works of Japanese Literature* published by Kaizōsha. Second, he wanted collections of Japanese folksongs, and again he listed several publications, including an anthology by Yanagita Kunio. He also wanted translations of foreign poetry; he was especially looking for a collection of the work of François Villon. Now he was not changing song, but the changed or various forms poetry could take through history were still of intense importance to him, as was his commitment to Marxism, even after half a year in isolation from the political activity of literary production. On December 4, six months after his imprisonment and anticipating another anniversary (for according to the old way of reckoning, he would turn thirty the following month), the poet affirmed that he was a Marxist. His words evaded the censors, possibly because they made use of tradition. He remembered that Confucius had stood firm in his position of utilitarianism at the age of thirty, as the sage had foretold; he too would stand firm, although he had staked his position in a different place: "I wish to stand upon an immutable Marxism" (pp. 57, 71–72, 89–90).

On January 25, 1931, the poet did celebrate his thirtieth birthday outside of captivity, but the hiatus lasted only about a year, before he returned to jail in April 1932. Nakano's first response to his reincarceration in Toyotama Prison appeared in his first letter. Accompanying requests for literary criticism by Kobayashi Hideo and works by Zola and Tōson was the quiet statement, "this time it will be longer than the last time" (pp. 113–14). In the next six months he resumed the task of decoding the outside world. He continued to follow popular magazines, especially the prison organ *Hito*, and attempted to maintain a hold on print culture outside by asking his wife to copy the tables of contents of all of the complete works being canonized. His intense efforts to connect with political change through his close exegesis of all words and pictures allowed him are painfully evident in his twenty-first letter, of September 14, 1932: "There seems to be a great deal going on out there but I don't understand it very well" (pp. 117, 147, 154).

Nakano did not stop studying all printed material possible, but a reading of the letters beginning in 1933 reveals that while the letters continued to be about the work of revolution, they were by then written by a revolutionary on the defense. Shortly after his thirty-first birthday, Nakano's feisty irony took on a demoralized tone when he complained how mail going in both directions had been stopped by the authorities. He reached back to a picture from his childhood, to recall an illustration in *Chūgaku sekai*. A young man facing a mirror to shave had a remnant of fine hair under his nose, and beside this image were the English words "Something is better than nothing." His only interpretation of the picture then had been that the man was proud of this beard. Only later, as a junior high school student, when he had come across the same picture, had he been able to associate the image with the meaning of the words. Now he was saying that it was better to receive mail he was not allowed to read than for nothing to arrive at all. And no matter how blackened by the censor's ink, it was better to receive such a letter than no letter at all (p. 221). That plea had been dated February 10. Nakano's letter of March 4, 1933, would express a much more profound sense of loss, for he was responding to the news that his close friend, Kobayashi Takiji, the leading writer of the Culture Movement, had been murdered by the authorities (p. 205).[30] Nakano was greatly shaken and said so. He apologized to his wife for sending her home before the end of the visiting period; he had been stunned by the report, and even now he was having trouble believing the news. For once he was at a loss for words; the letters of condolence he had written had come out stilted, formal. He was overwhelmed by images

---

[30] Kobayashi Takiji died after being tortured at the Tsukiji police station on February 20, 1933. Kobayashi's body spoke of the torture, as Shea reports: "An examination of the body revealed a hole in Kobayashi's temple 'large enough to stick one's finger in,' laceration marks around the neck and wrists (the right forefinger had been bent back and broken), a bruised black and blue area on the back and from the abdomen down to the knees, both thighs swollen and purple from internal bleeding, and over twenty needle-like punctures on the same area." Shea, *Leftwing Literature*, pp. 338–39. Sawachi Hisae treats the death as a "public murder" used or possibly even brought about to demoralize the remnants of the movement. Nakano, *Itoshiki mono e*, p. 205.

of "little, silly things" about his friend—his loud voice in argument, how he would grimace with one eye and scratch his head (pp. 229–30). Nakano grappled with his loss by attempting to experience the moment as a transition for himself and for "us," his community of colleagues on the outside: "Let us remember Kobayashi's death and study hard. Those on the outside will no doubt be busier, and their work more difficult. But it is cause for rejoicing that the work continues to progress" (p. 231).

Work was to continue. One month after the brutal death of his colleague, Nakano set forth a plan of study that would help him come to terms with modern Japanese history, through the use of the *enpon* canon. He wanted to read the Japanese authors of Meiji, Taishō, and Shōwa Japan, the major works of foreign works of foreign authors translated into Japanse, and the anthologized "studies of Japanese, literature, world literature, and Meiji literature (p. 259).

Since the five letters Nakano wrote between June 8 and June 15 were lost, his response to the sensational press coverage of the public disavowal of the party by the two party leaders Sano Manabu and Nabeyama Sadachika on June 10 cannot be read. Nor did Nakano discuss the ensuing defections by Communist Party members, but his letter to his wife of March 13, 1934, reveals that he had not abandoned his efforts to explain how journalism joined politics to culture. His Taishō critique of the media had been premised on his ambivalent stance toward a powerful medium: The capitalist press produced stories and pictures for profit, but the reader was free to construct interpretations not explicit in the captions. Moreover, when Nakano had written "Paul Claudel" and "Picture of the Newly Arrived Ambassador to the City," an alternative press could use the same weapons to propagate its views, and even the bourgeois press was open to publishing the views of Nakano and like-minded revolutionaries. Nakano's statement on the Shōwa press in 1933 responded to a very different set of circumstances. There was now no pretense at freedom, nor was there any truth other than the truth of demagoguery found in the mass media. The graphic but ultimately benign sen-sen metaphor of a pleasant placebo no longer held; the stories forced on the public were made of stronger stuff. On March 13 he warned his wife to read critically and in the process referred obliquely to the press coverage of the fate of their political movement (pp. 268–69, 360).[31]

There was a communion here with the young man who had produced such angry verse about the power of the press, but there was also a profound break. In 1933, Nakano could no longer talk about controlling the press by subverting it to his own end either through the production of

[31] On the apostasy and the ensuing "defection" of over one-third of convicted Communists in prison, see Beckmann and Okubo, *The Japanese Communist Party*, pp. 245–53.

alternative articles or through an analysis of the political events buried
between the lines, as he had earlier in his prison stay. By the early spring
of 1934 both his psychological and physical resistance were down; he was
hospitalized in the prison infirmary with a severe case of tuberculosis.
One of the final prison letters, dated May 9, reveals that after twenty-five
months of perseverance, he set aside his self-designated prison work: "I
am trying not to read too much." In a second reference to the earthenware
figure, he suggested, "If that Korean doll can be used for money I guess
it's all right for you to sell it some time. But I guess you had better check
to see whether it can really be used for money (p. 391). The satirical quality of his fantasized advertisement and the optimism in his earlier letter
were gone, replaced by a new and uncharacteristic lack of certitude; this
was an acknowledgment of defeat. Less than three weeks later, Nakano
Shigeharu stood in court to state that he had been a member of the Japanese Communist Party and to promise that he would remove himself from
the Communist movement. The following day he was released from captivity.

Much has been made of Nakano's *tenkō*, or disavowal of political be-
liefs, and most of the analysis is premised on the autobiographical factic-
ity of his five works of fiction ostensibly dealing with this experience.[32]
Undoubtedly, Nakano offers clues as to his motivation for a public break
with his commitment of a decade. For example, the psychodynamics of a
son's reunion with his father are rendered in painfully poignant detail in
House in the Village. But what is relevant to the study of Nakano's changing song in the early years of Shōwa is one moment in the closing dialogue
between the hero of this work and his father. The old farmer has confronted his son to ask what he now plans to do with his life. He tells the
younger man that if he continues to write now, after his disavowal, everything he has written will be rendered meaningless: "If you want what
you have written until now to remain alive throw away your pen. Whatever you write will be no good. You'll only kill what you've written." He
urges his son to regain his health and to take up farming. When the son
replies, after tormented consideration, he follows Nakano's actions: "I

---

[32] Mitsuta Ikuo discusses all five *tenkō shosetsu*: *Daiissho* (1/35), *Suzuki. Miyakoyama.
Yasoshima* (4/35), *Hitotsu no chiisai kiroku* (1/36), and the contrasting *Mura no ie* (5/35)
and *Shōsetsu no kakenu Shōsetsuka* (1/36) in his essay "Tenkō shōsetsu gobusaku wo me-
gutte," in Mitsuta, *Nakano Shigeharuron*, pp. 175–204. Tsurumi Kazuko uses Yoshimoto
Ryūmei's essay "Tenko ron" to view Nakano as conflicted. She conflates the author and the
hero of *Mura no ie*, treating them both as elitist intellectuals in conflict with the popular
values personified in the figure of the hero's father. Tsurumi Kazuko, *Social Change and the
Individual: Japan Before and After Defeat in World War* II (Princeton: Princeton University
Press, 1970), pp. 60–64. For the most comprehensive overview of the scholarship on Nakano's *tenkō* see the extensive commentary in part 4 of Sugino Yōkichi, *Nakano Shigeharu
no kenkyū* (Kasama shōin, 1979), pp. 213–454.

understand very well, but I want to go on writing after all."[33] Here the identification of fiction with fact is warranted, for Nakano did go on writing after his release from Toyotama Prison. Within a month of his release, while home in his native village, he was working on a new translation of Lenin's letters to Gorky.[34] While even this act alone suffices to indicate that his apostasy had not deprived the writer of his commitment to revolutionary culture or even to communism, a series of essays appearing in the press even more openly resumed the critique of the state he had been developing in 1931 and 1932, before his two years in prison. Rather than suggest that Nakano's *tenkō* was a lie—a means to manipulate officials— the distinction made by Nakano's life-long comrade, Ishidō Kiyotomo, early leader and librarian of the Shinjinkai, should be accepted. Ishidō explained that his own so-called apostasy had been a turning away from the Japanese Communist Party, but not from his adherence to Marxism.[35] The same distinction can be made for Nakano—in 1934 he turned away from the institution but not the ideology. He remained an activist, revolutionary critic of the state.

Six months after Nakano had signed a piece of paper renouncing allegiance to the Japanese Communist Party, "Tashō no kairyō" (A few reforms)[36] appeared in the November 1934 issue of *Kaizō*. On the surface, this was a modest essay about everyday life in prison. (This may be why it is never mentioned in the numerous attempts to come to terms with Nakano's *tenkō*.) It is based on the author's own experience as he explained in his understated opening:

> In 1930 and from 1932 until 1934, for a total of 29 months, the last month of which was spent in an infirmary, I lived in the Toyotama Prison as an accused prisoner. Based on my one experience there I would like to write about one aspect of reform regarding the treatment of the accused in the prisons. (p. 5)

There is no thunder in these words; there is no revolutionary passion. The author says that he will leave the criticisms and calls for overhaul of the system to others. He is merely asking for small changes which should be possible given the present framework of the system, but a closer listening to the language reveals this low-key piece of journalism to be a highly ironic attack on state officials who have destroyed Nakano's organization, incarcerated him and his colleagues, and murdered Kobayashi Takiji. In his even-handed attention to quotidian detail, Nakano reveals to his readers the institutionalization of a system of repression.

Nakano shares intimate aspects of his prison experience, including the

[33] Nakano, *Mura no ie*, p. 88.
[34] This was published as *Reenin no Gorikii e no tegami* (Iwanami bunko, 1935).
[35] Interview with Ishidō Kiyotomo, Tokyo, August 30, 1986.
[36] Nakano, "Tashō no kairyō," *NSZ* 10:5–18 [*Kaizō* 11/34].

insight first offered in one of his letters: "Because the accused is cut off from the world, in jail the outside is called 'society.' " He elaborates as to how, as a prisoner committed to the work of reading, he had received mixed messages, which he passes on to his readers. For example, prisoners were allowed to read individual works by Tolstoy, but a one-volume anthology of Tolstoy's works had been forbidden. Moreover, the official house organ, *Hito*, had quoted Victor Hugo's hero, Jean Valjean, yet *Les Misérables* was on the list of proscribed books. Another segment protests that the quality of the food, including New Year's treats, declined between 1933 and 1934. In addition, the ends of the pickled radish had disappeared from the breakfast table. Here the writer issues a demand: he would like the pickles returned, and the bits of sand, stones, and tin removed from the food. In a brief discourse on hygiene, requesting plumbing, Nakano asks whether any other Tokyo community housing eight hundred people went without such amenities. His request for better medical facilities is couched within statistics explaining the paucity of doctors, but in fact revealing the extent of incarceration: there are, he notes, 155 jails in the country; including enforced labor and children, there are 53,373 people behind bars (p. 14).

Nakano took on the role of intrigued outsider in order to analyze the rapid ideological and cultural transformation which he had begun to chronicle in the early 1930s. He explained his position in an essay entitled "Kiroku no omoshirosa" (The fun of documenting),[37] published in the July 1935 issue of *Shinchō*. The function of history was to capture the past, but the journalistic document or record could grasp the present through the objective truth (p. 262).[38] And indeed, without underlining his topics, or his motives, in a series of such documents published in 1934 and 1935 he implied a break between Taishō society and the Shōwa state. Two decades later, Fujita Shōzō, theorist of the modern Japanese state, would adopt the evocative term *zuruzurubettari* from Fukumoto Kazuo to describe how within "Emperor System Society" there was no mediation between public and private, the social and nature, the whole and the individual, the state and the civil. Somehow—*zuruzurubettari*—the whole was stuck together. In the mid-1930s, rather than take on the subaltern function of accepting the change as ahistorical, Nakano attempted to explain the *somehow* of *zuruzurubettari*, wherein the state came to subsume society during the Shōwa era. He did this by exposing a new ideology of "Japaneseness" and those responsible for its mobilization and enforcement.[39]

[37] Nakano, "Kiroku no omoshirosa," *NSZ* 10:261–68 [*Shinchō* 7/35].
[38] Taking a swipe at Nishida Kitarō, Nakano claims that as a true Marxist, he premises his thoughts and actions on what is objective and necessary.
[39] Fujita Shōzō, "Shōwa hachinen wo chūshin to suru tenkō no jōkyō," in *Tenkō*, ed. Tsurumi, 1:35.

Nakano's most concerted attack on the new emphasis on being Japanese appeared in 1934, in "Fūshū no kangaekata" (Thinking about customs).[40] Therein, the author denied the binary conceptualization which asserted that Japanese customs could and should replace Western practices. He based his discussion on one observation of many regarding changes in village life: children's clothing had changed since his childhood, and since his imprisonment. But he was adamant that just because rubber shoes had replaced clogs, this did not mean that village practices were being "Westernized" any more than the replacement of oil lamps by electricity, the sword by the airplane, hand weaving by the textile factory, or annual tribute by taxes signified "Westernization." As an observer of social change, however, he was not unaware that a uniquely Japanese culture was being created, not by coercion, but through a series of social organizations and organizers dedicated to the construction of the false opposition between East and West, ignoring real change of a universal nature (pp. 36–38).

According to Nakano, all modes of cultural expression were being mobilized to proclaim the unique nature of everyday Japanese life. This is how he described the creation of this extended hegemony:

> Recently a new force is working on changes in Japanese customs which are based on a Japanese reality. A certain type priest, military man, and educator, one after the other is circulating through the agricultural organization and the village offices, and the elementary schools, to give lectures. Their one major argument is their attack on the change in customs and manners. (p. 37)

Here is the Japanese equivalent of Gramsci's association of church, trade unions, and schools as mediating institutions working for a dominant social group. Another culprit in the dissemination of an ideology of Japaneseness is the press—in the media, which offers him little information on world events, Nakano finds the same themes repeated. The celebration of native customs along with an ancient familism (kazokushugi) in the media can even incorporate Hitler:

> For example the real situation in Germany is just not clear. As soon as it is known that Hitler has taken power a certain type of magazine treats him like a hero, and in great festive spirit runs a serial on the story of his life. Small-time publishers rush to sell Hitler biographies. The ads for these things even make Hitler seem like a variation on yamatodamashi.[41] (pp. 45–46)

[40] Nakano, "Fūshū no kangaekata," NSZ 10:36–41. It is not clear when or where this essay first appeared.

[41] Nakano maps out how the new control of culture works: those who control the dissemination of information have access to information. In other words, organizations like Mitsui, Mitsubishi, and the Industrial Club have fine research centers, and the South Manchurian Railway, along with the Foreign and Home offices, have efficient research facilities. The

While Nakano gave credit to the press, he recognized that those in power realized that the media alone could not maintain order. The omnipresence of the police official hinted at the physical coercion the state could wield, should its ability to create consent weaken or, in Gramsci's terms, should there be a crisis of hegemony. In the essay "Keisatsukan ni tsuite" (On the police official), published in the March 1935 issue of *Shakai hyōron*, he picked up on the theme of "In Front of the Policebox" as he traced the completion of the transition into the Shōwa era. After noting that the press was filled, on a daily basis, with articles on the private, everyday life of the police, he blamed the Japanese literary tradition for not giving any space to this entity who mediated the relationship of the Japanese citizenry to state structures. Nakano then commenced to redress this wrong through a semantic run-through of all of the theoretical and historical meanings implied by the synonyms for police officer, encompassing all variations on the Japanese colloquial equivalents for "fuzz," "cop," or "heat" (p. 169).[42] His stated aim was to give credit where credit was due—to show the close relationship between police officials and the everyday life of the people. He wished, he said, to familiarize his readers with the police officer because the state was doing the same.[43] According to Nakano, what he was witnessing was the popularizing of the policeman. He found it absurd that the policeman was receiving such homage at a time when he was far from the most effective urban worker, as proven by the fact that theft had joined suicide as the leading speciality (*meibutsu*) of Tokyo. But something else was going on: Civilians who nabbed pick-pockets were being praised in the press, and similar headlines announced the policing of cafes, theaters, and dance halls by teachers organized to be on the lookout for errant young female students. Nakano's conception was, in other words, twofold. At the same time as the policeman was being made more familiar or populist, through human interest stories in the press another shift was taking place. If, on the one hand, the popularizing of the police (*keisatsu no minshūka*) was going on, on the other hand, he and his contemporaries were witnessing a process whereby the populace was being made into police (*minshū no keisatsuka*) (pp. 172–73, 175).

---

complete, unexpurgated version of a speech by Mao Zedong circulates within such circles; to the rest of society such a text appears as a curio—it is a thing of the past.

[42] Nakano, "Keisatsukan ni tsuite." *NSZ* 10:169–76 [*Shakai hyōron* 3/25]. The terms, expressing varying degrees of politesse and of the police hierarchy, were: *keisatsukan, keikan, junsa, omawari, omawarisan, shochō, buchō san, keiji, supai, deikei, deka, danna, dannasan.*

[43] Nakano continued his task of educating, by poking fun at songs commissioned by the Home Ministry, which had had the poet Kitahara Hakuchō compose "Dai Nihon keisatsu no uta" (The police song of Great Japan) and "Keisatsu kōshinkyoku" (The police march). Nakano, "Hiroi seken," *NSZ* 10:288–98 [*Shimpo* 7/35].

The press and the police bureaucracy were not the only target of Nakano's ire as he lambasted the ideology of Japaneseness being disseminated. Like Gramsci, he reserved the right to criticize scholars engaged in the process of creating consensus.[44] In a characteristically tongue-in-cheek assault in the January 1935 issue of *Sarariiman*, entitled "Nihon kenkyū" (Japanese studies),[45] Nakano pointed a finger at the Japanese intelligentsia by welcoming the recent development of interest in the study of Japan. By the end of the brief article he had made his agenda clear—he meant to put this newfound interest in the classics in a political and cultural context. This philosophical and sociological interest, he explained, corresponded to the need for the ruling powers to assert the unique place of Japan as the legitimate economic and political power in Korea, Taiwan, the South Pacific, Manchuria, and elsewhere. This revived fervor for the classics also had to be put in the context of new control at home, for the reappearance of the classics corresponded with the disappearance of banned publications and censored portions of texts (p. 58).

In 1936 Nakano Shigeharu proved without a doubt that he had not abandoned his Marxism, when he applied his resistance to the ideology of Japaneseness to the production of one of the most Marxist of his manifestos. This was "Kawase sōba"(The rate of exchange),[46] the very last of his political poems. More than his translation of Lenin's letters to Gorky, and much more than his series of newspaper articles or fictional confessions produced in 1935 and 1936, this poem publicly announced Nakano's continuing commitment to challenging the manipulation of cultural traditions through the production of revolutionary writing. If the translations of Lenin had shown that after his formal denial of association with the Japanese Communist Party Nakano was still committed to the ideals of the man who had created the theory of the place of the party for twentieth-century Marxists, this biting attack on state ideology proved that the poet's alleged apostasy in no way reflected an abandonment of his Marxist critique of the manipulation of culture and history for political ends. Nor had he abandoned his firm belief in the potential in poetry for creating a political, cultural alternative.

In this poem, Nakano Shigeharu was working with some of the most basic presumptions about political economy published in *Capital*, but most of all, "The Rate of Exchange" is about the power of ideology.

---

[44] Gramsci, *Prison Notebooks*, p. 12. Again, Joll clarifies: It is the intelligentsia who "provide philosophy and ideology for the masses and who enable the ruling class to exercise its 'hegemony' by supplying the system of belief accepted by ordinary people so that they do not question the actions of their rulers." Joll, *Antonio Gramsci*, p. 120.

[45] Nakano, "Nihon kenkyū," *NSZ* 10:57–58 [*Sarariiman* 1/35].

[46] Nakano, "Kawase sōba," *NSZ* 1:532–33 [*Chūō kōron* 4/36].

Whether or not Nakano was aware at the time that he was expressing themes from Marx's exploration of the institutionalization of consciousness, the poem defends an argument set forth in *The German Ideology*, one of the last works by Marx to be translated into Japanese. By 1936, *The German Ideology* had been available in Japan for several years. It is an unnamed source for Nakano's last Marxist manifesto in the form of a poem, for while "The Rate of Exchange" placed money in history just as "The Beach at Kitami" had historicized both nature and labor in nature, it was also an indictment of ideologues who served to reproduce the ruling ideas of the era—ideas about nationhood and the Japanese nation in particular. This aspect of the poem did not go unnoticed by the censors before it first appeared in the April 1936 issue of Chūō kōron, as made evident in the deleted phrasings which are italicized in the following translation:

THE RATE OF EXCHANGE

If Japan is
That different from all of the countries of the world
Even if Nihonjin
Is read as NIPPONJIN   The sound sounds good
If we're that different from all the foreigners in the world
Tell me how you tell yourself apart

If one yen is not two marks
And it happens that it's not a half a mark
If on the whole the yen is not a mark and not a pound or a ruble or any of
    these things
What is this darn thing called one yen

I know   The professors taught me
Said some long ago know-nothing barbarian uncivilized folks
Used some sort of clamshells for their cash
And now even the professors
Don't even know how many yen's a shell.

On the front *the chrysanthemum's 16 petals*
On the back *rippling waves and cherry blossom flowers*
This is then my own 10 sen
And thrown into the bargain a hole like they didn't used to have

And by the way why do the mails
If all foreigners are unrefined
Putting on the front of their coins kings and presidents and sickles and
    hammers
Arrive at these far destinations

Why do "cheap and quality Japanese goods"
Have their way in foreign markets?

Soon all sorts of geniuses
Trying to make theory from all this
Will be suffering for sure
But that is fruitless effort
They've got to learn the exchange rate
And I for one   Even if you don't know
I know the international clamshell exchange

In his Taishō writings Nakano had talked about cultural commodities, and this poem was also in part about money, which Marx had termed "one privileged commodity." In the third chapter of volume 1 of *Capital*, Marx had solved the riddle posed by money, by discussing its function, its naming, its production as coin, and the process whereby its exchange is universalized, before turning to his discussion of the transformation of money into capital.[47] In contrast, in "The Rate of Exchange" the Marxist poet plays dumb. He has neither a theory nor any theoretical questions addressing the historic production of money or its reproduction as money or capital. Adopting an almost child-like voice, he accepts the differences between nations and their currencies. But in the process of asking his own riddle, "What is this darn thing called one yen," he calls into question the naturalizing of such socially created distinctions. In his ostensible innocence, he is not aware of Marx's discussion of the naming of money which is the "value shape" taken on by human labor, although in the chapter on money in *Capital* Marx does provide one answer to Nakano's riddle by revealing that a yen *may* be no different from a mark or pound or a ruble. According to Marx, such cabalistic signs as yen, mark, pound, or ruble serve only to mystify.[48] Marx goes on to narrate how coining is "the business of the state," which is responsible for its minting and naming, before it enters into the international market of commodities along with other commodities it serves to represent.[49]

Marx's theory of the symbolism of currency is the premise behind Nakano's supposed search; he already has his answers. First of all, he realizes that the symbols on the currency—the kings and presidents, sickles and hammers—are no different from the chrysanthemum petals and the cherry blossoms. They are indeed cabalistic signs, but they can be de-

[47] Marx, *Capital* 1:94–145.
[48] Ibid., pp. 100–101.
[49] In the words of Marx: "The different national uniforms worn at home by gold and silver as coins, and doffed again in the market of the world, indicate the separation between the internal or national spheres of the circulation of commodities, and their universal sphere." Ibid., pp. 124–25.

coded fairly easily as parts of an ideology separating people from people. He appears facetious as he offers his own cabalistic resolution to his queries: He knows the "international clamshell exchange." But something very serious is implied by the naming of this whimsical institution, as recognized even by the censor who could only separate out the most obvious allusion to the Japanese state from Nakano's riddle. Nakano is referring to the existence of an international money exchange as part of a capitalist world market, the integrated nature of which is hidden by the mythologizing of ideologues, including scholars working for the state to reproduce an ideology that contends that Japan is "different from all of the countries of the world." Nakano's last Marxist manifesto in verse is not then really about money, its varying form, or its history past or present within a world market. He is, of course, placing the world market within history, just as Marx did in *The German Ideology*, but he is more concerned with the production of a nationalist ideology than with the circulation of money. Indirectly, by circumventing the state control of culture, he is restating Marx's view of the naturalization and nationalization of consciousness: "The ideas of the ruling class are in every epoch the ruling ideas: i.e., the class which is the ruling *material* force of society is at the same time its ruling *intellectual* force."[50] He is much more blunt about the "producers of ideas." These are the scholars—the professors who are quoted in the press. They have written the history, and they are the theorists or "geniuses" who explicate the present, telling him that Japan is different. This is the group Nakano addresses when he demands to know how they tell themselves apart; they are the ideologues who according to Marx "turn everything upside down" by constructing and universalizing ideas that serve their interests. They are convincing Nakano's contemporaries to believe in national differences when in fact, as stated in *The German Ideology*, "all civilized nations and every individual member of them [are] dependent for the satisfaction of their wants on the whole world."[51]

During the Taishō era, the nature of Japanese capitalist society had led Nakano to talk in terms similar to the language of his twentieth-century contemporaries Lukács, Bakhtin, and Benjamin. But now, the revolutionary consciousness of a proletariat was not at stake, a multiplicity of voices was no longer allowed to speak, and the glitter of the commodity was no longer an issue in an era when the reproduction of culture was increasingly controlled by a single source, which was generating ideology. In 1935, one year before "The Rate of Exchange" appeared, the Marxist theorist Tosaka Jun had written his powerful analysis, *Nihon ideorogii*

[50] Marx and Engels, *The German Ideology*, pp. 67–68.
[51] Ibid., pp. 68, 81, 101.

ron (On the Japanese ideology), self-consciously adopting the title from *The German Ideology*.[52] Whether Nakano had Tosaka's work in mind when he wrote his last Marxist manifesto in verse the reader cannot know, but the verse is clear proof that after the Taishō era, after his ostensible apostasy, Nakano Shigeharu remained a Marxist, concerned with the ideas he had made central to "The Beach at Kitami." He no longer belonged to a political movement, but he was just as committed to a materialist vision that placed his own society in a history of men producing their own material needs, and to an awareness of the historic dialectic whereby in Japanese history men and women were constantly transforming their surroundings and themselves. By writing this poem in defiance of the authorities who had forced him to renounce his political past as a Communist Party member, he was asserting his continuing adherence to a Marxist belief in the inseparability of culture from politics. Publication of "The Rate of Exchange" was an act of resistance that denied that the political realm had swallowed up culture in its entirety. He had been deprived of organized political activity, and cornered within an everyday life that was increasingly organized in the hegemonic interests of the state which would push its citizens into total war within one year, Nakano was still demanding that culture change politics. Two of the three columns that had organized the complex narrative of his life since his days as a university activist had all but been obliterated. He had a severely delimited everyday life, and political activism was outlawed, but he held onto the third arena, of literary production. He refused to end his work as a producer of literature, or to give up the insight gained from the songs of the factory girls—new lyrics constantly had to be produced to express and contest the changed nature of labor.

Nakano never said that "The Rate of Exchange" was his last Marxist or even his final revolutionary poem, nor would he ever acknowledge that it would be one of his last poems ever.[53] Why did the poetry stop? There is no way of determining why, although clearly, for the prewar era, there was a correlation between revolutionary political activity and the production of poetry. What is important in the context of Nakano's Taishō and early Shōwa consciousness is that as a Marxist, he was able to put his political commitment into a series of manifestos in verse and prose form for an entire decade. As evidenced in his prison letters, during the 1920s and into the 1930s, Nakano identified himself as a poet; this was his identity as a revolutionary. And when the possibility of revolution was closed off, the poems did end, although the manifestos did not; the song of re-

---

[52] Tosaka Jun, *Nihon ideorogii ron* (Iwanami bunko, 1977), p. 7.

[53] On more than one occasion, Nakano conjectured that he might begin to write poetry again. See, for example, Kitagawa, *Nakano Shigeharu*, p. 199.

sistance had merely changed in content and form. Nakano came closest to admitting that the production of poetry belonged to one discrete moment in his life in a short story appearing several months before "The Rate of Exchange." In a brief passage premised on his characteristic autobiographical blend of fact within fiction, he chronicled his move from the production of poetry to a concentration on essays for the canon, in a passage that in effect denied the publication of editions of his poetry in 1931 and 1936. The short fiction was entitled "Shōsetsu no kakenu shōsetsuka" (A novelist who cannot write novels),[54] but in the passage the author indicated that the story might really be about a poet who was no longer able to produce poetry:

> He got by more or less as a novelist. Used to be a poet. Wrote some poems which were kind of good, stuck in people's minds, but after that when he took up writing essays he could no longer do the poems. When he wrote one once in a while it looked like badly done prose and wasn't interesting. His essays were essays, but parts of them read like poems and they were not interesting. Then finally he'd become a novelist, without even having published a volume of poetry.[55]

[54] Nakano, "Shōsetsu no kakenu shōsetsuka," NSZ 2:133–52 [Kaizō 1/36].
[55] Ibid., p. 134.

Marxism Addresses the Modern

MODERN MARXISM IN SONG

On December 15, 1937, the Home Ministry issued an order forbidding Nakano Shigeharu, Tosaka Jun, and a third surviving Marxist writer, Miyamoto Yuriko, from putting pen to paper. By the following December Nakano had begun writing again. And neither the arrest of Tosaka on November 29, 1938, of Miyamoto on December 8, 1941, nor his wife's four-month incarceration beginning on August 19, 1940, would stop Nakano from continuing to produce. On December 8, 1941, he escaped the new wave of nationwide arrests accompanying Pearl Harbor because he happened to be away from Tokyo, but ultimately he could not circumvent control; his activities were monitored by police authorities until he was drafted in January 1944. On February 2, 1944, Nakano Shigeharu's head was shaven—the process of turning him into one of the military men he had written about in "The Photograph in the Newspapers" and "On Soldiers" had begun. In June 1945 he entered the 186th unit of the Eastern section of Setagaya as a soldier of the second rank and was shipped to a small village in Nagano Prefecture, but Nakano never saw battle. He was discharged on September 4, and as early as October 18 he appeared at a gathering of literary figures sponsored by the publisher of the popular magazine, *Bungei shunjū*. Appearing with Nakano were such survivors from Taishō and early Shōwa as luminaries from the world of mass journalism Kikuchi Kan, Nii Itaru, Miyamoto Yuriko, and Sata Ineko.

In November, the Japanese Communist Party was reconstituted and Nakano was chosen as a member of the committee of writers who would organize the New Japanese Literature Association (Shin Nihon Bungakukai). With the establishment of the association in December, he was picked for the central committee of the organization that would reformulate the program of the Proletarian Literature Movement of the 1920s and early 1930s. The battle to produce political literature had resumed, but in one important sense Nakano's changing song had ended, for his politics was no longer put into poetry. From 1937 through 1941 he had published five poems, and the three poems of the immediate postwar period were followed by the lyrics of two school songs for his hometown of Maruoka-machi. Before the war, Nakano had proudly repeated the criticism of a peer: "even when the guy writes an essay he's speaking in verse."[1] In the years after the war, Nakano would tell friends that he planned to take up his poetry again, but he never did; nor did he explain why.

Just as this book has asked why and how Nakano adopted Marxism to express his politics by reading his poetry, covering his essays, and touching on his fiction, a close reading of his postpoetry writings should uncover how his Communist politics reworked his Marxism in his later years. Such an endeavor might also reveal why the poetry ended in the early 1930s. His postwar autobiographical fiction cannot be projected back onto his everyday life to explain his early years as a Marxist, and neither can his early Marxist writings illuminate his later work. Following from the principle that texts produced during the same era must be used in a historical interrogation of that time, it is only appropriate to conclude this discussion of Nakano Shigeharu's changing song in the 1920s and earliest years of the Shōwa imperial reign by reconsidering the works reviewed herein alongside work produced by other Marxists of the era. Such a rereading can suggest answers to the two questions raised at the outset: "Why Marxism?" and "How to interpret the Taishō years?"

What was the appeal of Marxism? A reading of one of Nakano's earliest poems, written by a young composer of haiku who has not yet gone to the big city, does not give a direct answer, but it tells how much his consciousness did change after his discovery of Marxism. In the poem there are no conflicting voices, for "Daidō no hitobito" (The people on the road)[2] is not about relationships under capitalism. There is neither master nor slave, for the poet was neither Marxist nor Hegelian. Nor is there a fixed public space, for the poet treats of a time preceding the establishment of a national order, or a technology to communicate boundaries. The poem is as though told by a story-teller; it is composed of the stuff of memory. Its lies are not bound up in the mythology or reproductive technology of nation building; they are but the stories of traveling peddlers of dreams:

THE PEOPLE ON THE ROAD

They came from nowhere really
The man in threadbare crested jacket did his drawings from the
    Takashimaeki school of physiognomy
Opening his paper he drew an evil face and showed it to the people
He went on drawing one profile from top on down

---

[1] Nakano, "Geijutsu ni seijiteki kachi nante mono wa nai," *NSZ* 9:274 [*Shinchō* 10/29].
[2] Nakano, "Daidō no hitobito," *NSZ* 1:3–6 [The original version of this poem, which has not been preserved, probably appeared in 1923 in a provincial newspaper published in Kanazawa, according to the editors of Nakano's collected works, *NSZ* 1:549].

But the eyebrows and the eyes and the mouth
He went on drawing like they'd seen it from the front
He made a thin bound volume flutter
Saying that in them the fates of a lifetime large and small were writ
If you read it no doubt of success he said
Yet he who was selling it had on a threadbare crest
The young man in square student's hat and skirt yelled to be allowed to sell
  his medicine
He showed what the medicine made by the doctors is really like
He showed a piece of paper saying this is the certified amount
From the group surrounding him hands reached out to buy it
Under the row of cherry trees the man with square-cut hair who had spread
  a blanket began his magic
At the end he began to push spikes into his nostrils
Putting the long, shining, 5-inch spikes into his nostrils and then banging on
  them with his clog
Little by little the spokes went inside
After he had pushed them in he made some bubbling noises for them
When that dangerous art began the lookers were standing
But when that sort of art ended the lookers began to walk
Most without paying even change of one sen, began to walk silently

At the four corners there was a monkey-trainer
Beating a small drum sometimes he pulled the monkey close to him
Flicking the potato skins thrown by the lookers, the monkey ate them
  skillfully
—Today's the middle day of All Soul's Day[3]
Take in all you can
The monkey-trainer shouted without looking at the monkey's face

They came from nowhere really
Countless, they came
Whetstones
Safety razors
Golden rings
Sealskins palm seeds
Night is night and Korean candy
And then the lottery
They all of them had the blackest of face
They all had gold false teeth
Some wore lined clothing in the middle of the heat
Some stood in hemp sandals inside the wintry wind

---

[3] The festival referred to is Higan.

> They came from nowhere really
> And where I wonder did they return to stealthily
>
> It was not in day not in night they came
> And shooting pistols and yelling in loud voices they gathered up the people
> You cannot come inside here they said drawing circles with a stick
> They blabbered constantly continuing to talk
> When the lookers would laugh and look at them
> When without stuttering they could continue to talk
> That time was like their own happiest of time
> When the lookers had dispersed
> When the gathering of lookers was not going well
> They would talk to the man next to them in fact someone just like them
> Those few words
> Resounded sadly in the ears of the passing people
>
> Cold lands Hot lands
> Those few words which had gone round the provinces
> Talked themselves hoarse, sadly in the wind of the seasons and then
>   disappeared

This large road, unlike the highway in front of Nakano's policebox, moves through a dispersed provincial space transporting a marketplace. There is no national space; there are only regions defined in terms of their climate—the various lands of a story-teller. The boundaries within the market are tentative and temporary, drawn in the dirt by the individual, unallied hawkers, as they respond to the movement of the spectators. This is not the site of Bakhtin's fairground where "all 'languages' were masks and where no language could claim to be an authentic, incontestable face,"[4] for there are no voices to prefigure one unified, national discourse. In fact, there is no speech at all. The routines of the charlatans are paraphrased by the poet, and the crowd remains inchoate, voiceless, depicted only in silent movement as hands reach forward, or as they walk to another spot within the passing bazaar when the violence of the magician does not meet the demands of their desires. This is a festival day, but the time and place of the event are not predictable, because the vendors come from "nowhere really," at all hours of the day and night, to make their promises. Nakano did not answer the poem's question as to the undisclosed destination of the people of the road. Instead, he allowed them to fade away with their words.

Nakano composed "The People on the Road" before his study of Marxism, and the culture he composed was as removed from history as the lonely youth appearing in the earliest poems of the 1920s. He thus

---

[4] Bakhtin, *Dostoyevsky's Poetics*, p. 273.

could not explain where the people came from or where they were going. In stark contrast, the Marxist changing song of Nakano was premised on a firm conviction about destination and a commitment to the understanding of the process of the reworking of tradition aimed at either its reproduction or its revolutionary reconstruction. Why did Nakano make this transition—why Marxism? In the chapters tracing Nakano's changing song I have stayed away from any extended and ultimately fruitless investigation into intentionality, but instead have worked to define how he was a Marxist. A fuller answer to the question why can be sought where this interpretation began, in the library of Nakano Shigeharu.

A mere corner of Nakano Shigeharu's study is preserved in the photograph of the artist in the alcove, but his entire library is open to the reader who visits his hometown of Maruoka in Fukui Prefecture. Hundreds of books are arranged in a large room of shelves, and to look through this archive, made up of the modern and premodern classics of Japan and the West and all of the editions of Nakano's own writing, is to go beyond the analysis of titles encouraged by previous readings of the photograph of the artist in his study. Most of the books are annotated in Nakano's own hand, in brush and ink or in pen. To look through these works is to gain an understanding of not only where but how Nakano learned, for the cultural figures with whom he worked during his decade of changing song all have their place in this room. The collected works of his earliest mentor, Mūro Saisei, are shelved along with the 1926 edition of the works of Nagai Kafū, and ink marks in an index to the works of Akutagawa Ryūnosuke show that Nakano studied Akutagawa as closely as Akutagawa is said to have read Nakano's poetry. There are four editions of *The Sad History of the Woman Factory Hand*, including the 1925 edition which Nakano says caused him to turn his poetry to political ends. The student who wishes to trace influence in a writer's production can follow Nakano's markings in the margins of songs appended to these works.[5]

An edition of the works of Ishikawa Takuboku,[6] the poet Nakano sought to reclaim after his discovery of Marxism, stands out on one shelf. It does not belong to a set of *enpon*, the one-yen books made popular during the early 1930s when the categories of the Marxist and Modern canons were established in the series on great works. Nor does it belong to the postwar series of *zenshū*, "the complete works" of all authors placed in the archives of Japanese literature along the lines established during the 1930s (although Nakano did own three multivolume sets of the complete works of Takuboku).[7] This is a large, leather-bound volume

---

[5] Hosoi Wakizō, *Jokō aishi* (Kaizōsha, 1925, 1929, 1939). Nakano also owned two copies of the 1967 Iwanami edition.

[6] *Ishikawa Takuboku zenshū* (Kaizōsha, 1931).

[7] *Ishikawa Takuboku zenshū*, 16 vols. (Iwanami shoten, 1961); *Ishikawa Takuboku zenshū*, 8 vols. (Chikuma shobō, 1967–1968; 1978–1979).

published in 1931 and studied at length by Nakano, as is clear from the strokes of his brush. The markings in the margins of select works of poetry and passages of prose are Nakano Shigeharu's Taishō concerns. He has marked several of Takuboku's writings about the city, including the poems "Tokyo," "Fear of the Summer Streets," a poem about a mounted policeman in a city crowd, and a poem with the heading of "Untitled," which opens with an exclamatory awe at the number and variety of rooftops within the poet's vision and contains the following lines: "When I first came to the big city / and saw this scenery / And heard these noises / The heart of the weak countryboy trembled."[8] Of course, it is not clear when Nakano studied these pages, but the signature and date of November 1931 in ink on the cover would indicate that he read these works and Takuboku's advocacy of poetry, "Poems to Be Eaten,"[9] immediately before his long imprisonment. Nakano's markings constitute a defense for poetry within Takuboku's own defense. His ink emphasizes such passages as the Meiji poet's declaration that poetry is necessary for everyday life, along with Takuboku's criterion for poetry—it must be spoken by the Japanese people living in Japan at that time and using the language of that time. It may or may not be that Nakano Shigeharu read these writings by Ishikawa Takuboku when his own poetry was coming to an end. Yet, regardless of when Nakano highlighted this work, it may be concluded that he was retracing his own history during the 1920s, through the narrative of Takuboku's concerns about making poetry in a big city, at a time when his country was going to war.

On another shelf in the library, the notes in the 1932 edition of the theory of Marx and Engels on art[10] express Nakano's concern for incorporating theory within his own practice after his release from prison. The well-marked *Communist Manifesto*, from the 1950 edition of the collected works of Marx and Lenin, along with the set of works by Marx and Engels from that same year, attest to the continuity in Nakano's concerns.[11] The Taishō and pre- and postwar Shōwa histories of Nakano Shigeharu thus merge in this collection of works, but they are a library of works belonging to one man who turned to Marxism from his own literary tradition in order to change contemporary culture. The songs by the factory girls, the poetry by Takuboku, and the theory of Marx are a short-

[8] Ishikawa Takuboku, "Tokyo," in *Ishikawa Takuboku zenshū* (1931); p. 108, "Natsu no machi no kyōfū," pp. 131–32; "Mudai," p. 133. Takuboku's commentaries on history and politics were also duly noted by his successor, including a passage distinguishing war from natural disaster and asserting a cause and effect for every war in Japanese history. "Taikenkun ashimoto," ibid., p. 478.

[9] "Kuu beki shi," ibid., pp. 478–82.

[10] Marx and Engels, *Marukusu-Engerusu no geijutsuron* (Iwanami shoten, 1934).

[11] Marx, "Kyosanto sengen," *Marukusu-Lenin zenshū* (Ōtsuki shobō, 1950), 2:489–531.

hand to answer the question, "Why Marxism?" The answer is as much in these works Nakano studied as in the works he wrote as a Marxist in the 1920s. It is very similar to the answer given by the intellectual historian Maruyama Masao to the same question. Maruyama attributes its popularity to the structural, synthetic nature of the method of analyzing society which combined politics, law, philosophy, and economics, and to its assertion that science, which could never be value free, had an obligation to change and not merely to understand society.[12] It is also very different, and not only because this one, focused treatment of some of the corpus of works of one man is not comparable to Maruyama's panoramic vision of the modern era as it emerged from the premodern Japanese tradition of thought. It is similar, because Nakano, like the Japanese intellectual who is the subject of Maruyama's investigation, did find a framework in the categories of Marxism, allowing him to place the discord and tempo in his society within a context. It was also very different in the case of Nakano, for as a poet dedicated to the detail he respected in his Japanese predecessors, he was not interested in developing grand schemas. Marxism gave him a vision of the process of historical change, of the place of culture within history, and of the possibility for transforming culture and society in an era when new historic actors, the industrial workers, were raising their voices in opposition to the Japanese state. Marxism placed consciousness in history for Nakano. He chose poetry as one expression of consciousness, as his means of political organizing to push history forward beyond the antagonisms he chronicled. Marxism gave Nakano a means to understand the politics in his own domain in society, the realm of cultural production. Marx's concept of reification was as important a notion in the workplace in which the intellectual produced essays and photographs, as in the workshop in which labor confronted capital. Nakano took Marx's notions of dialectical materialism, of commodity fetishism, and of ideology, but he did not place them in a grand picture for his reader like Maruyama's theory-builders (or theory-borrowers). He was a poet. He chose to work out his political insights and commitment by rendering the relationships in Japanese society and culture made visible by a "Marxist way of looking" in the detail of poetry that could speak to the social divisions in Taishō society.

Just as there were clear transitions in Takuboku's consciousness as discussed by Nakano, so were there stages in the thought of Nakano Shigeharu as a Marxist revolutionary who as a vocal critic of Taishō society worked most powerfully in the medium of poetry. These stages do not

---

[12] For one discussion of the appeal of Marxism as a social science providing a framework or grid for the analysis of society and history, see Maruyama Masao, *Nihon no shisō*, pp. 55–57.

come from the institutional history of the Proletarian Literature Movement. They express the development of a Marxist poetics as applied to the reality of late Taishō culture and politics, a poetics practiced in Nakano's poetry and prose. Nakano's poems employed Murō Saisei's simplicity of language as their foundation and took language one step further by historicizing it. Through the mixing of words rooted in different historical eras of Japanese experience, Nakano was to spread before his readers the experience of profound, abrupt rupture in Japanese social relationships characterizing Taishō and early Shōwa history. Nakano's teacher, Murō, had also firmly established the quotidian as the subject for poetic discourse. Nakano took this concern with the detail comprising the fabric of daily motions, and just as he had transformed Murō's use of language through a historicization, he would take Murō's subject matter and politicize it. Human activity experienced in work and in domestic routine was placed within the social context of the class relationship. Nakano believed that the significance of Murō's poetic work lay in its connection of poetry to everyday life, and he would adapt this fusion of work and life to allow for his dual role as revolutionary and poet.

Hagiwara Sakutarō's infusion of feeling into words was a second source. Forming emotions into language became one of the central tenets of Nakano's theory of poetry, and anger the governing emotion of his revolutionary verse. Nakano had noted that Hagiwara's anger was aimed at the urban petit bourgeoisie. His own verse would also rage against the hypocrisy and repressiveness of urban bureaucrats and intellectuals. Nakano's poetry gave a dialogic form to Hagiwara's passion. This dialogism was the third element comprising Nakano Shigeharu's Marxist poetics. In sum, through the application of history to language, of politics to daily life, and of the dialogic to the passion provided by Hagiwara, he was to create and put into practice a Marxist theory of poetics. In his quest to grasp the tensions in the everyday lives of Taishō society, Nakano constructed a Marxist critique of poetry without the aid of any archives devoted to the problematics of a Marxist poetry and contributed a Marxist poetry to the Japanese canon.

As a poet who was also a Marxist during the 1920s, Nakano had no recourse to a canon on poetry that would aid him in combining his political commitment to poetic praxis because there was no Marxist theory regarding the relationship of Marxism to verse. There is one work, however, written at the time Nakano began to produce his poetry, that comes closest to a Marxist theory of poetry, although it is concerned with the more general term, "poetics." Bakhtin's essay, "Discourse in Life and Discourse in Art (Concerning Sociological Poetics),"[13] can be used to as-

[13] V. N. Volosinov, "Discourse in Life and Discourse in Art (Concerning Sociological Po-

sociate Nakano's Marxist manifestos in verse form with a Marxian theory of poetry. The Russian theorist argues that art is "immanently social," and that the poet works from within society (pp. 96–98).[14] (The poet's art does not comprise language to be analyzed in some sort of objective linguistic fashion, for "the poet, after all, selects words not from the dictionary but from the context of life where words have been steeped in and become permeated with value judgments.") After its production, the poem remains within a socially dynamic linguistic realm as the object of the utterance of the poem, the "hero," and the listener or reader continue to participate in an ongoing social dialogue of interpretation and exchange. In a passage that can easily serve as a gloss on Nakano's Marxist critique in "Notes on Arts Written on the Run" in which he enumerates the pairings of oppressor and oppressor who will reappear to challenge the reader of his poems, Bakhtin speaks of the language of poetry as a "scenario" of an event and calls for a method of reading poetry that recognizes how the social is made up of relationships. Bakhtin is not unaware of the commodification of art, Nakano's concern in his poetry and prose on the reproduction of culture. He remarks how under capitalism (he calls it the bourgeois economy) the book market "regulates" writers, but ultimately (and here he differs from Nakano) he sees the market as external to his inquiry into ideology. In poetry, he claims, "relations among *people* stand revealed, relations merely reflected and fixed in verbal material" (pp. 109–15). The relationships can only be revealed or come to life when the creator, the subject of the poem, and the reader engage in dialogue from within their socially informed positions and languages.

Bakhtin's theory illuminates Nakano's poetic practice, for as has been discussed, in his reproduction of Taishō culture, by quoting Western-language utterances by intellectuals, the specialized speech of the media, and the vocal protest of colonized students in Korea who have been denied their language, Nakano Shigeharu consciously created and reenacted dialogue at the same time as he aggressively drew his readers into participation, through a method of interrogation. The creation of the triangulated relationship demarcated by Bakhtin was as evident in the first stage

---

etics)," appendix 1 to Volosinov, *Freudianism: The Marxist Critique*, trans. I. R. Pitunik, ed. in collaboration with Neal H. Bruss (New York: Academic Press, 1976), pp. 93–116. I am following the position of Michael Holquist, that the essay written under the name of Volosinov was penned by Bakhtin. Holquist, Introduction to *The Dialogic Imagination*, p. xxvi.

[14] Bakhtin was commenting on the social nature of art and voicing his opposition to its fetishization. This position was in counterdistinction to his position in the 1930s, when he would use poetry as a foil for his theory of the novel, claiming that poetry was to be excluded from the dialogic realm. Bakhtin, *The Dialogic Imagination*, pp. 285–88.

of his changing song—in "Urashimatarō" when he challenged the reader teasing him with the words "you sing too"—as in the second stage, when he identified the reader with the hero, "Fatty," the journalist, and taught the mother and the reader to read the photograph on the subject of imperial expansion. During the third stage of his changing song, Nakano could not present his poetry as objects for the reader's consumption or even education; the listener was refused the privileged perspective of an audience. The poet presumed that the reader was implicated in the violent struggles of which the poetry spoke, and he demanded participation from different sectors of society. The journalists, the mother, the group of tenant farmers had different languages and different relationships with each other, with him, and with the state, and Nakano framed their words and their relationships in verse in order to advocate a revolution that would rearrange their relationships. In the words of the concluding section of Bakhtin's essay, "A poet uses a metaphor in order to regroup values and not for the sake of a linguistic exercise" (p. 116). This is especially true of Nakano's poems on cultural reproduction. When he wrote "The Imperial Hotel," he was not merely playing with urban imagery from postearthquake Tokyo. He wanted to rework values that enshrined the bourgeois West and entombed Japanese culture as timeless.

Nakano's Marxist approach to poetry and to Taishō culture and consciousness was a response to contemporary Japanese history, but it places him within the tradition of "Western Marxism" as recently redefined by Martin Jay.[15] Unlike Antonio Gramsci, Karl Korsch, Ernst Bloch, Walter Benjamin, and others, Nakano did not come of age in continental Western Europe, nor was his Marxism Eurocentric. Nonetheless, his rejection of economism made clear in his commitment to cultural revolution places him, along with the generation of Western Marxists, in opposition to the scientistic, determinist stance of the Second International. His critique converges with what Eugene Lunn has termed the "renaissance of a dialectical and Hegelian Marxism" shaped by Lukács, Karl Korsch, Ernst Bloch, and Gramsci.[16] Like Gramsci and Lukács, Nakano did choose to work through a Leninist party, although his work does not exhibit the pessimism found by Jay in Western Marxism. Nakano's changing song, possibly because he entered politics as a poet, was not marked by the shift

[15] Martin Jay's treatment of the term revises the original usage by Merleau-Ponty and takes into account Perry Anderson's framework. Jay, *Marxism and Totality*, pp. 3–16. Cf. Perry Anderson, *Considerations on Western Marxism* (London: NLB, 1976).

[16] Writing along the same lines as Russell Jacoby, Lunn distinguishes these thinkers from Marxists who believed in the historical inevitability of progress and socialism. Eugene Lunn, *Marxism and Modernism: An Historical Study of Lukács, Brecht, Benjamin and Adorno* (Berkeley: University of California Press, 1982), pp. 105–106.

from an untenable politics to culture.[17] An irony that belongs here is that Fukumoto Kazuo, who is most often associated with Leninism, and with whom Nakano has been associated in the histories, gave the Frankfurt Institute of Social Research, from which the Frankfurt School of Western Marxists was to emerge, its name, but this is but a footnote to history. What must be emphasized above all else, to reclaim Nakano from his image as a Leninist politician who happened to be a poet, is Nakano's concern for cultural questions in his theory and poetry. Like the Western Marxists, Nakano sought to explicate how culture under advanced capitalism could be used to prevent revolution through a cultural hegemony. In late Taishō Japan he was forced to study how such hegemony embraced a mass-produced print culture, an ideology of emperor worship, and a practice of state police surveillance to enforce it.

This book has been about the influence of Marx on Nakano, but it has equally been about this hitherto unexamined convergence. Nakano Shigeharu belongs alongside Lukács, Benjamin, Gramsci, and Bakhtin, not because he studied their words, but because like all of them he chose to create a Marxist theory of cultural practice. To call him a "Western Marxist" for these reasons would be patently Eurocentric. A more appropriate designation, which does not sacrifice the specificity of the Japanese experience, is to consider him a "modern Marxist" who directed his art against mass commodity culture and the transformation of the urban space of Tokyo by capitalist forces organizing an empire abroad and social forms at home. This is not to say that he was a modernist. While Nakano's attention to the question of fragmentation in contemporary society, as expressed in the title and style of more than one of his essays, articulates the belief that notions of a social whole cannot hold, this does not make his manifestos modernist. To treat him as such would invite associations with an avant-garde sensibility not exhibited by this Marxist. Nakano shared with the members of the European and the Japanese avant-garde movements a distaste for the place of art in bourgeois society, but his own position was in support of art as socially significant, and not as significantly altered in either form or function.[18] To call Nakano

[17] Jay's discussion of the Western Marxist preoccupation with questions of culture in the context of their recognition that theory and practice could not be unified is similar to Anderson's thesis that Western Marxists turned to culture only after the practice of politics was no longer possible. Jay, *Marxism and Totality*, p. 8.

[18] In his *Theory of the Avant-Garde*, Peter Burger associates Brecht with the avant-garde in two ways: "What they and Brecht share is, first, a conception of the work in which the individual elements attain autonomy (this being the conditions that must be met if alienation is to become effective) and, second, the attention he devotes to art as an institution." Nakano's concern with the *danpen* or fragment may be associated with the first attribute, and his concern with art as an institution in the *bundan* is parallel. Neither Nakano nor Brecht meets Burger's third criterion: they do not wish to destroy the institution of art. See Burger,

"modern" is to place him as a critic of new forms of culture governing everyday life in twentieth-century Japan and Western Europe after World War I. Like the European Marxists, Nakano turned his Marxist vision toward a critique of the mass media and to a modern, mass society in which class had become embedded. To call Nakano Shigeharu modern is to shift the history of Japanese Marxism away from its association with directives from Moscow and from alternative theories of historical development. At the same time, by calling him a modern Marxist, the study of the Taishō era shifts from a preoccupation with the social forces of democracy toward an inquiry into the multivocal forces of culture and strengthens the very strong connections between Nakano Shigeharu and the Marxist poet Bertolt Brecht. Brecht was the only modern Marxist to put theory into the practice of poetry. A comparison of his approach to poetry with Nakano Shigeharu's attitudes associates Western European and Japanese Marxism, which concludes the explanation as to why and how the Japanese poet turned to Marxism.

Like Brecht, Nakano recognized the productive aspects of art and confronted the challenge posed by the new, reproductive media. Brecht, like Nakano, envisioned the control of the radio by the listeners and spoke in almost identical terms, about "turning the audience not only into pupils but into teachers."[19] Nakano's view of a world split in two in his theory of art and the poems written during the third stage of his changing song validated Brecht's commitment to class struggle. Both Marxists felt that traditional culture had ended by the 1920s, and both men saw a new art capable of expressing a character's socially and historically determined behavior as a means to revolution. A Leninist Communist Party was presumably a means to such art, although in both cases a distinction must be made between an advocacy of Leninist politics and their own cultural practice.[20] While Nakano quoted from Lenin's essay supporting realism in literature, "Lev Tolstoy as the Mirror of the Russian Revolution," and produced poetry and fiction that was more representational than avant-garde, to call his art "Leninist" is to confuse his political affiliation with the ideas informing his literary production. At least as important an influence on both Japanese and German Marxists was the impetus provided by what Lunn terms the "new, urban technological society." Both men

---

Theory of the Avant-Garde (Minneapolis: University of Minnesota Press, 1984), pp. 88–89.

[19] Nakano's view of art does not correspond to the full definition offered by Lunn, who defines Brecht's view of art as an aspect of material labor; as a construction based on the formative principles of technological modes of production, such as montage; and as an activity that was tied to new mechanical media, such as film and radio. Lunn, *Marxism and Modernism*, p. 103.

[20] Ibid., pp. 132, 136.

accepted the inevitability of "reified experiences under advanced capitalist conditions"—Brecht in the context of Weimar Germany, Nakano from within Taishō Japan. There was no turning back. Brecht's commitment to the radical transformation of culture was Nakano's determination to "overcome Kabuki."[21]

For Brecht as for Nakano, art was a product of labor; it was produced by an intellectual alienated from his product but nonetheless capable of representing society from a "montage of shifting multiple viewpoints" that distinguished levels of utterance.[22] A major inspiration for both poets appears to have been the folk songs of women workers, as proven by reminiscence from Brecht's childhood wherein he provides his own version of Nakano's discovery of the *kaeuta*:

> The women workers in the nearby paper factory would sometimes fail to remember all the verses of a song and make improvised transitions from which much could be learned. Their attitude towards the songs was also instructive. They never let themselves be naively carried away. They would sing individual verses or entire songs with a certain irony, putting quotation marks, as it were, round a lot that was cheap, exaggerated, unreal. They were not all that far removed from those highly educated compilers of the Homeric epics who were inspired by naivety without being themselves naive.[23]

The poetry produced by both men was considered sufficiently threatening by the state to be confiscated,[24] and the potency of the verse must be attributed not only to the political sentiment but to the ability to deal with what one critic has called "precise, tangible facts."[25] For both poets the truth was concrete. This quote is as applicable to Brecht's use of documented sources as it is to Nakano's earliest essay on poetry as it is to the size of the buttons on the uniform of the Imperial University student much maligned in the poem by that name. Moreover, both poets meet Benjamin's praise for Brecht's unique "extreme sensibility for the city-dweller's special ways of reaction."[26] According to Benjamin, as early as 1928 and before any other poet, Brecht understood the sensibility of the inhabitant of the urban battlefield, as revealed in the poetry of "The

---

[21] Ibid., p. 145.

[22] For Brecht's analysis of the artist as a "brain worker," see ibid., p. 125. The quote is from p. 116.

[23] Bertolt Brecht, *Bertolt Brecht Poems 1913–1956*, ed. John Willett and Ralph Manheim with the cooperation of Erich Fried (New York: Methuen, 1976), p. 473.

[24] Brecht's first collection of poetry was confiscated by Nazi authorities when it first appeared in 1926, five years before Nakano's first collection was taken.

[25] Ibid., p. xx.

[26] Walter Benjamin, *Understanding Brecht*, trans. Anna Bostock (London: NLB, 1973), p. 61.

Handbook for City-Dwellers." The reader of Nakano Shigeharu's changing song should recognize a kindred sensibility in a segment of this poem:

TEN POEMS FROM A READER FOR THOSE WHO LIVE IN CITIES

I

Part from your friends at the station
Enter the city in the morning with your coat buttoned up
Look for a room, and when your friend knocks:
Do not, oh do not, open the door
But
Cover your tracks.

Eat the meat that's there. Don't stint yourself.
Go into any house when it rains and sit on any chair that's in it
But don't sit long. And don't forget your hat.
I tell you:
Cover your tracks.[27]

These first and third verses of Brecht's poem are a rendering of the scene in "Farewell Before Daybreak" written two years before Brecht's guide to urban survival for the revolutionary, for as Walter Benjamin noted, the poem is for the underground political worker.[28] Both Nakano Shigeharu and Bertolt Brecht were urban intellectuals making revolution through poetry. In their struggle against injustice, Nakano, like Brecht, chose to align himself with poetry. In verse, they reproduced the culture of their time and place to show how new traditions could continue to deny the inconstancy and changeability of the social order. They chose to turn the culture of reproduction against itself actively to reject a system offering things for sale to its citizens, instead of an honest accounting of history, in verse.

The poem "Uta" (Song),[29] which appeared in Roba two months after the frenzied lines of "Days" and two months before the work song "Cleaning," during the second stage of Nakano's changing song, is the poem most often associated with Nakano Shigeharu when he is placed in the canon of modern Japanese literature, but it has also baffled Japanese critics who have read the following words literally, as an injunction not to sing:

[27] Bertolt Brecht, Bertolt Brecht Poems, p. 131.
[28] Of all of the numerous poems on cities written by Brecht, Benjamin has picked the poem closest in imagery to "Farewell Before Dawn." Benjamin, Understanding Brecht, p. 60.
[29] Nakano, "Uta," NSZ 1:508–509 [Roba 9/26].

SONG

You, Don't sing
Don't sing of flowery grasses[30] or dragonfly wings
Don't sing of the wind's whispering or the smell of woman's hair
All those weak things
All those uncertain things
All gloomy things—brush them aside
Reject all elegance
Sing of solely the honest parts
Parts that will fill the belly
Sing of that very edge where it pierces from the chest
Songs that spring back from being knocked down
Songs that draw up strength from the depths of shame
Those sorts of songs
Clear out fumigate your heart
Fill out your lungs
Sing out in severe rhythm
Those sorts of songs
Pound into the chests of the people going by going by

Nakano was to castigate those literary analysts who had interpreted his remonstrances in such a literal fashion as to deny him an affection for nature or for beauty, but his clarification was no less ambiguous. According to the poet, in singing of the denial of beauty he had been talking about the topic in a new manner.[31] And indeed, it is undeniable that the poem exhorting the poet or the singer *not* to sing engaged in that very act. Lines from Brecht help untangle this subtle contradiction. In the second stanza of a poem entitled "To Those Born Later," Brecht asked, "What kind of times are they, when / A talk about trees is almost a crime / Because it implies silence about so many horrors?"[32] Both writers believed that the revolutionary poet's job was to witness in order to change history. While anger at the deprivation resulting from the violence in society was to be shaped into poetry, neither poet denied nature its place in history. It was not the poet who denied the beauty of wildflowers or dragonfly wings. Capital had stolen nature from labor, and the poem "Song"

[30] Nakano's term was *akamama no hana*, a reference to the colloquial term for the plant *inutade* or knotgross (*poligonum blumei*). The term *akamama* can also refer to *sekihan*, the red rice made with beans and eaten on auspicious occasions. In some regional dialects, *akamama* is also a euphemism for blood, in baby-talk. The poet could easily have been working with all of these meanings, including the seemingly jarring allusion to blood.

[31] Nakano, "Koyama shotenban *Nakano Shigeharu shishū* atogaki," NSZ 22:174 [*Nakano Shigeharu shishū* (Koyama shoten, 1947)].

[32] Brecht, "To Those Born Later," in *Bertolt Brecht Poems*, p. 318.

was Nakano's means of affirming this beauty for the worker, who could not see because he was locked within the walls of his workplace.

Nature was to be reclaimed within history, and "singing in severe rhythm" in the city was the means to this revolution. Nakano Shigeharu, like Bertolt Brecht, found his voice in poetry. As a Marxist he turned his lyrics into revolutionary practice because he believed that poetry that worked in a new language about new social and cultural forms could bring about change. Revolutionary consciousness called for the detail of changing song.

Talking about Taishō

An analysis of Nakano's literary production of the 1920s and early 1930s alongside the work of European Marxists has led to the conclusion that he was a "modern Marxist." An analysis of the site of production of these same texts, in their relationship to the works of contemporary Japanese Marxist and non-Marxist writers, opens the way to a new answer to the second question raised at the outset, because it suggests a reinterpretation of what has come to be called "Taishō Culture." In the marginal space allotted it, the cameo of Taishō Culture has appeared in passing as a glittering, decadent interlude of middle-class consumption. Lip service has been paid to the expansion of the mass media and new modes of leisure, but culture is without doubt an aside to the real narrative of political intrigue, military expansion, and social unrest characterizing the era between the two world wars in Japan, the era characterized as one of "Taishō Democracy." But now that Western scholars of modern Japanese politics have begun to replace notions of a democratic interlude of liberal party government with investigations into the structural continuities emerging from the Meiji constitutional settlement, thus opening the way for a new conception that could be termed "Taishō Bureaucracy," Taishō Culture must also be rethought.

The culture of the era has usually been discussed in binary terms, and most often in literary histories. Revolutionary artists engage in polemic parallel to the actions of apolitical authors—the contest is between proletarian writers and modernists. Alternatively, the citizens of Japan are said to have engaged in a "double life" made possible by the borrowing of non-Japanese habits of everyday life.[33] The left is separated from the avant-garde, East meets West, old joins the new. Moreover, only the middle class emerges as a consumer class. There is thus a glaring contradiction between such an accounting of culture and the commentary on the political and social events of the time, for the histories of Taishō, espe-

[33] See Seidensticker, *Low City, High City*, pp. 90–143.

cially the accounts of the years following the First World War, have chronicled the expansion of the Japanese industrial work force and their politicization as expressed in the rapid intensification of militancy in the workplace. Yet this worker, who is present in the obligatory references to the postwar rice riots and to the turn to the left of the labor movement, is absent when the histories take up culture.[34] An examination of the context and the content of the changing song of Nakano Shigeharu suggests an alternative view to the bifurcated visions of a middle-class world at play.

The mass-produced journals and new archival collections of the late Taishō era—rather than the organizations of the cultural left—have been considered here as the site of Nakano's Marxist manifestos. When these writings are viewed in the context of their original site, isolated from the complete works and debates reproduced in anthologies after the Taishō era, the either/or formulation of proletarian versus modernist culture will not hold. This is because more than one of his essays on proletarian culture, like his diatribe on "sen-sen culture" and much of his poetry, appeared in the nonpartisan mass media. A simple overview of the contents of such magazines as the admittedly left-leaning *Kaizō*, which published "Shinagawa Station in the Rain," reveals that Marxists from opposing camps and nonpolitical modern writers mingled to offer their views on class and culture in the pages of the same journal. For example, when the article "Marx's Story of Robinson Crusoe" appeared in the June 1929 issue of *Kaizō*, the same issue carried an excerpt from Kawakami Hajime's *Second Tale of the Poor*. Both Yamakawa Hitoshi and Yamakawa Kikue also had articles in that issue, as did Sakai Toshihiko, whose article, "A History of the Japan Socialist Movement Seen Autobiographically," contributed to the process of canon making. Placed among these articles by the Marxists was a collection of cultural commentaries on "Modern Life." Three months later, Kawakami was still updating his treatise on poverty in an issue introducing fiction by the modernist author Yokomitsu Riichi.[35] Clearly, Marxist and modernist voices contested within

[34] Minami Hiroshi, *Taishō bunka*. Even this classic, which aims to integrate the economic and political developments from 1912 through 1926 with the emergence of a middle-class culture organized around new conceptions of family life and leisure activities under the rubric of "culture," fails to come to terms with the relationship of the worker to the cultural shifts of the 1920s. A recent exception to this trend is Ishikawa Hiroshi, *Goraku no senzen shi*.

[35] Kawakami Hajime, "Dai ni binbō monogatari," *Kaizō* (September 1929): 45–55; Yamakawa Hitoshi, "Rōdōtō kataba/gyoshū punpun musanseitō no chihō jichitai shinshutsu / nanja ka no na ni oite," ibid., pp. 62–68; Yamakawa Kikue, "Musan fujin undō gaiken," ibid., pp. 94–97. For the section on modern life, see pp. 29–70. Yokomitsu's contribution was Yokomitsu Riichi, "Tokubyō to zengan," ibid., pp. 1–24. A segment of Tanizaki Junichirō's *Manji* also appeared in this issue, pp. 25–41.

mass culture in an intertextuality not investigated by historians of Taishō consciousness but duly noted by Nakano Shigeharu, who recognized that both "sides" were implicated in their production of "sen-sen."

Nakano's changing song also suggests another shift in perspective: The history of Japanese Marxist thought is reoriented by the discovery of Nakano's focus on the place of the commodity in his culture. When this concern with the fetishistic aspect of capitalist consumption is sought and found in the works of other Japanese Marxist writers of the time, the issue of "how many stages to a revolution" loses its position as the sole strategic concern for Japanese Marxist social theorists who have been isolated from Marxist producers and critics of culture in our histories; the hitherto disparate canonical texts of Japanese Marxism rearrange themselves in revealing ways. For example, Kawakami Hajime's manifesto, *Binbō monogatari* (Tales of poverty),[36] alluded to in the title of the *Kaizō* articles of 1929, reads not only as an exposé of poverty. The reader who returns to that text will discover an indictment of the commodity consumption of the Japanese. In the context of this new interpretation, a better title for the widely read classic might be *Narikin monogatari* (Tales of the nouveau riche). From this alternative perspective, Hayama Yoshiki's classic from the proletarian literature canon, *Umi ni ikuru hitobito* (Those who live on the sea),[37] cannot be examined for the realism exhibited in the reenactment of a strike. Instead, it becomes an exposé of the Meiji ideology of getting ahead (*risshin shusse*) and an indictment of the pleasures of Taishō commodity culture as experienced by workers under capitalism. Kawakami, the political economist, Hayama, the proletarian novelist, and Nakano, the poet and Communist leader, are associated as Marxists rather than as specialists.

Because of the sheer bulk of Marxist writings produced during the Taishō years, the inquiry is infinitely expandable, but one more example should serve to reorient investigations into the history of Japanese Marxism and Taishō culture and consciousness. The writings of a fourth Marxist, the feminist theorist Yamakawa Kikue, reinforce the thesis that Japanese Marxists used the discussion of the commodity in *Capital* in their attempt to make sense of Japanese capitalism. When this new perspective on the canon is directed at Yamakawa, her theory takes an important place in the cultural history of Taishō Japan from which she has been almost altogether excluded. In the essay "Keihintsuki tokkahin to shite

[36] Kawakami Hajime, *Binbō monogatari* (Kyoto: Kōbundō, 1917). *Binbō monogatari* was read by more than 100,000 readers in 1916 when it first appeared in the *Asahi shimbun* and was so treasured by intellectuals that it received thirty printings in book form by 1919.

[37] Hayama Yoshiki, *Umi ni ikuru hitobito* (Kaizōsha, 1926). See Iwamoto Yoshio's treatment of Hayama's historical accuracy in "Aspects of the Proletarian Literary Movement in Japan," in *Japan in Crisis*, pp. 170–73.

no onna" (Woman as special bargain item with premium),[38] Yamakawa writes from a strategy similar to Nakano's method of discussing art as commodity in his essay on Akutagawa, but unlike Nakano, this theorist does not resort to imaginary construction of historical artifacts. Instead of composing an advertisement, she opens her essay with a quotation from the classified section of the newspaper, noting that such announcements render life one large bargain sale. She then releases her attack on the contemporary traffic in women:

> Yet even in this marketplace of bargains dealing in even land, houses, telephones, stores, poultry farms, hospitals, companies, typewriters, clothing and furnishings—where all of these are sold at "exceptionally low cost" what appears to be the really good bargains are the human beings for sale—the women. (p. 2)

This Japanese Marxist then reads from the classified ads placed by women advertising their availability in the press. Like Nakano, and like Walter Benjamin, she respects the power of the photographic reproduction of culture, and she is able to produce a graphic analogy for her reader. She tells readers of the January 1928 issue of *Fujin kōron* (Woman's forum) that the pictures adorning such women's magazines are qualitatively no different from the pictures in the portals of brothels. Her semiotic approach to the ideological implications of style of dress and hair contribute to an understanding of what Yamakawa termed the "marriage race" in the Taishō era, and to the range of Marxist thought that extended beyond party politics.

Yamakawa, like Nakano and all other leading Marxist writers of the Taishō years, published their attacks on capitalism in the capitalist press; their ideas should not be isolated as belonging within a political and cultural movement constituted by Communist and non-Communist camps and occupying one corner of Taishō culture; their Marxist voices contended with non-Marxist views in the same cultural space. The way to avoid such binarisms is to imagine "Taishō Culture" as constituted by contending cultures.[39] This imagining of such a complex relationship between cultures, within one culture, is consonant with the heteroglossia in Nakano's poetry, which, when taken as a whole, comprises voices originating in very different cultures, within one national shared culture and language. Such a method of interpretation allows for an understanding of

[38] Yamakawa Kikue, "Keihintsuki tokkahin to shite no onna," in *Doguma kara deta yūrei*, vol. 5: *Yamakawa Kikueshū* (Iwanami shoten, 1982), pp. 2–8 [*Fujin kōron* 1/28].
[39] I have been influenced by Dominick LaCapra, who suggests that modern culture is composed of elite, popular, mass, and state cultures belonging to one history. See LaCapra, "Is Everyone a Mentalite Case," in *History and Criticism* (Ithaca: Cornell University Press, 1985), pp. 71–94.

the scenario wherein Nakano Shigeharu's bride of two months received word of her husband's arrest on April 4, 1932. At that moment she was performing the Charleston—she was dressed in the flapper's uniform of a "modern girl." It can be argued that Marxism could not be separated from the modern in Taishō culture wherein the modernist voice was being commodified in tandem with the Marxist work; Marxism intermingled with modernism and concern with modernity. This actress in flapper's garb in the Marxist, revolutionary theater was employing a custom appropriated from a mass culture. In other words, the Charleston was being employed "to overcome Kabuki," to assert new ways of moving in history in a cultural production aimed at the worker, who has been absent from the sketchy accounts of the history of prewar nouveau riche consumerism. Working-class culture is also present in Nakano's writing, in both the changed songs of the factory girls and the changed language and gesture alluded to in Nakano's fantasies of a new image for the worker in literature and drama. According to the picture of culture emerging from Nakano Shigeharu's changing song, the intellectual may be a producer, but the worker is also both a producer of culture through art and transformed everyday gesture, and a consumer of mass culture. Neither the contesting, intermingling Marxist or Modernist, middle-class consumer or working-class producer-consumer, can be isolated from the dynamic of historic participation in a Japanese culture that is neither essentialized and frozen within "tradition" nor fractured into a patchwork of the best or the worst of East and West. Nor, within Nakano's changing song, can Japanese history be denied its specificity. Nakano Shigeharu's changing song illustrates that working-class culture and cultural expressions of revolutionaries during the late 1920s and of state officials during the early years of Shōwa were informed by reworked indigenous traditions not found in Europe, and by reproductive capabilities of a far more universal nature. A final tension that works against an either/or opposition—this time between democracy or repression—is the coexistence, documented by Nakano's works, of the overt state repression of the late 1920s with a space for critical expression and unregulated leisure. The glaring absences in Nakano's writings, marked by asterisks and by periods of nonproductivity, coexist with the reproduction of such commodities as the Marxist and non-Marxist *enpon* in a "sen-sen" culture. Because of the intersection of state-managed and commodity cultures, the Japanese citizens of late Taishō Japan were to be both imperial subjects and consumers of capitalist commodities. This emergence of the citizen-consumer or consuming subject in Taishō culture may indeed be one example of the specificity of the Japanese experience Nakano sought to articulate in his Marxist critique.

The histories have given us an abbreviated version of Nakano's life and work: the young university graduate, the literary man, the intense political activist destined to become editor and leader of a series of revolutionary forums, and the representative of the Marxist literary movement during the 1920s. That narrative is not wrong. But the changing song of Nakano Shigeharu's Marxist manifestos leads to a different ending: In the closing years of the 1920s, Nakano Shigeharu engaged in revolution, through his writing, as a Marxist critic. He refused to corner revolutionary literature into a narrow space occupied by propaganda and bad proletarian art, for good proletarian art included folk-literature; its powerful treatment of emotions could not be diminished by simplicity. Nakano spoke in simple terms, "putting the complex into the simple."[40] His was a struggle to tell his people how images were being sold to them, and to show how they had the power to see through such lies if they would only look. Nakano's poetry would end, but even now it elicits responses. It remains, in defiance of any power silencing its poets. It denies that the way things should be are the way they always have been. The changing song of Nakano Shigeharu addresses the reader who would continue to give present meaning to the past.

[40] This phrase is from William Empson's treatment of proletarian literature in *Some Versions of Pastoral* (London: Chatto & Windus, 1950), p. 23.

Chronology

January 1902	(January 25) Nakano Shigeharu born in village of Takaboko, Fukui Prefecture.
April 1914	Nakano enters Fukui Junior High School.
September 1919	Nakano enters Kanazawa Fourth Higher School.
April 1924	Nakano enters German literature department, Tokyo Imperial University.
January 1925	Premier issue of *Razō*, with seven poems by Nakano, including "Urashimatarō" and "Kyō mo" (Again today).
May 1925	Last issue of *Razō*.
Summer 1925	Nakano enters Shinjinkai.
October 1925	Nakano helps to organize the *Shakai bungei kenkyūkai* at Tokyo Imperial University.
January 1926	Nakano moves into Shinjinkai dormitory; participates in Kyōdō Printers Strike (strike lasts 1/19/26–3/18/27).
February 1926	Nakano helps form the Marukusushugi Geijutsu Kenkyūkai.
April 1926	Premier issue of *Roba*, including "Kitami no kaigan" (The beach at Kitami).
September 1926	"Uta" (Song) appears in September issue of *Roba*.
October 1926	Nakano considered part of left literary establishment as indicated by participation in roundtable discussion published as "*Sayoku bundan shinsakka ron*," in *Bungei sensen* (November 1926).
November 1926	"Teikoku hoteru" I, II, (Imperial Hotel) in *Roba*.
November 1926	Nakano chosen as member of Central Committee of the Nihon Puroretaria Geijutsu Remmei ("Purogei"). Appearance of "Takuboku ni kansuru danpen" (A fragment on Takuboku), written version of talk given for Shinjinkai, in *Roba*.
February 1927	"Kisha" (Train), I, II, III, in *Roba*.

June 1927	Purge of Purogei, defections, and organization of Rono Geijutsuka Remmei ("Rōnō"). Nakano remains in Purogei.
June 1927	Nakano visits home of Akutagawa Ryūnosuke; moves into Purogei group house.
July 1927	Suicide of Akutagawa Ryūnosuke.
October 1927	"Geijutsu ni kansuru hashirigakiteki oboe-gaki" (Notes on art written on the run) in *Puroretaria geijutsu*.
November 1927	"Kobanmae" (In front of the policebox) in *Puroretaria geijutsu*.
February 1928	(2/27) Nakano's first arrest, while campaigning for Rōdō Nōmintō candidate, Ōyama Ikuo. Released March 5, after detention in five jails.
March 1928	Nakano's second arrest during "March 15 Incident." Taken from Purogei Group House and released soon thereafter. (3/25) Establishment of Zen Nihon Musansha Geijutsu Remmei (NAPF).
April 1928	Nakano chosen Standing Committee member of NAPF; edits first issue of *Senki*. Last issue of *Roba*.
June–November 1928	Nakano debates Kurahara Korehito in "Geijutsu taishūka ronsō" in *Senki*.
October 1928	"Geijutsu ni tsuite" (On art) placed in Marxist canon in *Marukusushugi kōza*, vol. 10.
February 1929	"Ame no furu Shinagawa eki" (Shinagawa Station in the rain) in *Kaizō*.
April 1929	Nakano's third arrest and same day release during April 16 round-up.
July 1929	"Seiji to geijutsu" (Politics and art) placed in Proletarian Literature canon in first folio of *Puroretaria geijutsu kyōtei*.
April 1930	(4/16) Nakano marries Hara Masano.
May 1930	(5/24) Nakano's fourth arrest, for contributing funds to Japanese Communist Party, upon return from speaking tour of Kansai (with Kobayashi Takiji and others) sponsored by Nihon Puroretaria Sakka Dōmei to benefit *Senki*. Released 12/28/30.

February 1931	Nakano canonized in vol. 62 (Proletarian literature) of Kaizōsha *enpon* series on modern Japanese literature (Gendai Nihon bungaku zenshū).
July 1931	Nakano further established in canon of modern Japanese literature in vol. 51 of Shūyōdō *Meiji Taishō Shōwa bungaku zenshū*; "Iyoyo kyō kara" (Finally from today) in *Nappu*.
Summer 1931	Nakano joins Japanese Communist Party; edits *Nappu*.
September 1931	Nakano's fifth arrest.
October 1931	Police impound *Nakano Shigeharu shishū*, anthology of poetry to be issued by *Nappu*. One copy saved by Itō Shinkichi.
November 1931	*Nappu* discontinued. (11/12) NAPF disbanded. (11/27) KOPF established. Nakano on Central Committee and member Publications Committee.
December 1931	Nakano canonized as leading proletarian poet in Hakuyōsha, *Nappu shichinin shishū* edited by Nakano.
January 1932	Nakano editor of KOPF publication *Taishū no tomo* and member of literary establishment in *Shinchō* New Year's round-table discussion.
April 1932	(4/4) Nakano's sixth and longest arrest in context of arrests of Writer's Federation Members and suppression of KOPF dating from end of March, on suspicion of breaking Peace Preservation Law.
May 1932–May 1934	Nakano in Toyotama Prison.
February 1933	(2/20) Murder of Kobayashi Takiji.
June 1933	"*Tenkō*" of Sano Manabu and Nabeyama Sadaki.
March 1934	(3/12) Official sentencing of Nakano to four years penal servitude; request for release denied.
May 1934	Nakano spends one month in prison infirmary. Requests for release denied. (5/26) Testifies in court to acknowledge membership in Japanese Communist Party, prom-

	ises to remove himself from Communist Movement, and is released from prison.
Summer 1934	Nakano returns to village of Takaboko and resumes translation of *Lenin's Letters to Gorky*; reestablishes his position as proletarian writer in August issue of *Bungaku hyōron*, in round-table discussion on direction of proletarian literature, along with Hayashi Fusao, Kubokawa Ineko, and others.
September 1934	Nakano reestablishes position in literary establishment in round-table discussion on realism with Kawabata Yasunari, Kobayashi Hideo, and others in September issue of *Bungakukai*.
October 1934	Nakano reestablishes position as critic in essay demanding prison reform in October issue of *Kaizō*, followed by essay "Keimushō de yonda mono kara" (From what I read in prison) in *Bunka shūdan* (December).
February 1935	Nakano writes "Keisatsukan ni tsuite" (On the police official) to appear in *Shakai hyōron* (March).
April 1935	Nakano writes *Mura no ie* (The house in the village).
May 1935	Arrest of Miyamoto Yuriko.
June 1935	Nakano appears with Tosaka Jun and others in round-table discussion on the arts to appear in August issue of *Yuibutsuron kenkyū*.
1935–1937	Nakano continues to publish essays and articles in such sources as *Kaizō*, *Shinchō*, and *Bungei*.
April 1936	Nakano's last political poem, "Kawase sōba" (The rate of exchange), appears in April *Chūō kōron*.
December 1937	Nakano, Miyamoto Yuriko, Tosaka Jun, and others forbidden to write (ban to be lifted 12/38).
May 1938	Nakano hired by Investigative Division of Tokyo Social Bureau to translate German labor laws.

December 1938	Nakano allowed to resume writing.
February 1939	Nakano's daughter, Ume, born.
Spring, Summer 1939	*Uta no wakare* (A farewell to song) serialized in *Kakushin*.
August 1940	(8/19) Hara Senko (Masano) arrested. Released at end of December.
July 1941	Hara Masano banned from stage for one month.
November 1941	(11/19) Nakano's father dies.
December 1941	(12/8) Nakano escapes nationwide arrests at onset of Pacific War because he is not in Tokyo.
January 1942–June 1945	Nakano under police surveillance; continues to publish.
September 1944	Nakano refuses factory employment chosen by authorities and instead enters employ of research institute of Musashi Metallurgy Company. Continues to write; employed as rolling machine worker.
June 1945	Nakano drafted and receives army rank of second class. Sent to Nagano Prefecture as member of Setagaya Eastern Division, 186th Division, Unit 27659.
August 1945	Nakano returns to Tokyo at end of war.
October 1945	(10/18) Nakano appears with Kikuchi Kan, Nii Itaru, Miyamoto Yuriko, Sata Ineko, and others at gathering sponsored by *Bungei shunjū*. (10/19) Nakano does first radio broadcast, on "Kuimono no mondai" (The problem of things to eat).
November 1945	Nakano reenters Japanese Communist Party.
October 1946	Nakano named director of Cultural Division of *Akahata*.
April 1947	Nakano elected to Diet House of Councillors as delegate from Japanese Communist Party. Continues to publish and engage in public debate regarding relationship of politics to literature.

Bibliography

WORKS BY NAKANO SHIGEHARU

Note: *NSZ* refers to *Nakano Shigeharu zenshū*. 28 vols. Chikuma shobō, 1980. Both here and in the footnotes, the periodical in which the work first appeared and original date of publication are placed in brackets following the location in *NSZ*. Poetry, essays and memoirs, fiction, translation, and letters are listed separately. The English-language translations of Nakano's poetry and prose are mine. Unless otherwise indicated, all Japanese works here and in the notes were published in Tokyo.

Poetry

Nakano Shigeharu shishū. Nappu shuppan, 1931.
Nakano Shigeharu shishū. Naukasha, 1935.
Nakano Shigeharu shishū. Koyama shoten, 1947.
Nakano Shigeharu shishū. Chikuma shobō, 1959.
"Ame no furu Shinagawa eki." *NSZ* 1:529–30 [*Kaizō* 2/29].
"Chōsen no musumetachi." *NSZ* 1:524–25 [*Musansha shimbun* 9/1/27].
"Daidō no hitobito." *NSZ* 1:3–6 [Original version most likely in Kanazawa provincial newspaper].
"Dōrō wo kizuku." *NSZ* 1:514 [*Musansha shimbun* 1/1/27].
"Hataki wo okuru." *NSZ* 1:499 [*Razō* 3/25].
"Heitai ni tsuite." *NSZ* 1:522–23 [*Puroretaria geijutsu* 8/27].
"Hibi." *NSZ* 1:508 [*Roba* 7/26].
"Hōritsu." *NSZ* 1:525 [*Puroretaria geijutsu* 9/27].
"Iyoiyo kyō kara." *NSZ* 1:530–31 [*Nappu* 7/31].
"Kawase sōba." *NSZ* 1:532–33 [*Chūō kōron* 4/36].
"Kisha." *NSZ* 1:515–17 [*Roba* 2/27].
"Kitami no kaigan." *NSZ* 1:504–505 [*Roba* 4/26].
"Konya ore wa omae no neiki wo kiiteyaru." *NSZ* 1:531–32 [*Chūō kōron* 9/31].
"Kyō mo." *NSZ* 1:497 [*Razō* 2/25].
"Mattero gokudō jinushimera." *NSZ* 1:528 [*Musansha shimbun* 9/5/28].
"Me no naka ni." *NSZ* 1:495 [*Razō* 1/25].
"Museifushugisha." *NSZ* 1:510 [*Roba* 9/26].
"Nami." *NSZ* 1:503–504 [*Razō* 5/25].
"Pooru Kurooderu." *NSZ* 1:513–14 [*Roba* 1/27].
"Shimbunkisha." *NSZ* 1:511–12 [*Roba* 11/26].
"Shimbun ni notta shashin." *NSZ* 1:519–20 [*Puroretaria geijutsu* 7/27].
"Shimbun wo tsukuru hitobito ni." *NSZ* 1:520–22 [*Bungei kōron* 8/27].
"Shinnin taishi chakukyō no zu." *NSZ* 1:507 [*Roba* 7/26].
"Shiranami." *NSZ* 1:493–94 [*Razō* 1/25].
"Sōji." *NSZ* 1:509–10 [*Roba* 9/26].
"Suihen wo saru." *NSZ* 1:497 [*Razō* 2/25].

"Tanbo no onna." *NSZ* 1:496 [*Razō* 2/25].
"Teikoku hoteru." *NSZ* 1:510–11 [*Roba* 11/26].
"Tokyo teikoku daigakusei." *NSZ* 1:506 [*Roba* 6/26].
"Tsume wa mada aruka." *NSZ* 1:494 [*Razō* 1/25].
"Urashimatarō." *NSZ* 1:403 [*Razō* 1/25].
"Uta." *NSZ* 1:508–509 [*Roba* 9/26].
"Yatsura no ikkakenzoku wo hakidashiteshimae." *NSZ* 1:527 [*Puroretaria geijutsu* 10/27].
"Yoakemae no sayonara." *NSZ* 1:505–506 [*Roba* 5/26].
"Yokari no omoide." *NSZ* 1:528–29 [*Musansha shimbun* 9/5/28].
"Yoru no aisatsu." *NSZ* 1:502 [*Razō* 5/25].

Essays and Memoirs
"Akutagawa Ryūnosuke." *NSZ* 19:213–17 [*Bungaku no mondai*. Bungei kōza, vol 1. Chikuma shobō, 1951.]
"Akutagawa shi ni koto nado." *NSZ* 9:102–12 [*Bungei kōron* 1/28].
"Ame no furu Shinagawa eki no koto." *NSZ* 22:77–78 [*Likan sanseli*, Summer 1975].
"Bungei sensen wa doko ni mon wo hirakuka." *NSZ* 9:137–44. [*Senki* 5/28].
"Bunka remmei no koto." *NSZ* 9:460–67 [*Kaizō* 11/31].
"Bunshō wo uru koto sono hoka." *NSZ* 9:264–72 [*Shinchō* 9/29].
"Chiisai kaisō." *NSZ* 19:199–204 [*Bungei shunjū* 11/34].
"Chosha ushirogaki: hitotsu no kōtōgakkōki to hitotsu no daigakuki." *NSZ* 5:407–13 [3/15/76].
"Chosha ushirogaki: mukashi no yume ima no yume." *NSZ* 6:389–95 [6/7/77].
"Chosha ushirogaki: seiriteki yōshōnenki to bungakuteki shōnenki." *NSZ* 1:485–91 [3/1/76].
"Danpenteki yosō." *NSZ* 9:113–16 [*Bungei shunjū* 1/28].
"E ni tsuite." *NSZ* 9:125–32 [*Puroretaria geijutsu* 2/28].
"Engeki ni tsuite." *NSZ* 9:117–24 [*Puroretaria geijutsu* 1/38].
"Fūshū no kangaekata." *NSZ* 10:36–41 [original publication not known].
"Geijutsu ni kansuru hashirigakiteki oboegaki." *NSZ* 9:68–78 [*Puroretaria geijutsu* 10/27].
Geijutsu ni kansuru hashirigakiteki oboegaki. Kaizōsha, 1929.
"Geijutsu ni seijiteki kachi nante mono wa nai." *NSZ* 9:273–88 [*Shinchō* 10/29].
"Geijutsu ni tsuite." *NSZ* 9:179–218 [*Marukusushugi kōza*, vol. 10, 10/28, under title "Geijutsuron."
"Handōki no sakka seikatsu." *NSZ* 9:309–11 [*Teikoku daigaku shimbun* 4/21/30].
"Hiroi seken." *NSZ* 10:288–96 [*Shimpo* 7/35].
"Hitotsu no genshō." *NSZ* 9:11–13 [*Teikoku daigaku shimbun* 9/13/26].
"Ichi rōdōsha to shite Roshia kakumei jusshūnen wo mukaeru." *NSZ* 9:92–94 [*Puroretaria geijutsu* 11/27].
"Ikanaru chiten wo susumitsutsuaruka." *NSZ* 9:82–91 [*Puroretaria geijutsu* 11/27].
"Iwanami bunkoban, *Nakano Shigeharu shishū* atogaki." *NSZ* 22:200–201 [1956].

"Iwayuru geijutsu no taishūkaron no ayamari ni tsuite." *NSZ* 9:151 [*Senki* 6/28].

"Kaiketsu sareta mondai to atarashii shigoto." *NSZ* 9:218–29 [*Senki* 11/28].

"Kako no shi no kenkyū." *NSZ* 9:440–56 [*Sōgō puroretaria geijutsu kōza*, vol. 4, 10/31].

"Keisatsukan ni tsuite." *NSZ* 10:169–76 [*Shakai hyōron* 3/25].

"Kiroku no omoshirosa." *NSZ* 10:261–68 [*Shinchō* 7/35].

"Kodomo ni miseru shibai no uchi." *NSZ* 9:294–98 [*Engeki* 10/29].

"Kondō Eizō shi ni tou." *NSZ* 9:78–82 [*Puroretaria geijutsu* 10/28].

"Kono goro no kansō." *NSZ* 10:41–46 [*Tokyo asahi shimbun* 11/29–12/1/34].

"Kure no kansō." *NSZ* 9:484–86 [*Bungaku shimbun* 12/5/31].

"*Kyōdō bōkeishi* ni arawareta funnu." *NSZ* 19:173–83 [*Roba* 10/26].

"Mō hitotsu no Tokyo kōshinkyoku e." *NSZ* 9:261–63 [*Yomiuri shimbun* 8/20/ 29].

"Mondai no nejimodoshi to sore ni tsuite no iken." *NSZ* 9:156–69 [*Senki* 9/28].

"*Nakano Shigeharu shi* jijo," *NSZ* 22:151 [*Nakano Shigeharu shishū*. Nappu shuppanbu, 1931].

"Nakano Shigeharushū." *Gendai Nihon bungaku zenshū*, vol. 62. *Puroretaria bungakushū*. Kaizōsha, 1931.

"Nakano Shigeharushū." *Shinkō bungaku zenshū*, vol. 10. *Nihonhen X*. Heibonsha, 1929.

"*Nakano Shigeharu zenshū* dai gokan sakusha atogaki." *NSZ* 22:87–96.

"Nihon kenkyū." *NSZ* 10:57–58 [*Sarariiman* 1/35].

"Nōmin bungaku no mondai." *NSZ* 9:355–63 [*Kaizō* 7/31].

"Puroretaria geijutsu to wa nanika?" *NSZ* 9:337–54 [*Sōgō puroretaria geijutsu kōza*, vol. 1, 5/31].

Puroretaria shi no shomondai. Edited by Nakano. Sōbunkaku, 1932.

"Saikin bungakujō no arekore." *NSZ* 9:522–26 [*Sarariiman* 2/15/32].

"Sanjūichinendo bungeikai no kaiko." *NSZ* 9:481–84 [*Shinchō* 12/31].

"Seiji to geijutsu." *NSZ* 9:253–61 [*Puroretaria geijutsu kyōtei*. Vol. 1. Sekaisha, 7/29].

"Shi ni kansuru danpen." *NSZ* 9:3–10 [*Roba* 6/26].

"Shi no shigoto no kenkyū." *NSZ* 9:369–82 [*Puroretaria shi* 7/31].

"Shijin to shite no Murō Saisei." *NSZ* 17:388 [*Nihon shijin zenshū* as "Murō Saisei. Hito to sakuhin"].

"Soboku to iu koto." *NSZ* 9:169 [*Shinchō* 10/28].

"Takuboku ni kansuru danpen," *NSZ* 16:3–12 [*Roba* 11/26].

"Taishū no kairyō." *NSZ* 10:5–18 [*Kaizō* 11/34].

"Toki no mondai I." *NSZ* 9:527–34 [*Taishū no tomo* 2/32].

"Tokyo. Saitama nōson shōnen no katsudō." *NSZ* 9:311–17 [*Senki* 5/30].

"Waga bungakuteki jiden." *NSZ* 22:3–12 [*Shinchō* 8/36].

"Wareware wa zenshin shiyō." *NSZ* 9:229–52 [*Senki* 4/29].

"Wasureenu shomotsu." *NSZ* 17:423 [Kokubun Ichitanō, ed., *Wasureenu shomotsu*. Meiji Tosho, 1959.]

Fiction

"Atarashii onna." *NSZ* 1:259–64 [*Bungaku jidai* 8/29].

"Dai isshō." *NSZ* 2:3–39 [*Chūo kōron* 1/35].

"Doitsu kara kita otoko." *NSZ* 1:420–33 [*Shinchō* 7/31].
"Harusaki no kaze." *NSZ* 1:203–14 [*Senki* 8/28].
"Hitotsu no chiisai kiroku." *NSZ* 2:99–132 [*Chūo kōron* 1/36].
"Kinensai zengo." *NSZ* 1:186–202 [*Puroretaria geijutsu* 1/28].
"Kōbanmae." *NSZ* 1:179–85 [*Puroretaria geijutsu* 11/27].
Machiaruki. NSZ 5:99–121 [*Shinchō* 6–7/40].
Mura no ie. NSZ 2:64–89 [*Keizai ōrai* 5/35].
Muragimo. NSZ 5:125–404 [*Gunzō* 1–7/54].
"Nami no aima." *NSZ* 1:349–67 [*Shinchō* 5/30].
Nashi no hana. NSZ 6 [*Shinchō* 1/57–12/58].
"Oroka na onna." *NSZ* 1:157–62 [*Shizuoka shinpo* 1/1/26].
"Shōsetsu no kakenu shōsetsuka." *NSZ* 2:133–52 [*Kaizō* 1/36].
"Suzuki, Miyakoyama, Yasoshima." *NSZ* 2:40–63 [*Bungei shunjū* 4/35].
"Teishajō." *NSZ* 1:249–58 [*Kindai seikatsu* 6/29].
Tetsu no hanashi. Nihon puroretaria sakka sōsho. Vol. 9. Senkisha, 1930.
Uta no wakare. NSZ 5:3–95 [*Kakushin* 4/39; 5/39; 7/39; 8/39].
Yoakemae no sayonara. Shinei bungaku sōsho. Vol. 25. Kaizōsha, 1930.

Translation

Lenin no Gorikii e no tegami. Iwanami bunko, 1935.

Letters

Itoshiki mono e. Edited by Sawachi Hisae. Vol. 1 of 2. Chūō kōronsha, 1983.

JAPANESE SOURCES

Akita Ujaku. *Akita ujgaku nikki.* Edited by Ozaki Kōji. Vol 2. Miraisha, 1965.
Akutagawa Ryūnosuke. "Bungeiteki na, amari ni bungeiteki na." *Akutagawa Ryūnosuke zenshū.* Iwanami shoten, 1978, 9:3–80 [*Kaizō* 4–6/27; 8/27].
———. "Zoku bungeiteki na, amari ni bungeiteki na." *Akutagawa Ryūnosuke zenshū* 9:81–87 [*Bungei shunjū* 4/27; 7/27].
Chūgoku mondai kōwa. Puroretaria kagaku kenkyūjō, 1930.
Fujita Shōzō. "Shōwa hachinen wo chūshin to suru tenkō no jōkyō." In *Tenkō.* Edited by Shisō no kagaku kenkyūkai. Vol. 1. Heibonsha, 1978.
Fukumoto Kazuo [Hōjō Kazuo]. " 'Hōkō tenkan' wa ikanaru shokatei wo toruka." *Marukusushugi* 18 (October 1925).
———. "Oshū ni okeru musansha kaikyū seitō soshiki mondai no rekishiteki hatten" (I–II). *Marukusushugi* 12–13 (April–May 1925).
Geijutsu to marukusushugi. Edited by Puroretaria kagaku kenkyūjō, 1930.
Gendai Nihon bungaku zenshū. 37 vols. Kaizōsha, 1926.
Hariu Kiyoto. "Shakaishugi no tetsugaku no juyō to tenkai no shosō." In *Nihon kindai tetsugaku shi.* Edited by Miyakawa Tōru and Arakawa Ikuo. Yuhikaku, 1976.
Haruhara Akihiko. *Nihon shinbun tsūshi.* Gendai jaanarizumu shuppankai, 1969.
Hayama Yoshiki. "Semento daru no naka no tegami." In *Nihon puroretaria bungaku taikei.* Vol. 2: *Undō seiritsu no jidai,* pp. 71–74 [*Bungei sensen* 1/26].

———. *Umi ni ikuru hitobito*. Kaizōsha, 1926.

Hirano Ken, ed. *Nakano Shigeharu kenkyū*. Chikuma shobō, 1960.

———. *Nakano Shigeharushū*. Chikuma gendai bungaku taikei, no. 35. Chikuma shobō, 1979.

Hosoi Wakizō. *Jokō aishi*. Iwanami kurashikkusu 6. Iwanami shoten, 1982.

Hosokawa Karoku, ed. *Nihon shakaishugi bunken kaisetsu*. Ōtsuki shoten, 1958.

Hotta Yoshie, "Ryōhei to Shigeharu." In *Nakano Shigeharu kenkyū*. Edited by Hirano Ken. Chikuma shobō, 1960.

Imai Seiichi. *Taishō demokurashii*. Nihon no rekishi, vol. 23. Chūō kōronsha, 1966.

Ishidō Kiyotomo. "Shinjinkai jidai no Nakano Shigeharu." *Shin Nihon bungaku* 388 (December 1979): 40–45.

———. *Waga itan no Shōwa shi*. Keisō shobō, 1986.

Ishidō Kiyomoto and Yamabe Kentaro, eds. *Kominterun Nihon ni kansuru teezeshū*. Aoki bunko, 1961.

Ishikawa Hiroyuki, ed. *Goraku no senzen shi*. Shoseki kabushikigaisha, 1981.

Ishikawa Takuboku zenshū. Kaizōsha, 1931.

———. 16 vols. Iwanami shoten, 1961.

———. 8 vols. Chikuma shobō, 1967–1968. Reprinted 1978–1979.

Isoda Kōichi. *Shisō to shite no Tokyo: Kindai bungaku shiron nōto*. Kokubunsha, 1978.

Kamei Hideo. *Nakano Shigeharuron*. Sanichi shobō, 1970.

Kamei Katsuichirō. "Nakano Shigeharu." In *Nakano Shigeharu kenkyū*. Edited by Hirano Ken. Chikuma shobō, 1960.

Kawakami Hajime. *Binbō monogatari*. Kyoto: Kōbundō, 1917.

———. "Dai ni binbō monogatari." *Kaizō* (September 1929): 45–55.

Kawashima Takeyoshi. *Nihon shakai no kazokuteki kōzō*. Nihon hyōronsha, 1950.

Keizaigaku zenshū. 67 vols. Kaizōsha, 1928–1934.

Kimura Hideo. *Nakano Shigeharuron: shi to hyōron*. Ōfūsha, 1979.

Kitagawa Tōru. *Nakano Shigeharu*. Kindai Nihon shijinsen 15. Chikuma shobō, 1981.

Koyama Hirotake. *Nihon marukusushugi shi*. Aoki shoten, 1956.

Koyama Hirotake and Kishimoto Eijirō. *Nihon no hikyōsantō marukusushugisha*. Sanichi shobō, 1962.

Kunimatsu Kōji et al., eds. *Rukaachi kenkyū*. Hakusuisha, 1969.

Kuno Osamu. "Nakano Shigeharu san no eikyōryoku." *Geppō* 1. Vol. 1 (September 1976): [appendix to *NSZ*].

Kuno Osamu and Tsurumi Shunsuke. *Gendai Nihon no shisō*. Iwanami shoten, 1956.

Kurihara Yukio. *Puroretaria bungaku to sono jidai*. Heibonsha, 1971.

Maeda Ai. *Toshi kūkan no naka no bungaku*. Chikuma shobō, 1982.

Marukusu-Engerusu Shoshi Henshū Iinkai, ed. *Marukusu-Engerusu hōyaku bunken mokuroku* (Kyokutō shoten, Nauka, Ōtsuki shoten, 1973).

Marukusu-Engerusu zenshū. 30 vols. Kaizōsha, 1928–1935.

Marukusugaku kyōkasho. 7 vols. Marukusu shobō, 1928–1929.

Marukusushi geijutsu riron. Sōbunkaku, 1931.

Marukusushugi kōza. Edited by Kawakami Hajime and Ōyama Ikuo. 13 vols. Ueno shoten, 1927–1929.

Marukusushugi rōdōsha kyōtei: Keizaigaku. Translated by Puroretaria Kagaku Kenkyūjō. 6 vols. Sōbunkaku, 1931–1932.

Marukusushugi rōdōsha kyōtei: Kokusai rōdōsha undōshi. Translated by Kitajima Takehira. 3 vols. Chūgai shobō, 1931–1932.

Maruyama Masao. *Nihon no shisō.* Iwanami shoten, 1961.

Marx, Karl, and Frederick Engels. *Marukusu-Engerusu no geijutsuron.* Iwanami shoten, 1934.

Masu medea tōsei. Edited by Uchikawa Yoshimi. Gendai shi shiryō 41. Misuzu shobō, 1973.

Matsumoto Kenichi, ed. *Gendai ronsō jiten: shisō to bungaku.* Ryūdō shuppan, 1980.

Matsuo Takayoshi. *Taishō demokurashii.* Iwanami shoten, 1974.

Matsuzawa Hiroaki. *Nihon shakaishugi no shisō.* Chikuma shobō, 1973.

Meiji bunka zenshū. 24 vols. Edited by Yoshino Sakuzō. Nihon hyōronsha, 1928–1930.

Minakami Tsutomu. "Nakano Shigeharu san no koto." *Shin Nihon bungaku* 388 (December 1979): 57–59.

Minami Hiroshi. *Taishō bunka.* Keisō shobō, 1965.

Mitsuta Ikuo. *Nakano Shigeharuron.* Yagi shoten, 1981.

Miyakawa Tōru. *Miki Kiyoshi.* Tokyo daigaku shuppankai, 1970.

———. *1930 nendai mondai no shosō.* Nosan gyoson bunka kyōkai, 1979.

Moriyama Kei. "Hattan: Gakusei jidai no Nakano Shigeharu san ni kansuru danpen." *Shin Nihon bungaku* 388 (December 1979): 35–37.

Murakami Nobuhiko. *Nihon no fujin mondai.* Iwanami shoten, 1981.

———. *Taishōki no shokugyō fujin.* Domesu shuppan, 1983.

Murō Saisei. "Shiyū no koto." In *Nakano Shigeharu kenkyū.* Edited by Hirano Ken. Chikuma shobō, 1960.

Nihon puroretaria bungaku taikei. 9 vols. Sanichi shobō, 1954–55.

Nihon rōdō nenkan. Ohara shakai mondai kenkyūjō, 1929.

Nihon shakaishugi bunken. Ohara shakai mondai kenkyūjō, 1929.

Nimura Kazuo. "Zasshi *Marukusushugi* no shippitsusha chōsa." *Shiryōshitsuhō* (Ōhara Shakai Mondai Kenkyūjō) 177 (November 1971): 1–16.

Noma Hiroshi, gen. ed. *Nihon puroretaria bungaku taikei.* 9 vols. Sanichi shobō, 1955.

Noro Eitarō, gen. ed. *Nihon shihonshugi hattatsu shi kōza.* 7 vols. Iwanami shoten, 1932–33.

Ōe Kenzaburo, "Nashi no hana no bunshō." In *Nakano Shigeharu kenkyū.* Edited by Hirano Ken. Chikuma shobō, 1960.

Okano Takeo. *Nihon shuppan bunka shi.* Hara shobō, 1981.

Ōkuma Nobuyuki. "Marukusu no Robinson monogatari." *Kaizō* (June 1929): 14–31.

Ono Hideo. *Nihon shimbun hattatsu shi.* Osaka: Mainichi shimbunsha, 1922.

Ōya Sōichi. *Shakai mondai kōza.* 13 vols. Shinchōsha, 1926–27.

Puroretaria Kagaku Kenkyūjō, ed. *Puroretaria kōza*. 4 vols. Kyōseikaku, 1930.

Sata Ineko. *Natsu no shiori*. Shinchōsha, 1983.

"Senzen no ankoku jidai no shihonshugi kenkyū no keizai shi hakkō: *Hattatsu shi kōza* kara *Keizai hyōron* e." *Keizai* 144 (April 1976): 12–50.

Shakai kagaku kōza. 13 vols. Seibundō, 1931–32.

Shakai keizai taikei. 20 vols. Nihon hyōronsha, 1926–28.

Shakai mondai kōza. Edited by Ōya Sōichi. 13 vols. Shinchōsha, 1926–27.

Shakai shisō zenshū. 40 vols. Heibonsha, 1929–1933.

Shimpojiumu, Taishō demokurashii. Nihon rekishi, no. 20. Gakuseisha, 1969.

Shinobu Seizaburō. *Taishō demokurashii shi*. Nihon hyōronsha, 1958.

Shiota Shōhei. *Nihon shakai undō shi*. Iwanami zensho, 1982.

Shirai Yoshimi. "Nakano Shigeharu ni okeru inazuma tetsugaku." *Geppō* 22. Vol. 10 (January 1979): 1–3 [appendix to *NSZ*].

Shisō no Kagaku Kenkyūkai, ed. *Tenkō*. 3 vols. Heibonsha, 1959–1962.

Sōgō jaanarizumu kōza. 11 vols. Naigaisha, 1930–1931.

Sugino Yōkichi. *Nakano Shigeharu no kenkyū*. Senzen/senchū hen. Kasama shoin, 1979.

Sugiyama Sanshichi. "Shikō jidai no Nakano Shigeharu." *Shin Nihon bungaku* 388 (December 1979): 37–39.

Takabatake Michitoshi, ed. *Yamakawa Hitoshi shū*. Chikuma shobō, 1976.

Takabatake Motoyuki. *Marukusu jūni kōza*. Shinchōsha, 1926.

Takemura Tamio. *Taishō bunka*. Kōdansha, 1980.

Tosaka Jun. *Nihon ideorogiiron*. Iwanami bunko, 1977.

Tōyama Shigeki. *Meiji ishin to gendai*. Iwanami shinsho, 1968.

Tōyama Shigeki, Yamazaki Shōichi, and Ōi Tadashi, eds. *Kindai Nihon shisō shi nenpyō*. Vol. 1 of *Kindai Nihon shisō shi*. Aoki shoten, 1957.

Tsurumi Shunsuke, "Taishōki no bunka." *Iwanami kōza Nihon rekishi, Gendai* 19, 2:288–323. Iwanami shoten, 1963.

———. *Ajia kaihō no yume*. Nihon no hyakunen, vol. 4. Chikuma shobō, 1962.

Uchida Jōkichi. *Nihon shihonshugi ronsō*. Seiwa shoten, 1947.

Umeda Toshihide. "Puroretaria kagaku kenkyūjō kankei shiryō no shōkai to 2, 3 no ronten." *Kenkyū shiryō geppō* 326 (January 1986): 26–49.

Yamada Moritarō. *Nihon shihonshugi bunseki*. Iwanami shoten, 1934, 1977.

Yamada Seizaburō, "Puroretaria bunka undō shi," in "Bunka undō shi," *Nihon shihonshugi hattatsu shi kōza*, vol. 3. Edited by Noro Eitarō. Iwanami shoten, 1932–33.

Yamakawa Hitoshi. *Aru bonjin no kiroku*. Asahi shimbunsha, 1927.

Yamakawa Kikue. "Keihintsuki tokkahin to shite no onna." In *Yamakawa Kikueshū*. Vol. 5: *Doguma kara deta yūrei*. Iwanami shoten, 1982 [*Fujin kōron* 1/28].

Yamamoto Fumio. *Nihon shimbun shi*. Kokusai shuppan kabushikigaisha, 1948.

Yamamoto Taketoshi. *Kindai Nihon no shimbun dokushazō*. Hōsei daigaku shuppankyoku, 1981.

———. *Kōkoku no shakai shi*. Hōsei daigaku shuppankyoku, 1984.

———. *Shimbun to minshū*. Kinokuniya shoten, 1973.

Yui Masao et al., eds. *Shuppan keisatsu kankei shiryō: Kaisetsu. Sōmokuji.* Fuji shuppan, 1983.

Yūki Ryōichi. *Ahh Tokyo kōshinkyoku.* Kawade bunko, 1985.

ENGLISH-LANGUAGE SOURCES

Anderson, Perry. *Considerations on Western Marxism.* London: NLB, 1976.

Arima Tatsuo. *The Failure of Freedom: A Portrait of Modern Japanese Intellectuals.* Cambridge: Harvard University Press, 1969.

Bakhtin, M. M. *The Dialogic Imagination.* Edited by Michael Holquist. Translated by Caryl Emerson and Michael Holquist. Austin: University of Texas Press, 1981.

———. *Problems of Dostoevsky's Poetics.* Edited and translated by Caryl Emerson. *Theory and History of Literature.* Vol. 8. Minneapolis: University of Minnesota Press, 1984.

Barthes, Roland. *Empire of Signs.* Translated by Richard Howard. New York: Hill and Wang, 1982.

Beckmann, George, and Okubo Genji. *The Japanese Communist Party 1922–1945.* Stanford: Stanford University Press, 1969.

Benjamin, Walter. *Charles Baudelaire: A Lyric Poet in the Era of High Capitalism.* Translated by Harry Zohn. London: NLB, 1973.

———. *Illuminations.* Edited by Hannah Arendt. Translated by Harry Zohn. New York: Schocken Books, 1969.

———. *Reflections.* Edited by Peter Demetz. Translated by Edmund Jephcott. New York: Harcourt Brace Jovanovitch, 1978.

———. "A Short History of Photography." *Screen* 13, 1 (Spring 1972).

———. *Understanding Brecht.* Translated by Anna Bostock. London: NLB, 1973.

Bennett, Tony. *Formalism and Marxism.* New York: Methuen, 1979.

Berman, Marshall. *All that Is Solid Melts into Air: The Experience of Modernity.* New York: Simon and Schuster, 1982.

Bloch, Ernst. *On Karl Marx.* New York: Herder & Herder, 1971.

Brecht, Bertolt. *Bertolt Brecht Poems 1913–1956.* New York: Methuen, 1976.

———. *Brecht on Theatre.* Edited and translated by John Willett. New York: Hill and Wang, 1964.

Brown, Edward J. *The Proletarian Episode in Russian Literature 1928–1932.* New York: Columbia University Press, 1953.

Buck-Morss, Susan. *The Origin of Negative Dialectics: Theodor W. Adorno, Walter Benjamin, and the Frankfurt Institute.* New York: Free Press, 1977.

Bukharin, Nikokai. *Theory of Historical Materialism, a Manual of Popular Sociology.* New York: Allen & Unwin, 1926.

Bukharin, N., and E. Preobrazhensky. *The ABC of Communism: A Popular Explanation of the Program of the Communist Party of Russia.* Ann Arbor: University of Michigan Press, 1966.

Burger, Peter. *Theory of the Avant-Garde.* Minneapolis: University of Minnesota Press, 1984.

Carroll, David. "The Alterity of Discourse: Form, History, and the Question of the Political in M. M. Bakhtin." *Diacritics* (Summer 1983): 65–83.

Chaigne, Louis. *Paul Claudel: The Man and the Mystic*. Translated by Pierre de Fontnouvelle. New York: Appleton-Century-Crofts, 1961.

Chujo Shinobu. "Paul Claudel Ambassadeur de France au Japan." *Claudel Studies* 11, 1–2 (1984): 32–55.

Claudel, Paul. *The East I Know*. New Haven: Yale University Press, 1914.

Davis, A. R., ed. *Modern Japanese Poetry*. Translated by James Kirkup. St. Lucia: University of Queensland, 1978.

De Becker, J. E., trans. *Annotated Civil Code of Japan*. 4 vols. London: Butterworth Co., 1910.

Eagleton, Terry. *Walter Benjamin: Or Towards a Revolutionary Criticism*. London: Verso Editions, 1981.

———. "Wittgenstein's Friends." *New Left Review* 135 (1982): 64–90.

Emerson, Caryl. "The Tolstoy Connection in Bakhtin." *Publications of the Modern Language Association of America* 100, 1 (January 1985): 68–80.

Empson, William. *Some Versions of Pastoral*. London: Chatto & Windus, 1950.

Ermolaev, Herman. *Soviet Literary Theories: 1917–1934*. Berkeley: University of California Press, 1963.

Fowlie, Wallace. *Paul Claudel*. London: Bowes & Bowes, 1957.

Gluck, Carol. *Japan's Modern Myths: Ideology in the Late Meiji Period*. Princeton: Princeton University Press, 1985.

Gramsci, Antonio. *Selections from the Prison Notebooks*. Edited and translated by Quintin Hoare and Geoffrey Nowell Smith. New York: International Publishers, 1971.

Harootunian, H. D. "The Problem of Taishō." In *Japan in Crisis: Essays on Taishō Democracy*. Edited by Bernard S. Silberman and H. D. Harootunian. Princeton: Princeton University Press, 1974.

Hegel, G.W.F. *The Phenomenology of Mind*. New York: Harper & Row, 1967.

Hoston, Germaine A. *Marxism and the Crisis of Development in Prewar Japan*. Princeton: Princeton University Press, 1986.

Iwamoto Yoshio. "Aspects of the Proletarian Literature Movement." In *Japan in Crisis: Essays in Taisho Democracy*. Edited by Bernard S. Silberman and H. D. Harootunian. Princeton: Princeton University Press, 1974.

Jacoby, Russell. *Dialectic of Defeat: Contours of Western Marxism*. Cambridge: Cambridge University Press, 1981.

James, C. Vaughn. *Soviet Socialist Realism: Origins and Theory*. New York: St. Martin's Press, 1973.

Jay, Martin. *Marxism and Totality: The Adventures of a Concept from Lukács to Habermas*. Berkeley: University of California Press, 1984.

Joll, James. *Antonio Gramsci*. New York: Penguin Books, 1977.

Kasza, Gregory J. *The State and the Mass Media in Japan, 1918–1945*. Berkeley: University of California Press, 1988.

Keene, Donald. *Essays in Idleness: The Tsurezuregusa of Kenkō*. New York: Columbia University Press, 1967.

Kinmonth, Earl. *The Self-Made Man in Meiji Japanese Thought: From Samurai to Salary Man.* Berkeley: University of California Press, 1981.

LaCapra, Dominick. *History and Criticism.* Ithaca: Cornell University Press, 1985.

Lefebvre, Henri. *The Survival of Capitalism: Reproduction of the Relations of Production.* Translated by Frank Bryant. London: Allison & Busby, 1976.

Lucie-Smith, Edward. "The *Cinq grandes odes* of Paul Claudel." In *Claudel: A Reappraisal.* Edited by Richard Griffiths. London: Rapp & Whiting, 1968.

Lukács, Georg. *History and Class Consciousness: Studies in Marxist Dialectics.* Translated by Rodney Livingston. Cambridge: MIT Press, 1968.

Lunn, Eugene. *Marxism and Modernism: An Historical Study of Lukács, Brecht, Benjamin and Adorno.* Berkeley: University of California Press, 1982.

Marx, Karl. *Capital.* 3 vols. Edited by Frederick Engels. New York: International Publishers, 1967.

———. "Contribution to the Critique of Hegel's *Philosophy of Right: Introduction.* In *The Marx-Engels Reader.* Edited by Robert Tucker. 2d ed. New York: W. W. Norton, 1978.

———. *The Eighteenth Brumaire of Louis Bonaparte.* In *The Marx-Engels Reader.* Edited by Robert Tucker. 2d ed. New York: W. W. Norton, 1978.

———. *Grundrisse: Foundations of the Critique of Political Economy.* Translated by Martin Nicolaus. New York: Vintage Books, 1973.

———. *Manifesto of the Communist Party.* In *The Marx-Engels Reader.* Edited by Robert Tucker. 2d ed. New York: W. W. Norton, 1978.

———. Preface to "A Contribution to the Critique of Political Economy." In *The Marx-Engels Reader.* Edited by Robert Tucker. 2d ed. New York: W. W. Norton, 1978.

Marx, Karl, and Frederick Engels. *The German Ideology.* Moscow: Progress Publishers, 1976.

Mayakovsky, Vladimir. *How Verses Are Made.* Translated by G. M. Hyde. London: Jonathan Cape, 1970.

Mitchell, Richard H. *Censorship in Imperial Japan.* Princeton: Princeton University Press, 1983.

Miyake, Yoshiko. "*Jokō aishi* or the Pitiful History of the Mill Girls: A Reality and a Discourse Produced by the Partnership Between Patriarchy and Capital." Manuscript, 1987.

Najita, Tetsuo, and J. Victor Koschmann, eds. *Conflict in Modern Japanese History: the Neglected Tradition.* Princeton: Princeton University Press, 1982.

Nakano Shigeharu. *Three Works by Nakano Shigeharu.* Translated by Brett De Bary. Cornell University East Asia Papers, no. 21. Ithaca: Cornell China-Japan Program, 1979.

Oshima, Mark. "Kabuki: Structure and Change in a Traditional Artistic Institution." Senior Thesis, Harvard College, 1983.

Petit, Jacques, and Jean-Pierre Kempf, eds. *Claudel on the Theatre.* Translated by Christine Trollope. Coral Gables: University of Miami Press, 1972.

Pronko, Leonard Cabell. *Theatre East and West: Perspectives Toward a Total Theatre.* Berkeley and Los Angeles: University of California Press, 1967.

Reischauer, Edwin O. "What Went Wrong?" In *Dilemmas of Growth in Prewar Japan.* Edited by James W. Morley. Princeton: Princeton University Press, 1971.

Rimer, J. Thomas. *Toward a Modern Japanese Theatre: Kushida Kunio.* Princeton: Princeton University Press, 1974.

Roden, Donald. *Schooldays in Imperial Japan.* Berkeley: University of California Press, 1980.

Rubin, Jay. *Injurious to Public Morals: Writers and the Meiji State.* Seattle: University of Washington Press, 1984.

Said, Edward. *Orientalism.* New York: Pantheon Books, 1978.

Seidensticker, Edward. *Low City, High City: Tokyo from Edo to the Earthquake: How the Shogun's Ancient Capital Became a Great Modern City, 1867–1923.* New York: Knopf, 1983.

Sekula, Alan. "On the Invention of Photographic Meaning." In *Thinking Photography.* Edited by Victor Burgin. London: Macmillan, 1982.

Shea, George Tyson. *Leftwing Literature in Japan.* Tokyo: Hōsei University Press, 1964.

Sievers, Sharon L. *Flowers in Salt: The Beginnings of Feminist Consciousness in Modern Japan.* Stanford: Stanford University Press, 1983.

Silberman, Bernard S. "The Bureaucratic State in Japan: The Problem of Authority and Legitimacy." In *Tradition.* Edited by Tetsuo Najita and J. Victor Koschmann. Princeton: Princeton University Press, 1982.

Silverberg, Miriam Rom. "Changing Song: The Marxist Poetry of Nakano Shigeharu." Ph.D. dissertation, University of Chicago, 1984.

Slonim, Marc. *Soviet Russian Literature: Writers and Problems 1917–1967.* New York: Oxford University Press, 1967.

Smith, Henry De Witt, II. *Japan's First Student Radicals.* Cambridge: Harvard University Press, 1972.

Thompson, E. P. *The Making of the English Working Class.* New York: Vintage Books, 1966.

Trollope, Christine. *Claudel on the Theatre.* Coral Gables: University of Miami Press, 1972.

Trotsky, Leon. *Literature and Revolution.* Translated by Rose Strunsky. New York: International Publishers, 1925.

Tsurumi, E. Patricia. "Female Textile Workers and the Failure of Early Trade Unionism in Japan." *History Workshop* 18 (Autumn 1984): 3–27.

———. "Problem Consciousness and Modern Japanese History: Female Textile Workers of Meiji and Taishō." *Bulletin of Concerned Asian Scholars* 18, 4 (October–December 1986): 41–48.

Tsurumi Kazuko. *Social Change and the Individual: Japan Before and After Defeat in World War II.* Princeton: Princeton University Press, 1970.

Uyehara, Cecil H. *Leftwing Social Movements in Japan: An Annotated Bibliography.* Studies on Japan's Social Democratic Parties. Tokyo and Rutland, Vt.: Charles E. Tuttle, 1959.

Volosinov, V. N. "Discourse in Life and Discourse in Art (Concerning Sociological Poetics)," appendix 1 to V. N. Volosinov, *Freudianism: The Marxist Cri-*

tique. Translated by I. R. Pitunik. Edited in collaboration with Neal H. Bruss. New York: Academic Press, 1976.

Walthall, Anne. "Japanese *Gimin*: Peasant Martyrs in Popular Memory." *American Historical Review* 91, 5 (December 1986): 1076–1102.

Watanabe Yozo. "The Family and the Law: The Individualistic Premise and Modern Japanese Family Law." In *Law in Japan: The Legal Order in a Changing Society*. Edited by Arthur Taylor von Mehren. Cambridge: Harvard University Press, 1963.

Waters, Harold A. *Paul Claudel*. In *Twayne's World Author Series*. Vol. 92. Edited by Sylvia E. Bowman. New York: Twayne Publishers, 1970.

Whitman, Walt. *Leaves of Grass*. Edited by Harold W. Blodgett and Sally Bradley. New York: W. W. Norton, 1965.

Wolin, Richard. *Walter Benjamin: An Aesthetic of Redemption*. New York: Columbia University Press, 1982.

Young, Robert. "Back to Bakhtin." *Cultural Critique* 2 (Winter 1985–1986): 71–92.

INTERVIEWS

Hara Izumi. Tokyo, Japan. October 30, 1982.
Ishidō Kiyotomo. Tokyo, Japan. August 30, 1986.
Odagiri Hideo. Tokyo, Japan. November 15, 1981.
Sata Ineko. Tokyo, Japan. November 3, 1982; August 16, 1986.

Index

Hayashi Fusao, 33n.32
Hegel, G.W.F.: on labor in nature, 69; on master-bondsman, 54; *The Phenomenology of Mind*, 54. *See also* Master-bondsman relationship
Heibonsha, 167
Heimin Shimbun, 46
Heine, Heinrich, 97, 191, 194. *See also* Nakano: prison reading
History and Class Consciousness. See Lukács, Georg
Hitler, Adolph, 201
Hito, 191, 196, 200
Hosoi Wakizō. *See Jokō aishi*
Housekeeper system, 33. *See also* Civil Code; Family system; Women
Hugo, Victor, 169; *Les Miserables*, 200

Ideology: Gramsci on, 88; Nakano on, 200–203. *See also* Marx, Karl, works: *German Ideology*; Nakano: on ideology of Japaneseness; Nakano, works: *Fūshū no kangaekata, Kawase sōba*
Ideology of Japaneseness, 200–203. *See also* Nakano, works: *Fūshū no kangaekata, Kawase sōba*
Imperial Rescript on Education, 15
Inferno (Dante), 194
Inoue Tetsujirō. *See Shintaishi*
Intellectual: as revolutionary, 66–67, 79. *See also* Intellectual labor; Nakano, works: *Hibi, Sōji, Yoakemae no sayonara*
Intellectual labor, 66–67, 87; Marx on, 82; Nakano on, 87–89, 98; Trotsky on, 79. *See also* Benjamin, Walter; Gramsci, Antonio; Nakano: on intellectual labor; Nakano: on reproduction of culture; Nakano, works: *Akutakagawa shi no koto nado*
Invasion of Manchuria, 185
Ishidō Kiyotomo, 33n.32, 35–36, 39, 41, 60, 163, 166; on Tenkō, 199
Ishikawa Takuboku, 8, 9; influence on Nakano, 213–14. *See also* Nakano, works: *Takuboku ni kansuru danpen*
Itō Hirobumi, 18
Itō Sachio, 94
Itō Shinkichi, 176, 190

Jacoby, Russell, 69

Japanese Communist Party: Nakano's membership in, 9, 12, 175, 198, 218; Nakano on, 175, 203
Japan Leveller's Society (*Suiheisha*), 55, 56n.25, 164
Japan Proletarian Arts League, 38–39, 44–45, 79. *See also* Nihon Puroretaria Geijutsu Remmei
Jintan (sen-sen), 17; advertisements, 24; as metaphor, 128, 163. *See also* Mass culture; Nakano: on culture of reproduction
Jokō aishi (The sad history of the woman factory hand), 49; class consciousness in, 108–9; Hosoi on ballads in, 106–8; influence of, on Nakano, 213; Nakano on, 49, 169–70; rule by machines in, 109. *See also Kaeuta*; Nakano, works: *Kisha*

Kaeuta (changed song), 4, 7, 72, 78, 106–7, 170, 207. *See also Jokō aishi*
Kaji Wataru, 97
Kamei Katsuichirō, 34–35, 39, 41
Kani Kōsen. See Kobayashi Takiji
Kanno Suga, 19, 26
Kantō earthquake, 32; and massacre of Koreans, 31
Kawakami Hajime. Works: *Binbō monogatari*, 226; *Dai ni binbō monogatari*, 225; *Keizaigaku zenshū*, 164; *Marukusushugi kōza*, 165, 169. *See also* Marxism: in Taishō culture
Key, Ellen, 164
Kikuchi Kan, 30, 209
Kingu, 125; inauguration and circulation of, 163, 167. *See also* Print culture
Kitahara Hakuchō, 202n.43
Kitamura Tōkoku, 40, 93
Kobayashi Hideo, 195
Kobayashi Takiji: canonization of, 167–68; *Kani kōsen*, 168; murder of, 196; Nakano on, 196–97
Kollontai, Alexandra, 126
KOPF. *See Nihon Puroretaria Bunka Remmei*
Korea: annexation of, 12, 18; massacre of Koreans, 31. *See also* Nakano, works: *Ame no furu Shinagawa eki, Chōsen no musumetachi*
Korsch, Karl, 59–60